Gertrud Tauber
Architects and Post-Disaster Housing

Architecture | Volume 24

Gertrud Tauber (PhD) works as architect, consultant and researcher. Her research interests include architecture, power and post-disaster housing; housing in rural areas in non-European countries; post-colonial discourses on modernism and the conception of space; local knowledge and local building technologies. She lives close to Innsbruck (Austria).

Gertrud Tauber

Architects and Post-Disaster Housing

A Comparative Study in South India

[transcript]

Bibliographic information published by the Deutsche Nationalbibliothek
The Deutsche Nationalbibliothek lists this publication in the Deutsche Nationalbibliografie; detailed bibliographic data are available in the Internet at http://dnb.d-nb.de

Cover layout: Kordula Röckenhaus, Bielefeld
Cover illustration: Gertrud Tauber, Shanmuga Nagar (Tamil Nadu), 2012
Proofread by Maria Lord
Printed by Majuskel Medienproduktion GmbH, Wetzlar
Print-ISBN 978-3-8376-2862-3
PDF-ISBN 978-3-8394-2862-7

To all the architects out there who courageously explore alternative roles.

Contents

PART I:
AFTER THE INDIAN OCEAN TSUNAMI OF 2004 | 73

PART II:
THREE CASE STUDIES | 85

Acknowledgements

The present book is the revised version of my PhD, submitted at the Department of Architecture, TU Darmstadt.[1] As with many academic books, this one has also been a long time in coming and has accrued many debts along way.

My first thanks go to the villagers of Keezhakazakudy-Tsunami Nagar, Shanmuga Nagar and Tarangambadi-Tsunami Nagar who welcomed me and my team into their houses, patiently listened to my many questions, and engaged in passionate argument over a wide range of issues. I thank each one of them for making my time in the villages so intellectually meaningful and personally transformative.

This project was made possible with a PhD scholarship provided by the Department of Higher Education, University and Research of the Autonomous Province Bolzano (Italy).[2] It enabled me to concentrate exclusively on this thesis, including my fieldwork in South India. I would like to stress here in particular their non-bureaucratic and practical approach to student funding.

I am particularly indebted to my supervisor Kosta Mathéy for his engaging support throughout the duration of this study. I am thankful for his input and the many questions that spurred me to seek answers and to clarify my thoughts. I am deeply grateful to my second supervisor Andrea Rieger-Jandl for enthusiastic and intellectually-enriching discussions and

1 | Title of the PhD: Which Role for Architects? NGOs, Architects and Post-Disaster Housing: A Comparative Study in Rural South India after the Indian Ocean Tsunami of 2004.

2 | Amt für Bildungsförderung, Universität und Forschung der Autonomen Provinz Bozen/Südtirol.

for inspiring suggestions. I am also indebted to my third evaluator Julian Wékel for his encouraging input.

I extend my deep thanks to Jens Dangschat, for inspiring comments on my early PhD proposal; to Gabriele Alex, for supplying me with impotant literature (particularly for the period of my fieldwork); to Daniel Münster, for his invaluable advice on the first draft of the household questionnaire; and to Andreas Hofer, for thought-provoking input and the encouragement to go further.

I benefited greatly form the comments I received and the discussions at seminars and conferences, where I had the opportunity to present parts of this research, including the conference on Taming the Mega-City (2011) at the TU Darmstadt, the seminar on Urban Violence and Land Use Transformation in Sub-Saharan Cities (2012) at the Global Urban Studies Institute International Academy, Berlin Free University, and at the 6th International i-Rec Conference on Sustainable Post-Disaster Reconstruction: From Recovery to Risk Reduction (2013) in Ascona, Switzerland. The latter was of particular importance as it took place during the final stage of this research. The feedback provided by a very heterogeneous audience (architects, social anthropologists, activists, NGO representatives, practitioners and government officials) with experience of post-disaster recovery, helped me to further sharpen the focus of this research. I am particularly indebted to the two anonymous reviewers (of the paper presented at the conference) whose comments encouraged me to delve into the subject; to Sushma Iyengar, Graham Saunders, Anthony Oliver-Smith and Thiruppugazh Venkatachalam for encouraging feedback and thought-provoking suggestions.

The people who supported me during my fieldwork in Tamil Nadu are numerous. First of all, I extend my deep thanks to Rev. Fr P. A. Jacob, S. Jeyaseelan, Rev. Fr V. Albert Thambidurai, Rock Poucheparadjou, and C. Packiaraj who assisted me and my family in finding a home, and who reached out whenever we needed help. I am indebted to M. Iqbal, his family and R. Kasthuri who generously supported us throughout our stay and made us feel at home in Kottakuppam.

I am deeply grateful to the team that assisted me during the four months in the field and engaged empathetically with the subject of this research. Thanks to M. Siva, F. Jayachandran, M. Maria Antony Raj, M. Soundharajan, and A. Stalin for translating the household questionnaire, collecting the numerous household questionnaires, translating the many discussions with the villagers, and for the many inspiring and personally-enriching hours and days spent together.

I owe a special thanks to all the NGO representatives, architects and engineers who spared their time for my many questions and shared their vast experience. Their thought-provoking input has significantly contributed to the shaping of this study. Indeed, without the architects' reflections chapter International Voices would not have been possible. In alphabetical order they are: L. S. Anthonysamy, Ar. P. Anbukarasi, Jean Louis-Bato, Rajendra Desai, Rupal Desai, Rev. Fr Arul Devadoss, S. Jeyaseelan, M. J. Joseph, X. Joseph, S. L. Karunakaran, Benny Kuriakose, Satprem Maini, Purnima McCutcheon, Arun Menon, J. P. Nelson, Rock Poucheparadjou, J. S. Rajasingh, Fr Ratchagar Rayappan, Vivek Rawal, K. Sakti, Graham Saunders, Daniel Schwitter, S. Selvadas, Cameron Sinclair, S. Siva, Florian Steinberg, S. Vasanth, Sandeep Virmani, and Antje Wemhöner.

Many profound thanks to Claudia Neunteufl, for accurately checking my data-set and supporting me in elaborating the data diagrams; to Maria Lord, for the patient and thoughtful proofread of my English; to 'my' librarian Astrid Böck (Technical University Vienna), for very effectively assisting me in getting the many books from numerous European libraries; and to Axel Swoboda, for helping me with the layout of this book.

Working with transcript Bielefeld has been a pleasure. I thank project manager Annika Linnemann and the team, for the enthusiasm, accuracy and speed with which they got my book through the various stages of the publication process.

It is difficult to account for the ways family members and close friends shape one's pursuits. I am deeply thankful to my mother Helene Engl-Tauber, for encouraging me to pursue my own path; to my father Josef Tauber, for introducing me to the peculiarities of the 'traditional' building culture that has shaped the built environment of my native region;[3] and to my sister Elisabeth Tauber, for being an empathetic mentor throughout. I thank her in particular for encouraging me to pursue this research and offering wise counsel and intellectual sustenance during many periods of doubt over the manuscript.

My sincere thanks to Elisabeth Vogel, who has, over long conversations, been a patient listener and inspiring critic; to Suely Garcia, for her wisdom and guidance in challenging times; to Ursula Klein for her un-

3 | See Tauber *et al.* 2012.

daunted belief in this project and her emotional and intellectual support over the years; to Rüdiger Rausch for his empathy; to Hans-Horst Semler for enthusiastically listening; to Inge Skrebensky and Evi Semler for lovingly taking care of my son, Jakob, during the many hours I spent in front of the computer, writing up this study.

My son, Jakob, has been the best distraction from the self-containment of academic research. He has been a living reminder that doctoral research is only a small part of what makes life meaningful. And more than anyone else, I thank András Semler who has supported me wholeheartedly over the years with generosity, patience and thoughtful criticism, for helping me with my recalcitrant computer, and who has never lost confidence in the successful completion of this undertaking.

Abbreviations

ACC	Autoclaved Aerated Concrete
ADB	Asian Development Bank
CEDAP	Centre for Eco-centric Development and Peoples' Action
CPWD	Central Public Works Department
CI	Caritas Internationalis
CSEB	Compressed Stabilised Earth Blocks
CRZ	Coastal Regulation Zone
DDA	Donor-Driven Approach
GIZ	Deutsche Gesellschaft für Internationale Zusammenarbeit (Germany)
IFRC	International Federation of Red Cross and Red Crescent Societies
IRS	Indian Rupees
INGO	International Non-Governmental Organisation
KfW	Entwicklungsbank (Germany)
MoU	Memorandum of Understanding
MSSS	Madras Social Service Society
NCPDP	National Centre for Peoples' Action in Disaster Preparedness
NGO	Non-Governmental Organisation
ODA	Owner-Driven Approach
PMSSS	Pondicherry Multipurpose Social Service Society
PRA	Participatory Rural Appraisal
PMC	Project Management Consultant
PWD	Public Works Department
RBC	Reinforced Bonded Concrete
RCC	Reinforced Cement Concrete

SDC	Swiss Development Cooperation
SIFFS	South Indian Federation of Fishermen Societies
SKAT	Swiss Resource Centre and Consultancies for Development
TN	Tamil Nadu
UN	United Nations
UNDP	United Nations Development Programme
UNTRS	United Nations Team for Recovery Support
UToP	Union Territory of Puducherry
WB	World Bank

Note on Terminology

In this study the term 'fishers' is used as the best gender-neutral plural for people working in the local fishing industry.

The term 'village' is used whenever it refers to a 'revenue village'. In India, a 'revenue village' has definite, surveyed boundaries. It may comprise several 'hamlets' but the entire village will be treated as one unit for the presentation of the data. The term 'hamlet' will be used to refer to separate parts of a village.

Preamble

In February 2005, approximately one and a half months after the Indian Ocean tsunami of 2004 had hit many regions in Southeast Asia, I set off to Tamil Nadu to work as a member of the 'shelter team' in the reconstruction programme launched by the NGO Caritas India and its partners. I was appointed by Caritas Austria, one of Caritas India's funding partners, and I arrived at Chennai at a time when the world was still shaken by this terrible disaster. The question of how best the many villages and urban areas affected should be reconstructed was debated heatedly. I entered, as a young architect and for the first time, a chaotic and emotionally-charged working environment, one in which I would stay and work for more than two years.

Our team, two Indian engineers and myself, were assigned responsibility for guiding seven local partners (NGOs) through their efforts to errect post-disaster housing in the villages affected by the tsunami. In total, thirty seven villages in ten districts spread along the coastal belt of Tamil Nadu were provided with housing, and the projects ranged from reconstruction in-situ to relocation. During these years, our team was confronted with numerous challenges and constraints at various levels and various stages of this large reconstruction programme. However, there were two factors that impeded the programme most. Firstly, none of the local partners had experience in the construction of post-disaster housing as they focus on socio-economic issues. Thus, they needed to be introduced, first of all, to this specific building system and its procedures, and the fundamental themes related to it. Secondly, a premise of the reconstruction programme formulated by our team was that there had to be close cooperation between the architect and the villagers, particularly during the planning stage (see Caritas India 2005a). I soon realised, however, that the premise of 'close cooperation between the architect and the villagers' was easier said than done.

Tamil Nadu has many well established and experienced architects. While most of them focus exclusively on projects related to the urban context, only a few have experience of working on rural environments, not to mention post-disaster housing. Nevertheless, local architects were appointed by the bodies charged with the reconstruction and they were assigned responsibility for the planning and management of the projects.

The architects were of considerable value for the NGOs as they provided vital skills for the numerous practical and technical tasks to be handled during the building process. Still, were they of value for the villagers? Did the architects contribute to the realisation of housing projects that responded to the villagers' needs and aspirations?

What I witnessed and experienced first-hand helped to formulate my thesis that to be of value for the people in a delicate context such as that of post-disaster housing involves a great deal more than the mere application of creative urges and (technical) skills provided by formally trained architects. Two questions were raised by my experience. Which skills are required in this specific working context? Which role(s) should an architect take on so that people (with different socio-cultural backgrounds) benefit from it/them?

After having been confronted with these questions earlier during the course of a pilot housing project with a gypsy community in Northern Italy (Tauber 2005), and again during different development projects after my work assignment in Tamil Nadu, they led me to pursue a PhD, aiming to find out a great deal more.

Introduction

Some Facts

Globally, natural disasters are on the increase: storms, floods, famine, cyclones, drought, typhoons, earthquakes, mudslides and avalanches. According to the International Federation of the Red Cross and Red Crescent, 'an average of 354 natural disasters occurred throughout the world each year from 1991 to 1999'[1]. 'In the past decade an average of 456 disasters have been recorded annually, out of which only 29 were covered by the media in the West.'[2] Looking at the geographical distribution of these, 'Asia was the continent most often hit by natural disasters in 2011 (44.0%), followed by the Americas (28.0%), Africa (19.3%), Europe (5.4%) and Oceania (3.3%). This regional distribution of occurrence resembles the profile observed from 2001 to 2010' (Guha-Sapir *et al.* 2012: 2).

During the past two decades, non-governmental organisations (NGOs) have increased their profiles at local, national and international level, and they have also become recognised as important players in the field of post-disaster recovery and reconstruction (see Lewis *et al.* 2009: 1). The increase in the number and scale of the disasters has pushed NGOs to seek, among other experts, the skills of professionals of the built environment (see Lloyd-Jones 2009, Aquilino 2011, Desai 2011). Architects, engineers

1 | http://www.christianaid.org.uk/emergencies/prevention/facts.aspx (accessed on 02.09.2013).

2 | Data presented by Graham Saunders, Head, Shelter & Settlements, IFRC at the 6th International i-Rec Conference on 'Sustainable Post-Disaster reconstruction: From Recovery to Risk Reduction', in Ascona/Switzerland. Date of Presentation: 27.05.2013.

and land-use planners have been appointed as consultants, managers, planners and designers at local, national and international level. Nevertheless, the literature has so far neglected to examine the distinctiveness of this working context and to ascertain, based on empirical data, the skills required to realise the goal put forward by the NGOs, the creation of people-oriented housing. This research addresses this imbalance by examining permanent housing funded by international NGOs, implemented by local NGOs and planned by local architects in rural post-disaster environments affected by the Indian Ocean tsunami of 2004.

Post-Disaster Housing: A Challenging Working Context

One of the most challenging and at the same time most important tasks in post-disaster reconstruction is to organise the building process and the procedures related to it (Davidson 2010). According to Davidson, the degree of success of the project depends to a large extent on the skilful interplay and relationships between the multiple actors involved. Designing the process and defining the roles and responsibilities of the numerous actors (the people affected, NGO personnel, public authorities, professionals in various fields, and skilled and unskilled labour) in this particular context is, though, a delicate endeavour for a number of reasons.

Firstly, disasters create social disorder. They represent a time of chaos and sometimes of upheaval (see Luig 2012: 15). Some want to reconstruct the previous state of affairs. Others hope for a new beginning, for the opportunity to have a second chance in life (see Hoffman 1999: 150), and the building industry is called upon to provide more than just the provision of basic housing and services. The act of 'rebuilding is closely bound to how society frames its own values and re-establishes itself' (Duffy *et al.* 2013: 117). Potential participants (people affected, international, national and local NGOs, bi-lateral and multilateral agencies, and public authorities) in the process have many differences regarding their socio-cultural backgrounds, working cultures, powers and visions (see Boano *et al.* 2012), and conflict inevitably arises over what and how to reconstruct.[3]

3 | It is important to emphasise here that the actors (the people, NGOs, and government) are not seen as homogenous groups that share the same socio-eco-

Politicians, bureaucrats, middle men and entrepreneurs dream of the creation of entirely new villages (and/or cities), enforcing radical concepts of modernisation. 'Modern' technology is used, real and imaginary, 'as a symbol to reassure people that their new homes would be safer and more secure than those they had lost' (Desai 2011: 84). As a result, 'modern' construction technologies are in, and 'traditional' building techniques are out. 'Modern' settlement layouts and house styles are synonymous with a better future, while 'traditional' habitat structures and house layouts are equated with 'backwardness' (see Jigyasu 2002, 2006, 2010, Desai 2011). In other words, post-disaster reconstruction is characterised by disorientation, and bitter and tenacious negotiations over space, identity, and resources (see Boano *et al.* 2011, Luig 2012). Structures of power and inequality are revealed (see Luig 2012: 15) at local, national and international level, and the question of who decides what for whom (see Turner 2009 [1976]) becomes fundamental.

To complicate matters further, there is no clear project initiator, the equivalent of a building owner in a traditional building process (Davidson 2010: 99), in charge of specifying the project's brief. Public authorities, NGOs, bi-lateral and multilateral agencies all claim their right to co-determine the parameters of the reconstruction programme in general and the housing projects in particular.

Moreover, there is 'no pertinent earlier experience available due to the unique circumstances that characterise each disaster (location, gravity, time, socio-political context, etc.)' (*ibid*). Thus, each reconstruction process (and the procedures related to it) has to be designed from scratch.

Furthermore, providing housing is one of the most demanding activities after a disaster, because it operates in conditions of uncertainty, in regions struck by conflicts, in remote and environmentally delicate locations, and within severe budgetary constraints (see Wu *et al.* 2004, Steinberg *et al.* 2010). Added to this, the many actors involved (the donors, politicians, public and private agencies, international, national, and local NGOs, and the people affected) want results immediately, and time is of the essence.

---

nomic background, values and ideas (see also Guijt *et al.* 1998, Hüsken 2010, Sökefeld 2012). However, as this study is concerned with their interplay at various levels it will continue to refer to the people (and/or villagers), NGOs, and the government.

Acknowledging the socio-political dynamics of post-disaster contexts, and taking into consideration the intricacies on the ground, the NGO's approach to reconstruction and the role of the architect assigned responsibility for the planning and designing of the new houses (and habitats) become central. The following chapter will argue why.

NGOs, Architects and Post-Disaster Housing: Why Rethink the Role of the Architect?

Non-governmental organizations (NGOs) are high-profile actors in the field of international development, both as providers of services to vulnerable individuals and communities and as campaigning policy advocates (see Lewis *et al.* 2009). They began attracting attention during the late 1980s, and they appealed to different sections of the development community for different reasons. NGOs appealed to some western donors, who had become frustrated with the bureaucratic and inefficient government-to-government project-based aid then in vogue (see Lewis 2009: 16). NGOs provided 'an alternative and more flexible funding channel, which potentially offered a higher chance of local-level implementation and grassroots participation' (*ibid.*). According to Michael Cernea, NGOs embodied 'a philosophy that recognizes the centrality of people in development policies' and this, along with some other factors, gave them certain 'comparative advantages' over government and the public sector (1988: 8). NGOs were seen as fostering close cooperation with the people since they were more locally rooted organisations, and as a result, closer to marginalised groups than most public authorities were. Poor people were often found to have been bypassed by existing public services and programmes due to the fact that many public institutions 'faced resource shortages and their decision-making processes were captured by elites' (Lewis 2009: 16). Others also claimed that NGOs generally operated at a lower cost, and they were seen as 'possessing the scope to experiment and innovate with alternative ideas and approaches to development' (*ibid.*: 17).

While there have been many advocates for NGOs that stress their strengths, NGOs have also been subjected to fierce criticism. Different scholars have argued that the NGOs' claims can not be substantiated in many ways (see Tendler 1982, Tvedt 1988). Michael Edwards (1999), a writer and activist sympathetic towards NGOs, argues that few NGOs have developed structures that genuinely respond to the needs of the people, and even though they talk of 'partnership', the control over financial resources and decision making remains to a large extent unequal. With the rise of NGOs working in the context of post-disaster reconstruction during the past decade (see CHAPTER Some Facts) they have challenged the work of the public sector. At the same time, their own shortfalls have been exposed, and awareness has grown of the fact that there is a 'need for NGOs to be accountable to key stakeholders, both to consolidate their ethical position and to foster credibility' (Meding *et al.* 2009: 38).

A series of reports by ALNAP[4] has found that 'shelter and housing work is the least successful form of aid when compared to other humanitarian intervention sectors' (quoted in IFRC 2003: 4), and Cuny's (1983) groundbreaking post-disaster housing analysis for Oxfam America has not lost any of its relevance. Cuny found that most NGOs rush to build housing without any experience of the construction industry whatsoever, lacking a subtle approach and long-term commitment. Furthermore, he has shown that the majority of NGOs lack an understanding of the complexities of post-disaster housing, and they fail to link post-disaster housing to the local building process, a critical parameter for an integrated approach. As a consequence, many permanent houses provided by NGOs are deemed to be inappropriate and they remain, in the worst case, unoccupied (see Barakat 2003, Steinberg 2007). NGOs have trusted in the expertise provided by formally trained architects, assuming that the use of these professionals leads to the realisation of people-oriented post-disaster housing.[5] However, studies have highlighted that despite their involvement projects continue to fail, culturally and technically (see Ortiz 2002, Karunasena *et al.* 2010, Boano *et al.* 2011, 2012, Tauber 2013, 2014). What are the reasons?

---

4 | The Active Learning Network for Accountability and Performance in Humanitarian Action (ALNAP) is an interagency forum dedicated to improving learning among agencies working in humanitarian response (see http://www.alnap.org/).

5 | A frequent answer given during the interviews carried out with NGO representatives in decision-making positions was: 'We expect architects to realise people-oriented projects because they are not only concerned with technical issues, unlike the engineer. Architects plan for, and work with, people, and they know how to do that.'

The relevance of built-environment professional expertise in disaster response in general, and of architects in the reconstruction of permanent housing in particular, seems obvious on the face of it. Indeed, the value and significance of involving architects has been stressed by various researchers (Aquilino 2011, Harris 2011), and a guide for humanitarian agencies has been published, aiming to demonstrate the 'value of using built environment professionals' (Lloyd-Jones 2009: 5). Being general in scope, this guide deals broadly with disaster risk reduction and response. It mentions the typical built environment professionals (engineers, planners, architects and surveyors) and their skills, attempting to delineate their roles in terms of a typical set of activities. The architect's activities (and his/her value) were defined in terms of the following fields: 'design and building technology for dwellings (including open spaces), supervision and advice as the buildings are constructed, providing training in construction, retrofitting and maintenance, overseeing the delivery of dwellings, and identifying the contribution communities can make (and feed that into cost model)' (*ibid.*: 29).

The importance of appointing professionals of the built environment is emphasised by these scholars, and the NGO's choice of, and reasoning for, appointing architects seems to derive from an approach which owes much to the formal sector (see CHAPTER Building Cultures). However, the literature has neglected to examine the degree of 'success'[6] of these professionals in general and of the architect in particular. To be more precise, it is not known if formally trained architects have contributed to the realisation of people-oriented housing from the perspective of the villagers themselves. Hence, there is a need for a realistic picture, as argued here, of the potential and limitations of this professional in rural post-disaster environments, based on empirical data.

6 | The term 'success', as used here, refers to the inhabitants' degree of satisfaction regarding their new house (and new habitat in case of relocation). 'Success' was defined by the villagers based on the following parameters: size of the plot, size of the house, orientation and type of sanitary facilities, availability of a *puja* (prayer) room, provision of an outdoor kitchen, possibility of future extension of the house and the hamlet, quality of construction, possibility of self-repair, participation in decision-making stages, close interaction with the planner of the new house (and habitat), and carrying out of *pujas* during the building process (see CHAPTER The Household Interviews).

This study attempts a first step in this direction. Based on quantitative and qualitative data obtained in the villages, it seeks to shed light on the intricacies of the reconstruction process as a whole in rural environments and on the challenging task of identifying and assigning adequate personnel and their roles during a complex building process. Aiming to assess the degree of success of the architect involved, it is interested in the three questions of what, which and when? What was the architect's scope of work? Which results were obtained at project level? When was he/she involved during the course of the building process? In doing so, the study seeks to identify, first of all, the gaps in skills and planning during the course of the building process and the fundamental parameters which have an impact on the degree of success. From this it aims to explore the challenges architects are faced with at village level, to find out the different skills and capacities required to overcome them, and to ascertain if formally trained architects are adequately equipped for these tasks. Furthermore, this study aims to identify the fundamental parameters that are useful for defining the role and scope of work of the architect in a context as intricate as that of building permanent houses.

According to Davidson, the success of a project depends, to a large extent, on the relationships between the multiple actors involved, and their roles during the course of the building process. Hence, the challenge is, amongst others, 'to "design" the relationships of the various actors involved in the best interest of the recovery effort' (2010: 88). Deciding what is to be produced and who is to participate in reconstruction is difficult since conditions are not stable.[7] Moreover, the actors involved (the people affected, local and central governments, NGOs and international agencies and, of course, professionals of the built environment, builders, and skilled and unskilled labour) possess as many differences as they have different socio-cultural backgrounds, with different languages, technical, cultural and economic values and working cultures. They may be commercial or non-commercial, and they may be driven by priorities imported

7 | Davidson outlines the challenges (and the differences) of the management and procurement processes during the course of building projects under relatively stable circumstances and during unstable conditions, i.e. post-disaster reconstruction. The premise is that construction and reconstruction problems are by their very nature *wicked*, and that organizing for their 'solution' is of itself a major design problem (2010: 90).

from elsewhere or from another context. Thus, the questions of 'who does what, why and when' (*ibid*: 108) need to be answered afresh and sensitively in each context.

Taking into consideration the tricky task of defining the role and scope of the work of the actors involved, this study has four main aims:

- To analyse the reconstruction process comprehensively (who did what and when) in order to illustrate the distinctiveness and complexity of a rural post-disaster housing project, and to examine if the involvement of formally trained architects has proven to be significant for the goal put forward by the NGOs, the realisation of people-oriented housing.
- To ascertain which skills and capacities are required at project level, and why?
- To help NGOs and architects working in this particular context act more cautiously, and prudently, when designing and taking on roles during the building process.
- To provide a foundation for educational institutions for the design of a specific training course for architects who intend to work in the context of (rural) post-disaster reconstruction.

I seek to approach these aims by analysing the three case studies against the following background:

- The rural environment

Rural habitats in India follow their own logics with regard to the use (and meaning) of open and private spaces, of neighbourhood, and of construction materials. Each area within a hamlet has certain peculiarities. Temples spaces, trees, the different styles of houses and their location reflect a very strong hierarchy, which is specific to each and every village. In the creation of rural habitats 'folk beliefs, caste, kinship, family, marriage, rules of inheritance of property and of succession, etc., play an important role' (Chandhoke 1990: 3).

- The rural building culture (in normal times)

In rural India building a house takes place in the informal sector: people build the houses either by themselves or, if the financial means are available, this process will be guided (and executed) by local professionals (masons, carpenters) (Davis 1999, Ifthekar 2011). The building cultures in place in rural contexts follow their own logics. They differ from formalised and institutionalised building cultures in many ways, yet share the same aim: the realisation of a built environment (see CHAPTER Building Cultures). In this context, formally trained architects do not play any role whatsoever during the building process. They are 'outsiders'.[8] Still, in the aftermath of the Indian Ocean Tsunami of 2004 the values of a formal building culture and its professionals were, in many cases, superimposed on those of the villages.

- Formally trained architects

Current architectural education does not equip the professional to work in contexts that differ from his/her own socio-cultural environment (see Rieger-Jandl 2005, Davis 2006, Latter 2006). 'Traditional' architecture and construction technologies are seen as being 'primitive' by architecture schools (see also Oliver 1999, 2003, Asquith *et al.* 2006, Asquith 2006, Davis 1999, 2006, Latter 2006), and there is the assumption that the future has nothing to learn from the past. Experimenting with and developing new and 'modern' construction materials as well as technologies is an essential part of architectural education today (see Davis 2006). Moreover, architecture departments in universities do not introduce aspiring architects to the skills and methods of other disciplines (for example sociology or social anthropology), nor do they integrate building know-how available outside the academic circle into their courses. Architecture today is mostly taught as an individual pursuit and expression of the designer (see Davis 2006, Latter 2006). None of these premises and attitudes provide architects with the skills required for a working context as intricate as that of post-disaster housing.

- The labour market

Investigations during the course of this study have revealed that only a few colleges world-wide (see CHAPTER A Challenging Task Ahead) offer specific training courses for architects with a focus on post-disaster reconstruction. Hence, NGOs face difficulties when identifying adequately skilled professionals. This situation is further aggravated after major disasters, when many agencies compete for human resources (see Harris 2006).

---

8 | Interview with the Indian engineer, Rajendra Desai, who has worked extensively in the context of post-disaster housing over the past two decades. Personal communication on 22.12.2011 (Internet phone).

- The NGO as provider and employer of architects

As has been mentioned already, many NGOs participating in reconstruction operate outside their traditional field of expertise (see Barakat 2003, Steinberg 2007). Thus, they are neither familiar with the building industry and the themes and procedures related to it, nor with the challenging task of designing the building process and assigning the 'right' personnel. Reconstruction can be undertaken in a number of different ways. The case studies under examination in this study were all implemented within a donor-driven scheme. Below, the characteristics of this scheme will be explained in more detail.

NGOs as Provider: The Donor-Driven Approach

There is a growing body of literature concerned with the merits and drawbacks of different reconstruction schemes (Twigg 2000, Barakat 2003, Harvey 2005, Duyne-Barenstein 2006, Karunasena *et al.* 2010). Broadly, there are two main reconstruction approaches: the owner-driven approach (ODA) and the donor-driven approach (DDA).[9] The owner-driven approach enables people to undertake the building work themselves, with external financial, material and technical assistance. This approach can include the repair and reconstruction of houses. The criteria for financial support are based on damage assessments. This approach does not, necessarily, mean that the people build their houses on their own, rather, within this approach they retain, to a large extent, control over the entire building process.

Contrary to the owner-driven approach, in the donor-driven approach the project is fully managed by the agency and its personnel, from inception to completion. In many cases, planning (designing) is carried out by architects, construction by contractors, and supervision by engineers (and/or architects). Traditionally, governments and private agencies providing housing have assumed that this approach is the quickest and most

9 | These two approaches can be further divided, and thus many more exist in the literature. However, it is not the scope of this thesis to describe the various types of approaches in detail (their merits and faults). For further reading on this subject the following studies are suggested: Barakat (2003), Duyne-Barenstein (2006), Karunasena *et al.* (2010), Lyons (2009, 2010).

effective way to reconstruct houses. However, studies have shown that this claim could not be sustained in many respects and for a number of reasons (Oliver-Smith 1991, Barakat 2003, Duyne-Barenstein 2006, Lyons 2010, Karunasena *et al.* 2010).

First, the donor-driven approach tends to be top-down and to exclude people from the entire reconstruction process (Lyons 2010). Moreover, comparative studies highlight that this approach has been less successful than the owner-driven approach with regard to a number of significant parameters, namely: 'a) durability of house, b) availability of space, c) incorporation of people's requirements, d) flexibility for future changes, e) location of the house, f) size of land, g) overall facilities provided, and h) response time[10]. Only two parameters scored higher ratings for the donor-driven approach, namely aesthetics and functionality' (Karunasena *et al.* 2010: 180). This is 'not surprising because donor-driven housing projects were generally designed by professional architects' (*ibid.*). Despite these deficiencies, the donor-driven approach has been the most widespread in many post-disaster contexts, for the following reasons. After major disasters, funds have increasingly been channelled through large international agencies (see Steinberg 2007, Lewis 2009), and thus, local governments have been inclined to outsource the reconstruction of permanent houses to private agencies and NGOs (see Duyne-Barenstein 2010). Further, as the majority of NGOs have no experience in the field of housing in general, and in the provision of large-scale permanent housing in particular, they tend to adopt the donor-driven approach in order to externalise or reduce risk and construction time (see Lyons 2010).

After the Indian Ocean tsunami of 2004, the donor-driven approach was applied in most of the affected regions. While in some contexts different approaches were possible (for example in Sri Lanka), in others (for example in TN and the UToP, India) the state government outsourced reconstruction as far as possible to private agencies and NGOs (see Duyne-Barenstein 2010).

Due to the flow of grant funding (see CHAPTER Locating the Field), many NGOs expanded their initial commitment from emergency aid to the provision of housing. While they had previous experience when responding to emergencies, reconstruction work has been very taxing for

10 | The term 'response time' refers to the time-span required before construction can begin.

most of them, as many operated outside their traditional sphere of expertise and thus they lacked experience and skills (see Steinberg 2007: 157). Moreover, the scale of reconstruction and the management of large-scale projects as a whole were often far beyond the capabilities of both experienced and inexperienced organisations.

To get some idea of the scale of involvement it is interesting to look at a few NGOs such as the International Federation of Red Cross and Red Crescent Societies (IFRC), the international Caritas confederation, Oxfam, or the Indian NGO Mata Amritanandamayi Math. The IFRC, for example, provided 30,265 houses in Sri Lanka, 21,342 houses in Indonesia, and 1,514 houses in the Maldives (IFRC 2011: 12). In Sri Lanka alone the houses built by the IFRC represent '30 per cent of the total number of houses that were damaged or destroyed' (IFRC 2009: 8). The international Caritas confederation built permanent houses in India, Sri Lanka and in Indonesia. In India, a total of 13,472 permanent houses were constructed in the states of Tamil Nadu, Andhra Pradesh, Kerala, and in the Union Territories of Puducherry and the Andaman & Nicobar Islands. 13,391 houses were built in Indonesia, and 6,800 houses in Sri Lanka (Caritas Internationalis 2007: 5). Oxfam built a total of 2,900 houses in Indonesia, Sri Lanka and India (Oxfam 2009), and the Indian NGO Mata Amritanandamayi Math constructed 6,200 houses in India and Sri Lanka.[11] The following figure provides an overview of the different types of agencies involved.

11 | http://archives.amritapuri.org/tsunami/tsunami.php (accessed on 01.02.2013).

Figure 1: Different types of development agencies, potential partnerships and flow of resources

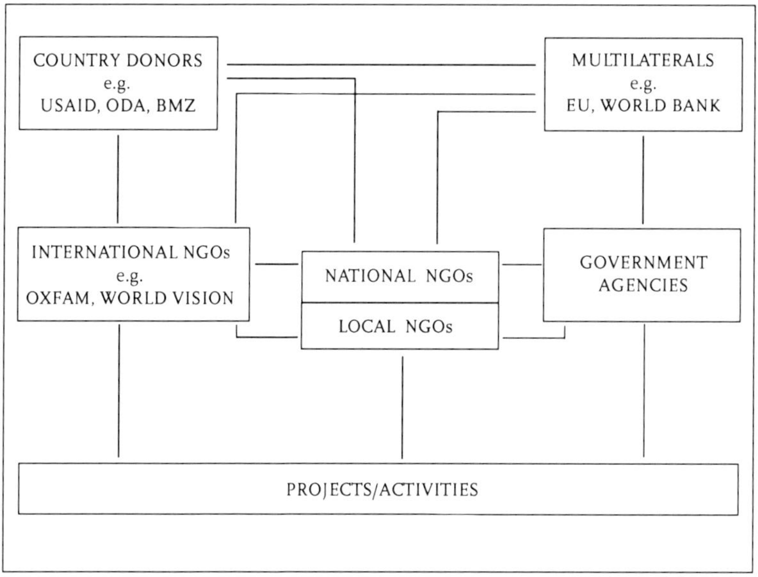

Source: adapted from: Gardner *et al.* 1996: 9

Common to all the three NGOs examined here was that they were new to the field of post-disaster housing, and they were all funded by international NGOs. However, they approached the task of reconstruction in the villages using different building processes, methods and strategies.

Most importantly, the architect's role and scope of work varied significantly, from 'project management consultant', to 'draftswoman', to 'surveyor-anthropologist'.[12] The following study will investigate whether the different roles (and scope of work) facilitated the realisation of people-oriented housing.

12 | It was found important to name the different types of architects and to highlight possible roles for the purpose of this study. The name 'project management consultant' was given by an NGO (see Caritas India 2005a: 3). The names 'draftswoman' and 'surveyor-anthropologist' were assigned by the author based on their scope of work for that particular project.

Locating the Field

Southeast Asia after the Indian Ocean Tsunami of 2004

On 26 December 2004 a severe earthquake measuring 8.9 on the Richter scale hit northern Sumatra. The earthquake resulted in one of the most powerful tsunamis in recorded history, affecting many countries in Southeast Asia, with Indonesia, Sri Lanka, Thailand and India being among the worst affected. Large-scale housing had to be provided in the aftermath of the tsunami. In Indonesia, for example, it was estimated that around '101,000 housing units needed replacement (88,000 in Aceh; 13,000 in Nias), and some 95,000 units needed to be rehabilitated (71,000 in Aceh; 24,000 in Nias)' (Steinberg 2007: 151). In Sri Lanka early estimates suggested 'the total number of houses fully or partially damaged to be around 113,000. Revised figures published by the Department of Census and Statistics at the end of August 2005 recorded over 77,561 houses to be affected by the tsunami out of which 41,393 houses were fully destroyed and 36,168 partially damaged' (ADBI 2005: 29). In Thailand 3,302 houses were reported to be completely destroyed, and another 1,504 damaged. In total it was estimated that 3,558 new houses would be needed (ADBI 2007: 11). In India, it was reported that 153,585 houses were affected (ADB 2005: 50) in the states of Andhra Pradesh, Kerala, Tamil Nadu and the Union Territories of Puducherry and the Andaman & Nicobar Islands.

The Indian Ocean tsunami of 2004 brought an unprecedented gathering of donor organisations to locations throughout South and Southeast

Asia.[1] It has been suggested that the high-level of aid offered to tsunami-affected areas was prompted by extensive world-wide media coverage (Clarke *et al.* 2010: 10). In Indonesia, for example, 'some 200 NGOs were contributing to housing construction in the field' (Steinberg *et al.* 2010: 10). While 'some NGOs adapted to [the] tasks, several were initially unable to produce housing of solid and permanent construction [...]' (*ibid.*: 11). Often projects are unsustainable: at best, houses are remodelled by their occupants; at worst, they are simply rejected and abandoned. This is because, in many cases, the delivery of housing lack proper planning (Barakat 2003). Furthermore, cultural and social concerns were not taken into consideration (Boen *et al.* 2005), and the scope reduced, predominantly, to mere technical matters such as building designs, the choice of construction materials and construction technologies (Lizarralde *et al.* 2010).

Why Tamil Nadu and the Union Territory of Puducherry?

In India, the waves, triggered by the tsunami, lashed over 2,260 kilometres of the coastlines of Andhra Pradesh, Kerala, Tamil Nadu, and the Union Territories of Puducherry and the Andaman & Nicobar Islands.

Nearly '80 per cent of the human and material losses were concentrated in the state of Tamil Nadu' (Duyne-Barenstein 2010: 162), with a total of '13 districts, 238 villages and 418 hamlets affected' (Government of TN 2008: xvi). The Union Territory of Puducherry[2] (including Karaikal) recorded a total of 19 villages and 38 hamlets which had been affected (Government of Puducherry 2006). Tamil Nadu (hereafter TN) and the Union Territory of Puducherry (hereafter UToP) together have about 1,000 km of coastline. Hundreds of fishing hamlets are dotted along the coast, and the fishers were, being located very close to the sea, among the worst hit. This region was selected as the arena for this study for two reasons.

First, governments outsourced reconstruction as far as possible to private agencies and NGOs (see Duyne-Barenstein 2010, 2011a, b). In TN

1 | Multilateral development agencies such as the UNDP, the World Bank, the Asian Development Bank, local, national and international NGOs, bilateral donor governments, national, and local governments.

2 | Pondicherry was renamed Puducherry in 2006 (The Hindu 2006).

72 NGOs participated in the reconstruction process constructing 32,552 houses out of 53,562 houses during the first phase (Government of TN 2005c: 49).

Figure 2: Degree of destruction in the states affected in India

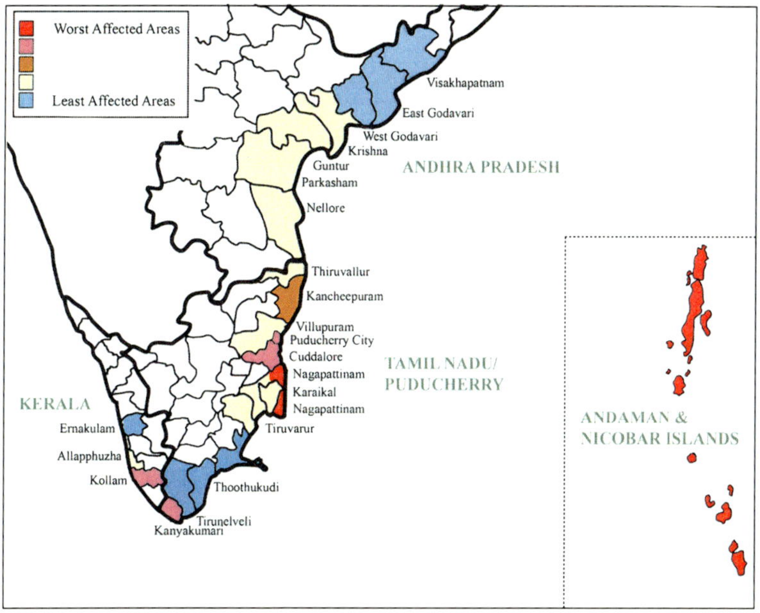

Source: adapted from UNTRS 2006b: inside front cover

In Nagapattinam district, for example, 43 NGOs provided housing in 80 hamlets (*ibid.*: 50). In the UToP 14 NGOs constructed approximately 10,131 houses, out of 12,380 in total (Government of Puducherry 2006). Most projects were implemented as public-private-partnerships. The NGOs involved, however, did not have to follow, unlike in the other states in India, a model-house design predefined by each respective government. They were free to assign architects, to develop the master plan of the hamlet and the house layout, as well as decide on the construction technologies of the new houses. This provided an opportunity to study the merits and drawbacks of different process-designs applied by various NGOs when assigning different roles to architects. More than four years after the completion of the projects selected for this study it was possible to examine the degree of success of assigning architects to work on post-disaster housing.

Second, many disasters affect rural environments.[3] However, the literature has so far neglected to study rural contexts (see CHAPTER Existing Literature). Thus, this research presents empirical data obtained in three hamlets located in the most affected districts of rural TN and the UToP. Case Study 1, Keezhakazakudy-metu (Tsunami Nagar), is located in Karaikal district. Case Study 2, Shanmuga Nagar, is situated in Cuddalore and Case Study 3, Tarangambadi (Tsunami Nagar), in Nagapattinam district.

Figure 3: Research area and location of the three case studies

3 | Some examples of post-disaster large-scale housing programmes undertaken within the past 10 years are: the Bam/Iran earthquake 2003 (rural), the Indian Ocean tsunami 2004 (urban and rural), the New Orleans/USA hurricane Katrina 2005 (urban), the Pakistan earthquake 2005 (urban and rural), the Pakistan floods 2010 (rural), the Chile earthquake 2010 (urban), the Haiti earthquake 2010 (urban), and the Japan tsunami 2011 (urban and rural).

Existing Literature on the Role of Architects in Designing Post-Disaster Housing

A debate around the role and the relevance of architects in the context of post-disaster housing has emerged only recently, and has been, so far, controversial. On the one hand, it is argued that the assignment of this professional is an adequate response to post-disaster housing due to their 'training, competence and ingenuity' (Aquilino 2011: 8). On the other hand, architects have been criticised in post-disaster scenarios as 'silent perpetrators of unsustainable solutions that focus solely on physical deliverables, rendering them as "useless"' (Boano *et al.* 2011: 293). While both arguments are justified, it is critical to examine the architect's role in a more balanced way, as it is not a simple question of yes, architects are needed, or no, architects are useless, rather, it is a question of identifying and assigning them an appropriate role within a specific local context.

Reconstruction has already been described as one of the most demanding forms of activity after a disaster, because it operates in conditions of uncertainty, in regions struck by conflicts, in remote locations, and within severe time and budgetary constraints (see CHAPTER Post-Disaster Housing). According to Martin Sökefeld, the 'complexity derives from the fact that none of the institutions involved actually constitutes a clearly bounded, unified actor' (2012: 187). Many actors are involved in a dense and 'constricted environment characterised further by the primacy of speed, performance and numbers' (Boano *et al.* 2011: 293). The likely result of this is that one person, or profession, alone can not make that much of a difference. In such a complex situation, which role should an architect adopt?

Architects are, as argued by some researchers, indispensable professionals in post-disaster housing, and they are needed 'more than ever' (Aquilino 2011: 8). According to Aquilino, their know-how is critical in three main ways. First of all, 'well trained architects who are actively building and have wide-ranging experience' are needed, for 'their ability to erect secure, durable structures and because they are expert contract managers capable of calculating needs, resources and budgets' (*ibid*: 9). 'Representation' is the 'second area: architects working in close collaboration with communities can help them act on their own behalf [...] They can represent community consensus on viable projects to intransigent or indifferent governments, and this, in turn, promotes local independence. It is terribly difficult for communities to successfully represent their own best interests in the face of intractable politics' (*ibid.*). The third function is 'vision'. Architectural expertise can help to 'imagine a better future' (*ibid.*). Harris also notes that they are, in addition to being designers and builders, 'also expert contract managers able to see the arc of a project. They are the part responsible for taking the budget and resources available to a credible, pertinent, long-term built solution, along an optimal path' (2011: 13). Moreover, as Harris further argues, architects are adept at planning methods that take into consideration community consultation and planning. 'Project design is imbedded not only in building design but in how the whole construction process is coordinated. This is where architects become not only relevant, but vital' (*ibid.*: 15).

So, if architects are adept at this type of work and are involved in many NGO- and government-funded projects, why do post-disaster projects so often fail in terms of their practical usability and acceptance by the people?

Considering the complexity of the tasks to be fulfilled, the pro-architect positions of Aquilino (2011) and Harris (2011) are problematic for various reasons. First of all, they depict a truly flat and idealised image of the architect. The architect is portrayed as *the* suitable professional, regardless of his/her training (which differs from university to university), regardless of his/her socio-cultural background, and regardless of his/her working experience (which may range from interior design to urban planning), regardless of the particular context of a post-disaster project with its peculiarities, unique qualities and requirements. Moreover, their argument about the architect appears to be derived very much from a formal-sector approach in place in 'western' societies, ignoring 'non-western' societies,[1] their realities, and forms of knowledge and wisdom. In fact, in most countries (and in particular in rural environments) construction occurs in the informal sector, whereby artisans, village elders, informal professionals such as masons and carpenters guide this activity (see CHAPTER Building Cultures). Their insights and expertise (and the fact that architects can gain from their on-the-ground embedded experience and know-how) are completely neglected. This ignorance, and the one-way, top-down concept of an omnipotent architect has often led to technically and culturally inappropriate projects. Finally, the pro-architect view turns a blind eye to the necessity of multidisciplinary cooperation in the course of reconstruction, to ensure a holistic response. Know-how and the tools of cultural and social disciplines, of land-use planning, of engineering, of geology, and of organisational management are required in order to handle the many levels of complexity, and to build, as an ultimate goal, people-oriented houses. Hence, it is pretentious (and naïve) to assume that *the* architect is the answer to the problem.

There is the need, as discussed by others, to reflect on the traditional role of the architect as defined in 'western' societies (see CHAPTER The Illusion of Certainty), particularly because providing post-disaster housing poses immense challenges.

Ortiz calls for an 'urgent need to make profound changes in the formation of the architect' (2002: 19) involved in post-disaster housing, by comparing the technocratic and 'dictating' (2002: 15) role of (high-profile) architects during the reconstruction programme in Kobe after the earthquake of 1995 with the architect as 'facilitator and committed supporter of the affected population' (*ibid.*) in the case of Mexico City after the earth-

1 | The term 'western' as used here refers to Stuart Hall's discourse on an idea, the concept of 'the West'. It allows us, according to Hall, to characterise and classify societies into different categories, i.e. 'western' and 'non-western', and it provides a standard or model of comparison (1992: 186). This image, or idea, works in conjunction with other images or ideas, for example, '"western" = urban = developed; or "non-western" = non-industrial = rural = agricultural = underdeveloped' (*ibid.*). It provides criteria of evaluation against which other societies are ranked and around which powerful positive and negative feelings are clustered. 'The meaning of this term is, therefore, virtually identical to that of the word 'modern'' (*ibid.*).

quake of 1985. In the first case, the 'reconstruction plan would be imposed without further consideration in order to achieve a rapid, efficient and economically reasonable reconstruction' (*ibid.*: 16), whereas in the case of Mexico City the NGOs, architects and other professionals together with the inhabitants 'occupied the streets en masse to fight for their rights' (*ibid.*: 16–17). As a result, the government opened up dialogues and devised a participatory reconstruction strategy.

Sanderson (2010) provoked an interesting debate questioning the relevance and the appropriateness of the knowledge of formally-trained architects in dealing with these challenges. Architects are, according to Sanderson, often the last people needed in disaster reconstruction, as they are taught to focus on the product (a building) and thus 'ownership of the design rests with them and fellow professionals' (2010: 2). Hence, as argued by Sanderson, many projects planned by architects have been inappropriate and not in line with the users' needs. Above all, the results can be 'painful' when, as in the case of New Orleans after hurricane Katrina in 2005, high profile architects produced 'funky housing types' (*ibid.*).[2] Unless architects move beyond their traditional role as designers of buildings in places of relative certainty to become 'facilitators of building processes that involve people in places of uncertainty and rapid change they will remain on the margins of humanitarian response' (*ibid.*: 3).

In their paper 'Architecture at Risk (?): The Ambivalent Nature of Post-Disaster Practice', Boano *et al.* question the state and the role of architecture, calling for a 'renewed anthropocentric post-disaster practice' (2012: 1). They examine the 'ambiguously risky role of silently complicit architects and conventional architectural practice in the delivery of post-disaster housing, as well as the expedient nature of recovery and provision that tends to threaten the value of architecture, which is often seen as object-centric in such contexts' (*ibid.*: 2). Architecture, according to Boano *et al.*, has the potential to – when critically reflecting back on itself and looking away from the objective design and provision of space – enable

2 | In 2007 the NGO Make it Right was founded by the American actor Brad Pitt with the aim of building 'healthy homes, buildings and communities for people in need. Make It Right is building 150 safe, sustainable homes in New Orleans' Lower 9th Ward, the neighbourhood most devastated by Hurricane Katrina. To date, 86 homes are built.' Renowned architects were invited to plan the houses. http://makeitright.org/where-we-work/new-orleans/ (accessed on 14.03.2013).

'individuals to intervene within the building process with their own set of ideas, aspirations and articulation of spatial values' (*ibid.*: 9). However, in the context of post-disaster housing architecture tends to be 'physically objective and superficial: a merely service oriented practice inescapably located in the disaster relief industry paradoxes of speed, numbers and turn-key typologies' (*ibid.*). Should this signal a total dismissal of the discipline?

Post-disaster housing is embedded in a predominantly hegemonic, top-down, and technology-driven context (see Boano *et al.* 2011). The parameters of the spaces to be reconstructed are defined by those in power, namely politicians, 'experts', technocrats and the decision makers of the agencies providing assistance. The voices of those without power are excluded, and 'the production of space is an inherently conflictive process where competing forces and contentious actions both for and against the status quo are manifested' (*ibid.*: 293).

If architects wish to contribute significantly to post-disaster housing they need to shift their role to what is needed in a given situation. What would such a shift in the architect's role look like? Adopting a theoretical framework of postcolonial discourse[3] in the case of post-disaster Chile, Boano *et al.* discuss a 'possibly innovative way of looking at experts as *trans-*

3 | Postcolonial theory refers to, most simply, the rereading of history to reveal the economic, cultural, linguistic and social strategies used in order to create and maintain an unequal distribution of power between the colonised and the coloniser. The discourse, however, does not refer to the past, but to the effects that colonialism continues to have in the world today. 'the postcolonial is a discourse of the minorities which offers the possibility to question, or challenge, traditional assumptions - attitudes and ideologies - according to which certain groups are inherently superior to others' (Hérnandez 2010: 15). Indian-born Homi K. Bhaba, one of the leading exponents of postcolonial theory, points out, for example, that 'international aid to the poor countries of the developing world does not necessarily lead to the eradication of poverty, nor is the aim of such aid to alleviate the uneven distribution of power in the world. On the contrary, the practices of 'conditionality' with which economic, educational and technological assistance is offered to nations in the developing world (or Third World) guarantee that the First World nations retain their position of power' (*ibid.*). Why should this discourse be relevant for architects? According to Bhaba, architecture was one of the principal means used by colonisers to impose a new social and political order and

lators, aiming to include the voices of those excluded by dominant forms of knowledge production' (*ibid.*: 295). The 'expert' as translator should, according to Boano *et al.*, interpret the 'needs of the affected population, rather than imposing power and dominance' (*ibid.*: 296).

Whilst I agree with the necessity of questioning the role of formally trained architects in the context of post-disaster housing, the debate as a whole has been, so far, narrow in the literature, as it has been based on 'western' ideological preconceptions (where architecture is the domain of architects, whatever his/her role may be), rather than on local practices, requirements and operational necessities. Moreover, the search for an adequate response to the question has been theoretical (Lizarralde *et al.* 2010, Aquilino 2011, Harris 2011, Boano *et al.* 2012), in that it has been related to urban contexts only (Ortiz 2002, Boano *et al.* 2011). Yet, the debate has neglected to address the theme in relation to rural post-disaster environments, and to examine precisely the tasks to be handled at various operational levels, and the relevant expertise required during the course of a project.

This study addresses this imbalance and complements the existing corpus of work by taking into consideration the following ideas.

Architects 'contribute to only three per cent of the world's built environment' (Aquilino 2011: 8), and their contribution is found, to a large extent, in urban contexts only (this is even more the case in so-called developing countries). In India, for example, the construction of housing in rural areas 'is a labour shared by the community, where the making and reshaping of homes is a consequence of the strong ties of kinship, the family and caste organization [...] Moreover, the severity of the environment [...] and the limitation of resources, impose restrictions that have kept most of the conventional architects away' (Bhatia 1991: 202–203). To this day, formally trained architects hardly play any role whatsoever in rural housing (see CHAPTER Building Cultures). Thus, entering rural (post-disaster) housing means, for most architects, breaking new ground. Therefore, it is all the more critical to fill the gap in the literature by giving a realistic picture of the potential, and at the same time the limitations, of formally trained architects in rural post-disaster contexts.

'architects are largely complicit with the above-mentioned structures of socio-cultural and political hegemony' (*ibid.*: 16).

Secondly, I aim to demonstrate that the suitable role for an architect can not be determined in isolation from a given context, since the architect is one out of many actors, intertwined in a net of conflicting human relationships. 'Working with others that we disagree with, that we do not understand, that we do not have much respect for, or that we might even dislike is just plain hard' (Briand 1999: 8), and, thus, operating inclusively, a premise for the realisation of people-oriented projects, is difficult. In a working environment such as that portrayed here, architects deal with far more than the facts at hand and technical or managerial matters. They are expected (by their employer) to approach the many problems they face neutrally, rationally, and technically (based on their training, knowledge and expertise). That the architects themselves are part of an essentially political policy-making process is ignored. For whom do they think and on behalf do they speak, after all?

NGOs assume the appointment of the 'expert'[4] to be the appropriate response to the many problems posed by the disaster (see CHAPTER The Illusion of Certainty). However, as I will argue here, one of the reasons for the failure of the projects (from the villager's perspective) is *because* of this paradigm at agency level. While architects may provide skills and techniques of relevance during the course of a project, how, why, at which stage and for whom these 'experts' may be a valuable resource is yet to be examined comprehensively (including from the villagers' perspective).

Finally, I believe that it is critical that the debate around the role of the architect is embedded in practical post-disaster architectural theory, which is both grounded in practice and which helps to explain and understand practice. Theory should be related strongly to reality. I concur with Alvesson and Sköldberg's view that 'empirical material can inspire ideas and theories, endowing them with credibility, clarifying them and, in the case of theories, making them more stringent' (2000: 275). Empirical data

---

4 | The term 'expert' used here and throughout this study refers to professionals who are considered to possess expertise in a certain discipline (in this case architecture), by virtue of, usually formal, training/education and practice. Even where quote marks are not used, I continue to question the term itself which defines some types of knowledge as expertise while discrediting other forms of knowledge (see CHAPTER The Illusion of Certainty).

can be useful to deepen and also to revise theory; empirical methods may expose themes of relevance that have, so far, been neglected in theory.[5]

It was my own experience as a project manager in post-tsunami TN, and the many stories on the reality of post-disaster reconstruction told by architects (and engineers), which inspired me to go beyond a mere theoretical discussion of the role of architects in rural post-disaster housing. If post-disaster architecture theory is to be of real use to NGOs and architects, it needs to address practice as it is actually encountered. In this way the empirical material I have drawn from practice should be seen as one component of my efforts to make the case for a particular way of understanding the complex reality of involving architects in an intricate environment, such as that portrayed in this study. It is hoped that insights from practice will contribute to stronger and deeper theory, useful to both NGOs and architects who aim to build people-oriented post-disaster housing.

5 | The French sociologist Pierre Bourdieu (1930–2002) sought to connect his theoretical ideas with empirical research grounded in everyday life, and his work can be seen as a sociology of culture or, as he labelled it, a 'Theory of Practice'. His contributions to sociology were both evidential and theoretical (that is, calculated through both systems), see Bourdieu (1977, 1992).

Building Cultures

> [A]lthough individual building cultures handle different issues in similar ways, different cultures vary in the way they work.
> Howard Davis, 1999: 26

> As an imperialist fantasy, the normative models of modernism have excluded from the annals of 'modern' the ordinary, the irregular, and the changing vernacular, even within the coterie of 'modern' nations.
> Jyoti Hosagrahar, 2005: 6

> No college teaches you sensitivity for 'traditional' building cultures.
> Rajendra Desai[1]

The 'Modern' and the 'Traditional'

One of the major challenges in post-disaster reconstruction is, as argued in this study, the design of the building process with regard to the roles and responsibilities of the various actors involved in it in general, and the architect in particular (see CHAPTER NGOs, Architects and Post-Disaster Housing). Who provides adequate expertise, at which level, in which phase and for which task during the project? In this particular working environment 'modern' and 'traditional' building cultures, as this study seeks to show, clash. In many cases, 'modern' values and procedures discredit

1 | Indian Engineer. Interview on 22.12.2012 (Internet phone). For more details about Rajendra Desai see Appendix A: Profile of the Interviewees.

and overrule 'traditional' ones, and as a consequence, valuable knowledge resources and wisdom available within 'traditional' building systems are expelled from the rehabilitation process. This is argued here to be one of the reasons why in many post-disaster contexts the chance of realising a successful project is at risk of failure.

The aim of this chapter is to illustrate, first of all, the logic behind different building cultures, which vary in systematic ways from context to context, and over time. While they differ in many respects,they share the same goal: the creation of living spaces, structures and buildings (see Davis 1999).[2] The formal and institutionalised building culture in which architects (amongst other professionals of the built environment) take on a leading role, represents just one building culture out of many. Many buildings are constructed without the involvement of institutions and formally trained professionals. The lack of centralised planning, authorities and bureaucratic control over the building process is common to many building cultures, particularly in rural environments and informal urban settlements around the world. Artisans, village elders, masons and carpenters provide the knowledge, the techniques and the social habits that cover the entire building cycle (see Fathy 1973, Bhatia 1991, Schaur 1991, Davis 1999, Asquith *et al.* 2006, Marchand 2009).

According to the American professor of architecture Howard Davis, any building culture is the coordinated system of knowledge, rules, procedures, and habits that surround the building process in a given place and time (1999: 5). A building culture is characterised by 'fundamental human relationships and social habits, and not all building cultures require large and formal institutions' (*ibid.*: 27). According to Davis, within a building culture, construction is rarely a solitary act, isolated from the 'material, social, and aesthetic world around it' (*ibid.*: 5). It is embedded in a web of human relationships which are in turn characterised by the 'predictable ways people carry out their jobs and the predictable ways they deal with each other' (*ibid.*). The participants in the building culture share 'common understandings that may be only partly understood by the large culture outside them. But at the same time, the building culture is a part of the larger world' (*ibid.*), sharing ideas, practices, forms of education and

2 | In this chapter I refer extensively to 'The Culture of Building' (1999) by Howard Davis as he describes, for the first time, the built environment as the result of many different building processes in place around the world.

training, and attitudes about buildings and the environment. The product of different building cultures is 'the built world as a whole – the world of houses and warehouses, churches and libraries, schools and factories, barns and shops, the monumental and the everyday, the imported and the vernacular, the famous and the unknown' (*ibid.*: 8). In short: the built world is much larger than the world architects are usually concerned with, but part of the one which makes up people's everyday experience of open spaces, streets, buildings, villages, neighbourhoods and cities.

I will, hereafter, focus on the two building cultures encountered in the course of this study, namely, the 'modern' one, whereby the building process is guided by formally trained professionals (architects, engineers), and the 'traditional' one of the research area of this study, in which the building process is guided by the people themselves and by rural professionals (craftsmen).[3]

Architects are part of an institutionalised building culture which emerged alongside industrialisation (see Hughes *et al.* 2013) in the West, and during colonialism in the rest of the World.[4] The demarcation of the 'profession's boundaries included the development of exclusive claims to professional expertise, the encouragement of clients' use of architects, the adoption of legislation to control both means of entering the profession [...] and the exclusive right to practice by the members of the profession (the requirement that only licensed architects can design buildings)' (Davis 1999: 121). During the course of the 19th century professional organisations were established and pushed for – and attained – statutory registration, so that no one could be called an 'architect' without meeting the standards of education and competence, as determined by an institution. A degree from an architecture school became one of many other important standards defined (*ibid.*). While earlier the person called 'architect' could have had any background (craftsman, builder) and come from different places

3 | It is important to stress here that I do not intend to categorise and isolate different building cultures, as all building cultures are part of the larger (built) world, and they are exposed to the ideas, habits, and institutions of other building cultures. They are both autonomous and inter-dependent at the same time (see Davis 1999, Hosagrahar 2005).

4 | For example, the Sir J. J. College of Architecture located in central Mumbai and affiliated to the University of Mumbai (India) established in 1913, which became Asia's first architecture school.

and operate without formal training, 'it gradually became the role of institutions to determine who would have that privilege' (*ibid.*). As a result, the architect – having undergone this formal training at schools – successively assumed a dominant role in the building process, and has, ever since, held 'positions of considerable esteem and influence within the domain of the built environment [and] also within wider society' (Hughes *et al.* 2013: 29). Within this 'modern' building culture, the privilege to rationalise about architecture and to define what architecture is remains, to a large extent, with its institutions and its professionals.[5]

In a 'traditional one-on-one architect-patron relationship' (Davis 1999: 73) the architect is chosen by a client based on the quality of his/her previous work, mouth of word recommendation, or, in most cases, by his/her architectural style, as this may be an important means of expressing the image and status of the client.[6] The client and the architect together define the project brief, based on the client's wishes. The architect designs the building in consultation with the client. This consultation consists – in general – of a series of presentations of drawings and/or three-dimensional models at different stages of the project. The client is asked to comment on the design, and, based on his/her feedback, there may be revisions. In this situation, the architect is in 'control and may tend to only want to make changes that do not fundamentally alter the basic conception of the project' (*ibid.*: 73). After the design process is completed, construction is

5 | Within the built environment there are a number of professionals that have to undergo higher education. Hartenberger *et al.* list the following professions: 'architects/designers, landscape architects/town planners, construction engineers, construction managers/project managers, specialist consultants (e.g. sustainability assessors/auditors), quantity surveyors, facility managers, construction product engineers, construction process technicians, mechanical engineers (e.g. for heating, ventilation and air conditioning), plant, energy and waste technicians. A longer list could include: property and land economists, asset managers, valuation professionals, (real) estate agents, specialized financial and insurance consultants, specialized lawyers' (2013: 62).

6 | I focus here exclusively on the planning and construction procedures of a single-family house (as opposed to large scale projects) so to compare this building culture and the villages' building culture.

handed over to a general contractor, or construction is divided into several stages, and the different work allocated to specialist trades.[7]

The building cultures of the villages portrayed in this study and the nature of their building operations are characterised by a lack of bureaucratic institutions, formally trained professionals, and authorities exerting overarching control.[8] Knowledge of building is widely shared. The informal building process in place in the villages may be guided by the family members themselves, who pass this knowledge on to their children by involving them in house construction year after year. Or, if their economic background allows, the construction process is guided by the village 'architect', the mason, who has learned his skills either through his father, or through an apprenticeship (master and apprentice).[9] A mason is chosen on the quality of his previous work, or because he is known by friends and neighbours. This familiarity helps to 'make the contract sure' (see Davis 1999: 41). The conception of the building and its execution are not separate in terms of time and people. The entire process is either in the hands of the family members themselves, or of the mason along with the house owners. When masons are involved, they work with contracts, for fixed amounts. Design decisions about the house are made between the house-owners and the mason. The mason oversees the entire process of construction, he hires his own helpers, and he is responsible for the progress of the work. Very often, the mason's contract is a labour contract, and the family is responsible for procuring the construction materials. In

7 | Within institutionalised building culture Davis presents the following subcultures: 'Speculative commercial and office development, and standard buildings for large corporations; buildings designed by architects for particular clients (public and private buildings); residential development by merchant builders; small-scale building and self-building, without architects' services; and manufacture of building components and buildings' (1999: 67–68).

8 | Depending on the economic background of the family, they may have access to public housing schemes. This process will not be described here as it follows the logic of a formalised building culture (however, one house is constructed irrespective of the house-owners wishes), and, as far as the villages of this study are concerned, a negligible number of houses had been constructed under the public housing scheme before the tsunami of 2004.

9 | In other parts of India, for example, it is the carpenter who takes on the role of the 'architect'.

the villages there is a good deal of repetition of common building designs, but at the same time there is also a lot of difference in the way details are realised (*ibid.*: 37–42).

The construction of the house is, moreover, a ritualised process and marked by ceremonies (see Glaeser 1995). Since a house costs a lot of money, usually a life's savings, building a house is one of the most important social events in the village context. It has to be pursued 'in conformity with one's personal destiny and with the blessings of gods and goddesses "in heaven"' (Glaeser 1995: 251). This can be achieved only with the approval and consent of astrologers and priests 'on earth'. The 'right' place, and also the 'right' surroundings of the house to be built are of equal importance. Thus, at various stages of the construction process, religious ceremonies (*pujas*) are carried out. For example: work only starts on an auspicious day, which is identified by the *swami*, based on the horoscope of the house-owner. Before digging the foundations, the foundation–stone ceremony is performed. Another ceremony is performed before work actually commences (*manaj puja*). Thereby, the soil of the site is blessed (*bhumi puja*). The house-entering ceremony (*grahapravesam*) takes place upon completion (*ibid.*: 249–250).[10]

While the two building cultures differ in many respects, two essential parameters are inherent in both of them: they are embedded in profound human relationships, which are characterised by mutual trust and the legitimisation of expertise (see the following chapter); and the people involved in the entire process concur in terms of social values, building procedures, and the functionality and the image of a house. These aspects are, amongst others, essential prerequisites, as will be shown in the course of the study, for the degree of success of a project.

In the aftermath of the Indian Ocean tsunami of 2004, however, the built world of the villages was, as a whole, stigmatised as 'backward' by the government (see CHAPTER The Revised Policy). Rural building experts were excluded from, and formally trained professionals of the built environment assumed control over, the government's decision-making process. Many NGOs involved in the scheme adhered to this top-down and

10 | It is not possible to identify traditional house-building customs which are equally valid for all villagers. Religious requirements and ceremonies may even be individually fixed, for a single person or family, by priests or astrologers.

exclusionary approach, while only a few challenged it by incorporating rural building expertise into the building process.

The Illusion of Certainty: The Notion of the Architect as 'Expert'[11]

> The certified professional makes a fool of himself, and often does a great deal of harm to other people, by assuming that he knows more than the 'uneducated' by virtue of his schooling.
> John F. C. Turner 1972: 146–147

> This modernist way of thinking prevents the architect from listening, asking questions and reaching out to other sources of knowledge, which is, however, essential in this context.
> Sandeep Virmani[12]

Late modernity is a world populated by expert systems, expert knowledge and an increasing awareness among ordinary people that the world is an unpredictable and increasingly dangerous place (Giddens 1990, Beck 1992). As a consequence, expert knowledge is expected (by various legitimising audiences) to formulate ideas and to provide solutions in response to the challenges of a rapidly changing world. But who is an 'expert', and who defines, above all, who an 'expert' is and what he/she can or cannot do?

There is an extensive literature on the sociology of the professions, aiming to define the characteristics of a professional (see, for example, the summaries by Elliott 1972, Sharma 1997, Evetts 2003). According to Evetts (2003), for example, a profession has exclusive ownership of an area of expertise and knowledge, the power to define the nature of problems as well as control over the access to solutions, a supportive professional community, autonomy, and works for the public good.

---

11 | 'Illusion of certainty' was borrowed from Woods 2006.

12 | Indian architect. Interview on 09.08.2013. For more information on Sandeep Virmani see APPENDIX A: Profile of the Interviewees.

Professionalism is, of course, a social construct that has changed over time. Expert knowledge requires audiences who legitimise its output of knowledge (McNeill *et al.* 2013), and a common characteristic of all types of expertise is that it always depends on the relations between cognitive authority and audiences (Turner 2004). There are, though, different types of audiences and processes which lead to the legitimisation of experts' knowledge, and also different kinds of dynamics that may lead to very different relations between experts and the source of legitimacy of their expertise (see Arce *et al.* 1992, Wood 1998, Mosse 2013, McNeill *et al.* 2013). Below, I will first take a closer look at how the role of 'experts' has been discussed in the literature in relation to development cooperation in general. Thereafter, I will outline specific instances in which 'experts' and their legitimising audiences of 'modern' building cultures largely disempowered 'traditional' professionals as 'non-experts' during the reconstruction process after the tsunami of 2004, with the result that many projects failed to meet the people's needs.

Some studies of development cooperation have questioned the role of 'experts' as agents of change and transformation (see, for example, Betke *et al.* 1978, Lachenmann 1991, Escobar 1995, Chambers 1997). Particular studies (Betke *et al.* 1978) have dealt with the selective perception of 'experts' of the complex realities of 'non-western' societies. These critiques focused particularly on the adoption of elite perspectives towards societies, instead of dealing with the 'life-worlds' (Schutz *et al.* 1973) and the needs of ordinary people. The German sociologist Gudrun Lachenmann (1991), for example, studied how expert discourses constitute a specific reality, showing how these discourses systematically exclude forms of knowledge and practice that do not conform to the technocratic paradigm of 'experts'. As a result, development discourse and practice create, according to Lachenmann, 'systems of ignorance' by disconnecting expert knowledge from other forms of knowledge (see also Hobart 1993). The ignorance of alternative interpretations of the world leads, as a consequence, to poor decisions and interventions.

According to the German social anthropologist Ute Luig, hegemonic structures of knowledge and access to resources can best be observed and studied during phases of reconstruction, as these phases are 'arenas of negotiations, of cooperation in forging new alliances, but also of conflicts and bitter struggles' (2012: 15). They involve 'the politics of space and identity' and they 'reveal structures of hierarchy and inequality in societies' (*ibid.*). Housing is one of many arenas of reconstruction where hegemonic structures unfold, and where the question of 'who decides what for whom' (Turner 2009: 11) becomes central.

After the Indian Ocean tsunami of 2004, the 'expertise' of formally trained professionals has permeated rehabilitation policy and the reconstruction process as a whole in a striking fashion. Was their involvement part of a political agenda propagating the restoration of safety, and a better future, in a time characterised by social disorder, chaos, and sometimes also by upheaval (see Luig 2012: 15)?

Public and private agencies drew extensively on 'experts' (local and international alike), assuming that they knew, due to their professional education, what was best for the people. They were the authors of numerous policies, guidelines and tools on and for the rehabilitation programme, constructing and transmitting what 'sustainable' and 'people-oriented' housing is.

Architects were appointed in order to ensure the realisation of the programmes as formulated by the headquarters of the NGOs. The unsustainable nature of many of the projects which were implemented, however, is particularly surprising. I will argue here that it is partly *because* agencies drew extensively on the use of formally trained architects, assigning roles and responsibilities unquestioningly during the project and irrespective of the building culture they were confronted with. Building professionals of 'traditional' building cultures, namely craftsmen, village elders and the users themselves (see Davis 1999), were largely excluded from the process and discredited. Government engineers, NGO representatives and formally trained 'experts' accused 'traditional' building cultures of producing 'weak', 'unsafe' and 'outdated' houses (see Jigyasu 2006), and as a consequence, 'traditional' know-how with regard to land-use, local climate, appropriate construction materials, layout of the house and the settlement were largely ignored (see Jigyasu 2010). Decision makers from public and private agencies conceived post-tsunami reconstruction as an opportunity to 'modernise' rural settlements (see Subramanian 2009: 248) with the support of formally trained 'experts'.

Architects (among other professionals of the built environment) were assigned responsibility for numerous tasks such as the planning and the designing of new habitats, new houses and public buildings, for developing alternative construction technologies, for managing contracts, and for supervising the quality of construction. Above all, they were expected to realise 'sustainable' (with regard to culture, technology and the environment) as well as 'disaster-resistant' settlements and houses. Could architects comply with these demands? Did they really have all the answers to the many tasks to be carried out? Or, did they also have to pretend, in order to meet their employer's expectations?[13]

Architects enjoyed a good reputation at institutional level, their expertise had been legitimised by the agencies providing housing. According to the villagers, however, many projects failed on a fundamental level, such as the size of the plot and the house, the location and the orientation of the house within the new settlement, the layout (arrangement of rooms) of the house, the appearance of the house, the choice of construction materials, and the quality of construction. Working in a rural post-disaster environment was a new experience for many architects. The myriad and diverse tasks were far beyond their experience, and the answers provided were thus, very often, inappropriate. Architects relegated the skills of rural experts to a level unworthy of consideration, ignoring the fact that in these environments, craftsmen have developed appropriate habitat designs and technologies over centuries (see Jigyasu 2002, 2010). At village level it is the craftsman who enjoys an excellent reputation, and whose skills are sought when constructing a house. In fact, the majority of the villagers interviewed during the field survey commented that they would have chosen (if they had had a free choice) to work with the mason during reconstruction as, according to them, 'he designs and builds based on wishes and needs, and he does good quality work' (see CHAPTER The Key Qualities of 'Their Architect').

It has already been shown that profound human relationships, mutual trust and the legitimising of expertise are common to all building cultures, and are thus key, as well as other considerations, to a successful building process (see Davis 1999). Hence, one of the major challenges in a context where different building cultures clash, is, as argued here, the assignment of the 'right' personnel during the project.

The villagers' voices demonstrate that formally trained architects do not provide adequate expertise for the many challenges to be tackled during reconstruction (see Part II and Part III). More precisely, the villagers' responses demonstrate that calling in formally trained architects,

13 | I thank the architect Sandeep Virmani for pointing this issue out during our discussion.

unquestionably assigning them roles and responsibilities, irrespective of the peculiarities and abilities of the building culture in place, can have, as will be shown in this study, fatal consequences.

Research Method

> [T]he fieldworker cannot anticipate the developments in the field which will inevitably guide the course of the investigations. Hypotheses formed without regard to these considerations may turn out to be trivial if not banal [...] What most fieldworkers do is to go to the field with a grounding in the theory of the discipline, especially in the subarea of their interest, and with as much knowledge of the region as can be derived from secondary material. The field then takes over, and the outcome depends on the interaction between the fieldworker and the field.
> Srinivas *et al.* 1979: 8

The Research Plan

In the course of this study, different tools from various disciplines (sociology, social anthropology and architecture) were used to apporach such a multifaceted theme, that is to say the role and significance of formally trained architects in a rural reconstruction context. Moreover, various elements of the research process had to be identified: selecting the three case studies; making contact with the NGOs' key-personnel as well as with the projects' architects; gaining access to the sites selected; and, collecting and analysing quantitative and qualitative data. These elements were built into a three-stage research plan. The first involved studying secondary material; selecting the case studies; making contact with the NGOs' key-personnel and getting prepared for the field survey (the preparation of the household questionnaire and semi-structured interviews). The second was the field survey itself (from November 2011 to March 2012), collecting quantitative and qualitative data (the household questionnaire, informal interaction, participant observation, and in-depth semi-structured interviews). The final stage was the screening, computing and analysis of the quantitative and qualitative data, as well as the preparation of tables and diagrams.

For the field survey I found it important, with Srinivas (1979) in mind, to be open to what was there. 'It is the idea of the open-ended quest which permits a fieldworker to collect unexpected material pertaining not only to his chosen theme of research but to other themes as well' (Srinivas *et al.* 1979: 8). As a result, methodological tools from the disciplines of sociology and social anthropology were used to explore the field. Household questionnaires were designed to collect quantitative data (closed questions), on the one hand, and to explore qualitative data (open questions) on the other. In addition, qualitative data were gathered by means of informal interaction with the villagers and participant-observation during the course of the field survey. To complement this study, in-depth, semi-structured and recorded interviews were carried out with architects, engineers and NGO representatives (in decision-making positions). Furthermore, critical information was gathered from government notifications and acts, as well as from the projects' documentation, maps, architectural plans and drawings of the old (where still existing) and new hamlets and houses. However, the selection criteria for the case studies will be outlined before describing the approach and the methods in detail.

Selection of the Case Studies

The opportunity to do research in rural TN and the UToP provided an arena in which the impact of post-disaster housing could be studied across a range of different projects (see CHAPTER Locating the Field). Many projects were implemented as public-private-partnerships (government/NGO) in which NGOs were free to develop the master plan of the new village (in the case of relocation) and the layout, design and construction technologies (materials) of the new houses. The government, on the other hand, provided new land (in the case of relocation) and infrastructure services such as roads, electricity and water. NGOs did not have to follow a model-house design predefined by the government[1] (see CHAPTER The Reconstruction Policy). A variety of approaches were possible within the same legal context and, thus, this region proved to be ideal for the research focus of this study. The problem facing the selection was not that it was difficult to identify projects as such. Rather, the problem of selection had two related concerns. First, there was the question of how the three projects should be identified; second, on what criteria should they be selected (see Burgess 1994: 131).

Considering the abundance of projects available in this region (see CHAPTER Why Tamil Nadu?) it was, first of all, crucial to collect data about the key characteristics of the NGOs and their projects. For the selection process it was of central importance to analyse the NGOs' goals, their approaches and the type of project(s) implemented. As a result, I was completely dependent on the availability of secondary material such as the NGOs' leaflets and folders, the NGOs' websites, their project reports, their case studies and their evaluations. Furthermore, reports published by the UNDP, Asian Development Bank and World Bank were critical for the identification of the variety of projects carried out.[2]

Having studied substantial amounts of secondary material, it became evident that the case studies should not be taken as representative of the number of projects implemented in that region. Rather, they illustrated diverse approaches, the different profiles of architects and their respective results (based on the villagers' feedback) within the same legal, political and cultural context. Thus, the criteria upon which the selection was based, were:

- Location, rural
- Type, the new construction of permanent housing
- Planner, an architect
- Provider, an NGO
- Goal, people-oriented
- Status, completed and occupied

1 | In the states of Andhra Pradesh, Kerala and the Union Territory of the Andaman & Nicobar Islands NGOs providing houses had to follow a model house predefined by the respective governments.

2 | ADB (2005, 2008), ADBI (2005, 2007), SKAT (2008), UNTRS (2006a, b).

This set of criteria made it possible to limit the number of potential case studies available in this region. A final decision, however, was taken in the field after having visited various projects and after having interacted with the relevant NGO representatives. In this way, detailed information could be gathered about the NGO's approach and, most importantly, the architects' role and scope of work. Furthermore, this clarified if the NGO's staff on the ground were available for semi-structured interviews, and if data and project documentation were accessible. Moreover, I had to clarify whether the projects on the ground corresponded to what had been published in the secondary material.[3] I had short-listed eight NGOs: Architecture for Humanity, Oxfam, Care, Mata Amritanandamayi Math (Amma), Caritas India, Swiss Red Cross, SIFFS and BLESS. The three NGOs and the three projects chosen for the purpose of this study were selected for the following reasons.

Firstly, the NGO PMSSS was chosen as it is a partner of Caritas India and a member of the international Caritas confederation. Caritas India and its partners implemented 37 projects (relocation and in-situ) over eight districts, and architects were assigned for all the projects (in total eight architecture firms from TN and the UToP). This NGO network is well suited to the purpose of this study, not only because it demonstrates clearly the realities of a large and established NGO network (comparable, for example, to NGO networks such as the IFRC, World Vision, Oxfam and Care) in the context of post-disaster housing, but also because I have

3 | Before entering the field I had also listed the following case studies: Pillaichavadykuppam (Villupuram district), and Samanthampettai (Nagapattinam district). The two latter, however, had to be excluded due to the following reasons: In Pillaichavadykuppam a housing project was implemented by the American NGO Architecture for Humanity in cooperation with the local NGO LEAD. However, as it turned out when visiting the village, houses were only repaired and not newly constructed, and a community hall was constructed. As the construction of new houses is one of the selection criteria this project had to be excluded. Samanthampettai is a relocation project, implemented by the Indian NGO Mata Amritanandamayi Math (Amma). This project would have been in accordance with the selection criteria. But it became evident in the field, that the approach was very similar to the one in Keezhakazakudy-metu. Furthermore, I did not succeed in making contact with the NGO's key-personnel. Thus, this project had to be excluded from the shortlist.

'insider knowledge' of the process, having been closely involved from the beginning up to the completion of most of the reconstruction projects. Out of the 37 projects, Keezhakazakudy was selected as in this case the architect developed a cluster master plan (see Fig. 8, page 71), in contrast to the grid layout which was implemented by all the other relocation projects, aiming to provide a culturally sensitive solution. Grid layouts have been criticised as monotonous and culturally inappropriate to the context (see Boen *et al.* 2005, Duyne-Barenstein 2007, 2011a, b).

Secondly, the NGO BLESS was chosen as it was the only NGO that had opted for an alternative construction technology in one of its housing projects (see UNTRS 2006a: 14–15). In total, BLESS built four projects in Cuddalore district. While reinforced cement concrete (RCC) was used throughout TN and the UToP, for Shanmuga Nagar the NGO's representatives opted for compressed stabilised earth blocks (CSEB).

Thirdly, the NGO SIFFS was selected as their particular reconstruction approach had been highly acclaimed in secondary literature (see Government of TN 2008: 6, SKAT 2008). In total, SIFFS was responsible for four projects in Nagapattinam district with the financial support of Swiss Solidarity, the Swiss Red Cross, Terre des Hommes, Christian Aid UK, and Philips Electronics India Limited. Putting forward '2,000 houses in 2,000 designs' (SIFFS 2009: 6), SIFFS aimed to customise each house plan, based on the families' wishes and needs. Having adopted the same approach for all four projects, Tarangambadi was selected for this study as it was the biggest reconstruction project at a single location in TN (see *ibid.*: 4).

Finally, the mode of construction adopted by the NGOs was an important selection criterion. In the literature there has been an ongoing debate about the adequacy of assigning professional construction companies in this context (see Barakat 2003, Duyne-Barenstein 2008, 2011a, b). While NGOs and private agencies tend to assume that employing professional contractors is the quickest and most effective approach, researchers have shown that this is not necessarily the case (Duyne-Barenstein 2006, 2011a, b, Karunasena *et al.* 2010). Duyne-Barenstein argues, for example, that 'villages reconstructed by professional companies generally consist of grid-patterned row homes that pay little attention to the communities' social structure and settlement patterns' (2011b: 344). In post-tsunami TN, most NGOs employed professional contractors for the construction of the thousands of houses neded (*ibid.*: 353). For the purpose of this study, however, it was critical to select projects that differed with regard to the mode of construction in order to assess their implications for the degree of success of the project. In Keezhakazakudy-Tsunami Nagar the houses were built by professional contractors. Hence, a significant number of NGOs and their projects (Oxfam, Care, World Vision, Mata Amritanandamayi Math (Amma)) were excluded from the short-list before entering the field.

The three case studies finally selected are located in the most affected districts of rural TN and of the UToP, namely in Nagapattinam, in Cuddalore and Karaikal (see CHAPTER Locating the Field). The projects incorporate the following selection criteria:

- Keezhakazakudy-metu (Tsunami Nagar)

Rural; relocation and reconstruction of 200 new permanent houses; provided by a local NGO; planned by a local architecture firm; built by a professional contractor; completed and occupied since December 2007.

- Shanmuga Nagar

Rural; in-situ construction of 62 new permanent houses (31 detachted houses); provided by a local NGO; planned by a local architect; built by skilled (masons) and unskilled labour (villagers); completed and occupied since June 2007.

- Tarangambadi (Tsunami Nagar)

Rural; combination of relocation and in-situ construction of 1091 new houses (813 relocated and 278 reconstructed in-situ); provided by a local NGO; planned by a local architect; built in cooperation with a professional labour contractor; local builders; NGO staff and villagers; completed and occupied in various stages from May 2007 to December 2009.

Taking into consideration the number of projects put in place in the research area of this study (see CHAPTER Why Tamil Nadu?), the case studies portrayed here will not provide sufficient scope for a comprehensive picture of the operational designs, the roles and responsibilities of architects, and the results in the context of rural post-disaster housing.4 It

4 | After the tsunami of 2004 a number of projects with diverse approaches were implemented in the states and the Union Territories affected in South India, Indonesia, Sri Lanka and Thailand. Moreover, during the past ten years various regions from all over the world have been hit by disasters, and, based on the cultural, political and legal framework of these countries, different approaches were designed

is hoped, however, that this selection will help to highlight the challenges, the potentials and the limitations of using formally trained architects in a working environment such as that portrayed in this research.

Approaching the Field

A topic as far reaching as the one dealt with in this research clearly imposes challenges and also certain limitations. I approached the field with questions in mind that were to be explored, and – if necessary – dismissed. Nevertheless, this approach turned out to be challenging in many ways. I entered the field bringing with me my past experience as a project manager after the tsunami of 2004 in this region (see CHAPTER Preamble). This provided me with, first of all, a good background as I was very familiar with the geographical, cultural, political and post-tsunami context. Also, I was acquainted with the local NGO landscape, and with local research institutes involved in post-tsunami housing projects. This was beneficial in gaining access to secondary material, and for making contacts with the NGOs' key-personnel. Moreover, managing several permanent housing projects right from the beginning until their completion provided me with profound insights into the realities and challenges of NGOs and architects in an intricate set-up like that portrayed in this study. However, I realised that this context which was very familiar on the one hand, turned out to be very challenging on the other. Living in this region as a fieldworker meant leaving aside the perspective of a former project manager and being open to themes of relevance to the villagers. However, the main challenge was the fact that I do not speak Tamil. As a consequence, the possibility of spontaneously interacting with the villagers and taking notes (without a translator) was restricted and this, I understood, would limit my perspective. Hence, this raised the following questions: how does the household questionnaire, one of the main tools, need to be designed in order to facilitate an open-ended approach? What type of assistant would I need to support this survey?

I decided to draw up a questionnaire using a combination of closed questions to collect facts and figures, and open questions to explore the-

---

and applied by the various agencies involved in the reconstruction of permanent houses.

mes and issues coming out of the field (see Diekmann 2010: 33-34; Lamnek 2010: 113). According to Diekmann (2010) and Lamnek (2010), open questions encourage further informal discussions and the narration of incidents. Insights can be gathered which help to give a more inclusive understanding of the issues under investigation. In my case, however, the degree of success of this inductive approach also depended on the profile and attitude of my assistant(s), and on our capacity to handle the challenges described above in the course of the survey. As a result, I formed a team of PhD students from the Department of Social Works of Pondicherry University.[5] This was because, according to Goldstein (1994), social workers bring the necessary qualifications for this type of survey as they attempt to understand the human experience as it is lived, felt and known by its participants.

Intensive meetings with the team were carried out during November 2011 discussing in detail the research context, the draft questionnaire that I had prepared in advance and some of the terminology which was new to them. We decided to carry out a pilot study of 10 households in Keezhakazakudy-Tsunami Nagar so that any revisions and adjustments that were necessary could be made. The villagers' feedback was essential for the finalising of the questionnaire. Some of the questions had to be adapted and the questionnaire amended to be 'complete'. For example, questions were added relating to the preference for with whom to plan and build a new house, and why. Also, the questions relating to the degree of satisfaction and building customs were augmented, and, finally, open questions added relating to the interaction with the architect added. The revised household questionnaire was then translated into Tamil by M. Siva.

5 | As I could not identify an assistant who would be available throughout the whole four months of my field survey I had to form a team. The members of the team were: M. Siva, F. Jayachandran, M. Maria Antony Raj, M. Soundharajan and A. Stalin. They assisted me as follows: M. Siva (finalisation and translation of the household questionnaire); F. Jayachandran (surveyor in Keezhakazakudy-Tsunami Nagar, in Tarangambadi, and in Shanmuga Nagar); M. Maria Antony Raj (surveyor in Keezhakazakudy-Tsunami Nagar and in Shanmuga Nagar); M. Soundharajan (finalisation of questionnaire, pilot survey Keezhakazakudy-Tsunami Nagar, surveyor in Tarangambadi, and feeding of the data into SPSS); and A. Stalin (surveyor in Keezhakazakudy-Tsunami Nagar and in Shanmuga Nagar).

Beyond gaining clarity with regard to the questionnaire, the pilot survey revealed some more issues that had to be tackled. During our first interactions with the villagers I sensed that my colleagues did not translate everything, but summarised. I realised that sometimes feedback to open questions was not recorded. As I was 'illiterate' in the field I was fully dependent on the assistants for information. Thus, I stressed the importance of translating and taking notes of everything, even if they considered it to be 'trivial', 'unpleasant' or 'irrelevant' with regard to housing. Not sharing 'trivial' or 'irrelevant' information, I assumed, was, first of all, a matter of sovereignty; not sharing 'unpleasant' and 'negative' feedback a matter of courtesy. Pointing this out, I knew, was offensive as, after all, I had questioned their professionalism. Quoting the British anthropologist Okley, I had to explain, however, that 'nothing is irrelevant' (2011: 23). Only unfiltered information would enable me to adopt an explorative approach and, finally, lead to a sharpening of the research question.

I was in the field with the team throughout the survey. I accompanied them from house to house, listening, taking notes and taking pictures of the houses and hamlets (old and new). Informal discussions were carried out with villagers and traditional *panchayat* leaders. Moreover, we decided that after each day of collecting questionnaires we would sit together, go through them, correct and clarify – if necessary – uncertainties. This methodological approach turned out to be very constructive.

The Household Interviews

The survey was carried out from November 2011 to March 2012. The month of November was spent refining and finalising the questionnaire. Taking into account the availability of access to the villagers, the interviews were carried out mostly on weekdays starting in the morning, breaking for lunch and continuing during the afternoon. Households were chosen through random sampling (see Bortz *et al.* 2010: 25). It was hoped that, by not specifying whom we wanted to question, we would be invited to interview whoever was available. Hence, in total 40 households in Keezhakazakudy-Tsunami Nagar, 30 households in Shanmuga Nagar, and 40 in Tarangambadi-Tsunami Nagar were interviewed. The questionnaire was long but could normally be completed within an hour. However, in many cases this timescale expanded due to the informal discussions which took place. Before starting with the survey in the hamlets we introduced ourselves to the traditional *panchayat* leaders, informing them about the scope of the survey and the topics of the questionnaire. The survey was started only after getting the leaders' permission.

The questionnaire was intended to provide information about the socio-economic background of the household, the degree of destruction of the house, the villagers' living situation before and after the tsunami, their view on the running of the project, their degree of involvement in the decision-making process, their customs/values and traditions related to the construction of a house, their interaction with the architect, their opinion of the architect's role and performance, and their degree of satisfaction with their new house and their new hamlet. More specifically, the questionnaire sought information on the following issues:

- Living situation (see Waterson 1990, Carsten *et al.* 1995, Bourdieu 2005, Oliver 2003) before and after the tsunami: socio-economic background; degree of destruction; construction materials of their old house; use of public and private space in their old/new hamlet and in their old/new house; positive and negative features of the new house and the new hamlet.
- Satisfaction about the new house/hamlet: satisfaction with regard to location of the house; the size of the plot; the size of the house; the number of rooms; the sanitary facilities; the climatic conditions inside the house; the quality of materials; the design and the quality of construction.
- Customs/traditions related to the construction of a house (see Chandhoke 1990, Waterson 1990, Davis 1999, Oliver 2003): ceremonies carried out during the course of building a house; religious restrictions while building a house; whose advice, and what type of support, is sought during the course of building a house?
- Interaction with the architect: is the architect known; how often did interaction take place; what was this interaction like; could wishes and needs be shared; were wishes and needs incorporated into the plans of the new house (and the new hamlet); were the presentations of plans about the new hamlet/house understandable?
- Decision making process (see Davidson *et al.* 2007): who decided on the type of the project (relocation, in-situ, mix of the two); who decided on the new location; who decided which new features were to be inclu-

ded in the new project (i.e. construction technology, construction materials, layout of the house and sanitary facilities); who decided on the mode of construction (i.e. contractor-driven, owner-driven, or other)?

Also, I had some questions which sought the villagers' opinions. These were:

- What is your impression of the NGO involved in this project?
- Would you like to work with this NGO again? Why?
- What is your impression of the architect involved in this project?
- Would you like to work with him/her again? Why?

The answers to these questions, and to the following questions, were surprising: Do you know the architect who planned your village and your house? Did you interact with the architect? If you could choose with whom to build your house, whose support would you like to get?

First of all, the majority of the villagers said that they had never encountered the architect as a professional of the built environment (see CHAPTER Building Cultures), as in normal times, if sufficient financial means are available, a mason would plan and build their houses. Moreover, in two of the projects the villagers did not know that an architect had been involved in the project at all. Secondly, it became evident during which of the project phases, and in which areas, the NGOs and architects failed to interact with the villagers. The answers clearly illustrated which qualifications 'their architect' should bring to the project. They stressed that they would have preferred to work with their local mason as 'he is the one who designs based on wishes and needs, and he does good quality work'. These comments influenced my present research focus as I felt there was much information which no-one had studied in this respect.

Computation and Analysis of the Results

The data of the household questionnaires (in total 110) were analysed using SPSS Statistics.[6] Feeding in and coding the data was carried out

6 | SPSS Statistics is a programme package designed for statistical and graphical data analysis.

after having collected all the questionnaires. This tedious exercise proved to be a vital check on the accuracy of the survey. The data file was fully documented, thereby allowing the creation of properly labelled tables and statistics. Both the analysis of the data gathered through the field survey and the writing up of the results were completed in several stages. Gradually, the computations became more complex, and needed overseeing for other variables, amalgamating data and re-computing indices.

Moreover, as the questionnaire was a combination of closed (quantitative) and open (qualitative) questions two aims had to be achieved during the course of the analysis. First of all, the quantitative data of the villages needed to be evaluated (e.g. the degree of destruction of the house, time spent in temporary shelters, and type and construction materials of the old house). The insights this analysis provided proved to be critical for, amongst others, the discourse analysis. In some cases, the results did not correspond to the data published by the government. For example, the figures relating to the degree of destruction obtained in all three villages did not accord with the data announced officially (see also Duyne-Barenstein 2011a: 188; SIFFS 2009: 16).

In addition, the analysis was intended to highlight themes, issues and concerns raised by the villagers in response to open questions and/or during the course of informal interaction. The answers, however, were multifaceted and thus I decided to revert to one-to-one correlations (see for example Table 17: If you could choose with whom to build your house whose support would you seek? P. 179).

The results of both the quantitative and qualitative data analyses highlighted the differences (and/or similarities) between the three projects and generated crucial questions for further consideration. They are, however, 'descriptive' (Bortz *et al.* 2006: 25) and they are relevant only for the households interviewed. More precisely, they do not have any statistical significance as 'no statistically representative sample' (*ibid.*) was used.

Semi-structured Interviews with NGO presentatives, Architects and Engineers

In-depth, semi-structured interviews with other groups involved in the process, namely NGO representatives, project architects and engineers, were carried out in order to complement this research. Many NGOs had been involved in post-disaster housing for a long time. Others were new to this field and became involved only after the tsunami of 2004 (see CHAPTER NGOs, Architects and Post-Disaster Housing).

By chance, the three NGOs selected for this research were all new to the field. Key-personnel from each NGO were interviewed, as well as key staff from other NGOs experienced in post-disaster housing. I was interested in their experiences and in their views on the challenges of post-disaster housing and their opinions of the architect's role in this. What were their motives in carrying out projects in a particular way? Who were the NGOs key-personnel deciding on approaches, on methods and on the profile of the project architect? Which skills did they consider essential for architects in this context? Faced with the results, what – if anything – had they learned, and what would be changed when approaching future post-disaster projects?

In addition, the project architects were interviewed. I set out to comprehend how architects perceived their role, and the challenges and the needs of post-disaster housing. Moreover, the interviews with the project architects focused on their educational and professional backgrounds, past work experience, challenges and constraints in the context of post-disaster housing, and the skills required for working in this field. Furthermore, they were asked what, in their opinion, were the essential ingredients for the 'success' of a project, the methods used for interacting with the villagers and for planning the new hamlet as well as the new house. Moreover, I sought to identify the challenges they had to face during the course of the construction phase, and, more importantly, how they were handled. Those interviewed were highly experienced architects and those new to the field, senior as well as junior architects, locals (the majority), Indian and international architects.

In total 9 representatives of NGOs, 15 architects and 5 engineers were interviewed (most of them in English, and two in German) (see APPENDIX A). Wherever possible, the interviews were held in person. The majority of interviews (23) took place between July 2011 and March 2012 out of which four were conducted over internet phone. All of the interviews were recorded, and notes were taken during the course of the conversations. Insights gathered from these interviews proved to be critical for this study. They depicted the challenges and constraints that were faced, and differences between providers, professionals and villagers with regard to aspirations, values and needs as well as identifying negligence during the course of the project. Juxtaposing the villagers' feedback with the insights gained through these interviews proved to be vital for the identification of crucial project phases, vital themes, and the fundamental roles and skills required in this context.

During the final stage of the research (June–July–August 2013), another six architects, who have worked extensively in different cultural contexts around the world, were interviewed. The purpose of these interviews was to find out if the results of this study resonate with their experience, and if the findings can be considered as relevant at a global level. Three of the interviews were conducted over internet phone; they were recorded and notes were taken during the conversation. One interview was conducted on the phone, and notes were taken during the discussion. Two of these interviews were written conversations (email).

Analysis of Government Notifications, Acts, Guidelines and NGOs' Project Documents

The analysis of government notifications, acts and guidelines as well as the NGOs' project documents constituted a fundamental source for this research for two reasons.

First of all, elementary technical data were gathered (i.e. the number of NGOs involved in the programme, the number of villages and houses reconstructed, and the legal and economic parameters with regard to the housing programme in general, and the village projects in particular). Most of the projects were implemented as public-private-partnerships (between the state and NGO), hence, these documents proved to be vital in outlining the respective responsibilities of the two entities during the course of the project cycle.

Secondly, these documents proved to be a significant source for the discourse analysis of this research. State governments along with NGOs were the main providers of permanent housing. Decisions on the fundamental parameters for the entire housing programme as well as for each single project were taken at this level. Hence, these documents were analysed with regard to the aspirations, agendas and strategies of the public and private agencies involved, and their implications at village and project level (see CHAPTER Local Governments, NGOs and the Villages).

PART I: AFTER THE INDIAN OCEAN TSUNAMI OF 2004

Local Governments, NGOs and the Villages

International Aid and Local Response

India is a federal state characterised by a clear division of responsibilities between the central and the state governments. Even though the central government has an overall development policy and a supportive role, the main responsibility for rehabilitation after a disaster lies with the state governments. Immediately after the Indian Ocean tsunami of 2004, the central government of India declared that international humanitarian aid was not required for the recovery of the affected regions. This declaration, however, led to outrage among the aid community, who considered India's reluctance to accept international support an act of arrogance. However, the central government may have had good reasons for having reservations about external aid. First, beyond the coastal strip of land that was devasted by the tsunami, the inland economy and infrastructure were intact. The local construction industry was not at all affected, construction materials, skilled and unskilled labour were available, and the number of houses that needed to be reconstructed would be comparatively less than had been estimated immediately after the disaster. Second, before the tsunami of 2004, India had already suffered three major disasters,[1] and the contribution of international aid during the course of reconstruction was marginal.

A 'super cyclone', for example, hit Orissa in September 1999, 'destroying approximately 800,000 houses' (Duyne-Barenstein 2011b: 347). However, this disaster was not followed by a major governmental recons-

1 | The earthquake in Maharashtra 1993, the cyclone in Orissa 1999, and the earthquake in Gujarat 2001.

truction scheme, and only few NGOs provided permanent housing. Indeed, 'it is estimated that national and international NGOs constructed only 5,000 houses' (*ibid.*). People who lost their houses received a compensation grant, and, moreover, the government promised housing assistance through the Indira Awas Yojana (a regular public housing programme supporting households below the poverty line and for scheduled castes and tribes). Moreover, housing loans were provided through the Housing and Urban Development Cooperation organisation for the reconstruction of new houses.

In January 2001, two years after the Orissa cyclone, the state of Gujarat suffered a major earthquake which rendered more than '1 million people homeless' (*ibid.*: 348). There, the government adopted an 'owner-driven' reconstruction approach (see CHAPTER Why Rethink the Role?), providing financial and technical assistance and subsidised construction materials to enable people to rebuild the houses. 87% of the reconstructed homes (or over 197,000 houses) were built under this scheme (Duyne-Barenstein 2006: 5). This made it the biggest post-disaster housing programme ever undertaken in India. At the same time, Indian and international NGOs adopted the donor-driven approach, reconstructing entire villages. In the case of Gujarat, house-owners could choose between the owner-driven approach provided by the government and the donor-driven approach provided by an NGO.

Despite the declaration announced by the central government of India after the tsunami of 2004, international NGOs and private agencies were invited by various state governments to participate in the reconstruction. They flocked to the affected regions with grand aims (see Duyne-Barenstein 2010, Meding *et al.* 2009), and the reconstruction of permanent houses became a priority for both NGOs and their donors (see Telford *et al.* 2007). This, as will be shown in the following chapter, had major implications on the rehabilitation policies issued by the different state governments.

The Reconstruction Policies of Tamil Nadu and the Union Territory of Puducherry

The initial reconstruction policy announced in January 2005 had much in common with that of Gujarat in 2001. Housing reconstruction was either to be supported through financial assistance from the government or realised through public-private partnerships, envisaging a permanent resettlement of all coastal communites. However, several objections led to the revision of this policy.[2]

First, forced permanent relocation of all coastal communities to the hinterland led to immediate tension on the ground, and to stiff public resistance, particular among the fishers, as little consideration was given to their relationship with coastal land. Living on the shore, even in vulnerable thatched huts, greatly facilitates the fishers in earning their livelihoods, and coastal inhabitants belong to a population with strong historical attachments to place. Thus, shifting fishers inland disregarded the importance of coastal land as an asset, particularly for the most marginalised (see Subramanian 2009).

Second, identifying sufficient adequate land in the hinterland for the resettlement of all affected villages turned out to be impossible. Land was either not available within a distance to the coast acceptable for the fishers, or too expensive, or not adequate from a technical point of view. Moreover, in many cases resettling would result in conflicts with other castes residing inland.

Third, this policy focused on those most obviously affected: traditional coastal communities, mainly fishers. However, many inland villages were also affected. Their livelihoods suffered as they are involved in allied activities with the fishers as well as in agriculture. Fields were contaminated by salt water and crops were devastated by the waves. As the degree of destruction of houses was less (or even nil) compared to the hamlets located close to the sea, they were not considered at first for relief and reconstruction, neither by the government nor by NGOs and private agencies. These inland communities came out with a 'slew of complaints at the public hearing [...] of the Supreme Court Commission on Food Security on 20th March 2005 [...] 900 members of inland communities attended the hearing and expressed their concern about not receiving any help, and pointed out several issues such as their total loss of livelihood, unequal food distribution and water scarcity' (The Hindu 2005b).

2 | The reconstruction policies of both governments, TN and the UToP, are identical and will be treated as one hereafter (see Government of TN 2005a, b, c, d; Government of the UToP 2005a, b; The Hindu 2005a).

Fourth, the availability of sufficient private funds among the international aid community led the government to reconsider its own role in reconstruction, and, as a consequence, to revise the reconstruction approaches offered to the affected people. The revised (and final) policy was announced in March 2005, comprising the following core parameters:

- The role of the government and NGOs

The government withdrew from offering financial assistance (the owner-driven approach), and reconstruction was outsourced to NGOs as far as possible (the donor-driven approach). The NGOs focused on rural areas, which accounted for 70% of what was needed: about 30% of the affected houses were located in Chennai city, which were to be provided by the government (UNTRS 2008: 22).

- Public-private-partnership

Reconstruction was to be undertaken as a public-private partnership. Thereby, the government was responsible for the provision of new land (in case of relocation) and its basic infrastructure (water, electricity and roads). The NGOs, on the other hand, were accountable for the planning and the construction of the new houses. NGOs were invited to send their request for participation to the respective District Collectors:

'They may select a particular habitation with the plan for providing permanent housing [...] They are free to choose any habitation of any suitable size accommodating at least 50 families based on their capacity' (Government of TN 2005a: 2).

- Relocation and reconstruction in-situ

The forced relocation of all coastal communities was modified. It was optional for people having resided between 200m and 500m of the high water line, and those living beyond 500m of the high water line. They were entitled to assistance in-situ. People, however, who lived within 200m of the high water line were not entitled to housing assistance unless they opted for relocation:

'Those who weren't willing to relocate beyond 200m [of the high water line] were, however, allowed to repair authorized structures developed prior to 1991 in the

Coastal Regulation Zone [hereafter CRZ] without any government assistance' (Government of TN 2005c: 49).

In the case of relocation, the old house was to be relinquished to the government.

- Size of land provided by the government

The land for the houses to be relocated was to be given free of cost by the government:

'Three cents [121.401m²] [...] of land in rural and 1.5 cents [60.70m²] in municipal areas were provided, free of cost [...] For availing the new houses, old houses need to be relinquished to the government [...] The fishing community is being allowed to keep their boats, nets, etcs in this area with a view not to disturb their livelihood patterns' (Government of TN 2005c: 49).[3]

- Size of house

The house would have between 300–325 sq.ft. (27.6m²–29.90m²) of built space, and it would have disaster-resistant features (Government of TN 2005b: 3). General guidelines regarding the minimum investment per house and the construction standards to be guaranteed by the agency providing housing were laid down by the government. Design options were prepared by the Public Works Department (PWD), suggesting a framed structure with a RCC (reinforced cement concrete) column and beam tied at ground level, roof level and at all free ends (see Government of TN 2005d).

- First line and second line villages

The outcry of inland communities did not go unheard, and they were, ultimately, listed as second line villages, eligible for reconstruction support provided by NGOs and/or the government.

3 | 1 cent is equivalent to 40.467m².

The Revised Policy and Its Implications at Village Level

Even though the initial policy had been revised, it remained problematic for several reasons and had severe implications, as will be shown here, at village level.

First, the new policy made it necessary to reassess thouroughly the degree of destruction and to redefine the total number of new houses required, because not all houses were completely destroyed (as had been thought immediately after the disaster). Indeed, the initial estimate of the numbers of houses to be reconstructed was far beyond actual needs. It was found that a significant number of houses were not, or only partially, damaged and thus repairable (see SIFFS 2009, Duyne-Barenstein 2010). However, it was argued by the government that '87 per cent of the people were living in *kachcha* [houses and that] reconstruction would be an opportunity to upgrade these people's housing condition[s]' (Duyne-Barenstein 2010: 163). Thus, it was decided to replace all *kachcha* houses with *pucca*, disaster-resistant houses, either in-situ or in the areas of relocation. In India, the housing stock is divided into house types. According to the National Buildings Organisation the house types are defined as follows:

- 'the *pucca*: a unit whose predominant wall and roof materials are as follows: a) the wall consists of burnt bricks, galvanised iron (GI) sheets, stone cement, concrete, etc.; b) the roof consists of tiles, slates, corrugated zinc or metal sheets, ACC, RBC, RCC, brick, lime, stone, etc.
- the serviceable *kutcha* (*kachcha*): a unit with mud walls and thatched roof;
- the unserviceable *kutcha* (*kachcha*): a unit with thatched walls and thatched roof;
- the *semi-pucca*: all units which do not fall under any of the above three categories' (NBO and ESCAP 1984: 21).

The Hindi word *pucca* litterally means '"cooked" and refers to the use of fired materials such as bricks, blocks or tiles' (Khosla 1980: 60). *Kachcha* means '"raw", referring conversely to mud, thatch or country tiles' (*ibid.*). The words *pucca* and *kachcha* are officially used by the Government of India to differentiate between houses built out of industrially produced construction materials, on the one hand, and houses built out of locally available construction materials, on the other. The connotation of *pucca* is positive, being industrialised and 'modern'. On the contrary, the connotation of *kachcha* is negative, being vernacular and 'backward'. The negative attitude of the government (and other decision-making entities) towards 'traditional' construction materials and house designs led to 'a massive demolition of undamaged houses' (Duyne-Barenstein 2010: 169), that were well adapted to local climatic conditions and socio-cultural needs.

Second, even though relocation away from the sea to inland was not mandatory anymore, the final policy did not empower the coastal inhabitants to make a free choice about rehabilitation. They were neither given a choice regarding the agency which would reconstruct their village nor about the reconstruction approach as such. In fact, the decision to reconstruct a village was decided, in most cases, by the district administration together with the respective NGO.

Third, rural building cultures were not taken into account by the government when defining the parameters for reconstruction. Both the size of the plot and the house were defined without any thorough habitat assessment. The definition of this size was based on the assumption that fishers live in independent nuclear families. Between 300–325 sq.ft. per house is far too small for an average family as, traditionally, fishers live in joint families, with an average of five to eight family members. Moreover, 1.5 cents of land per plot in municipal areas renders future extension of the house impossible.

Fourth, the government had stipulated a housing density of 25 per acre (4046.9m^2) for a relocated hamlet in rural areas. Each house was to be built on three cents (121.40m^2) and the balance of 25 cents (1,011.67m^2) was to be assigned as common space. However, studies have shown that the size required for open space (in a fishers' hamlet) was much higher than that stipulated by the government (see SIFFS 2009). Moreover, this parameter neglected the importance of providing sufficient land for the future growth of the hamlet.

Fifth, even though NGOs did not have to build a model house as predefined by the government, in most cases the guidelines issued were applied and implemented without being questioned. The final reconstruction policy and reconstruction approach that were ultimately approved were top-down to their very core. The people affected had neither a voice when these crucial parameters were formulated, nor did they have a free choice about their type of rehabilitation, as the government had withdrawn from offering different reconstruction schemes. In a hegemonic context such as that portrayed here, the NGOs' design process and the architect's role gain significantly in importance. How did NGOs and architects react to the government's policy and approach rural reconstruction?

The Reconstruction Process: Defining Five Building Phases

The three case studies portrayed in this study illustrate different operational designs and different roles for the architect, and they will be examined by juxtapposing what was done, by whom, during the course of the entire reconstruction process. It will examine the architect's role over the course of the project cycle, and the project's outcomes. Thus, the aim of this chapter is to outline the five building phases during the course of reconstruction, to define what happened at each stage of the project (see also Davidson *et al.* 2007), and to illustrate how the various phases are interlinked.

- Phase I: Programme formulation

In this phase, the reconstruction policy, as discussed in detail above, was finalised by the relevant government (and in cooperation with bi-lateral and multi-lateral agencies, and international and Indian NGOs, in rare cases with the participation of the people affected).

- Phase II: Project formulation

At this stage, the NGO's approach and the design of the building process (including the assignment of personnel) was defined. The formulation of the parameters for each project was finalised (e.g. relocation or reconstruction in-situ, site selection, list of beneficiaries, number of new houses, number of houses to be repaired, size of the plot, size of the house, construction technology, sanitary facilities and mode of construction).

- Phase III: Planning

The drawing up of the master plan (in the case of relocation), and the house (or the house typologies) took place during this phase, based on the parameters defined in phase II.

- Phase IV: Construction

The method of construction (management of the construction stage, materials and logistics, standard of workmanship and handover) would have, in general, already been defined in phase II. Construction could be undertaken in different ways. For example, it could be outsourced to a private contractor (managing the entire construction phase), or it could be assigned to local craftsmen and unskilled labour, or it could be undertaken by the NGO (organising construction materials and/or skilled and unskilled labour) in cooperation with the house owners.

- Phase V: Post-occupation

Depending on the degree of satisfaction (and on their financial means), the house owners could start repairing, modifying and adapting their new house to their needs.

The table below illustrates to what extent the various reconstruction phases are interlinked. The parameters defined in phase I, for example, have, inherent implications for phase II, for phase III and, ultimately, for phase V. The parameters defined in phase II (Project Formulation) affect all following phases, namely planning, construction and post-occupation.

Figure 4: The five building phases and their interdependence in post-disaster reconstruction

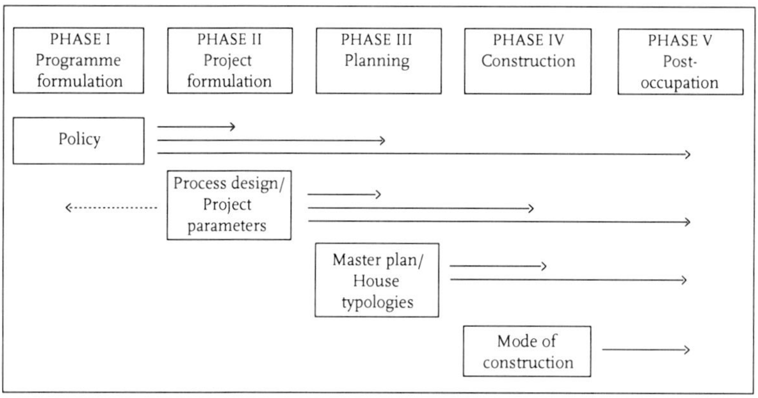

Taking into consideration the many tasks to be handled during the various building phases, NGOs faced (and face) challenges when identifying suitable staff. At first sight, and from a 'technocratic'[4] perspective, the

4 | The term 'technocratic', as used here, describes development interventions that are '"depoliticized" [and] the classic conception implies an authoritative elite that possesses expert positivist knowledge' (Wilson 2006: 502).

table suggests that appointing architects may indeed be an appropriate response, as the tasks fall within their traditional domain of expertise. However, as NGOs and architects enter a different building culture, they must agree to follow that culture's logic and values, and confide in its own experts (see CHAPTER Building Cultures). This study argues that, during the course of the building process, the roles, the scope of work and the procedures must be agreed upon by both the NGO and the villagers, and the reconstruction building process adapted accordingly.

The following case studies will analyse the five building phases in detail with a specific focus on the role and scope of work of the architect. Each of the projects will be examined by juxtaposing what, how and at which stage things were done by the project architect with the results obtained in the village. However, as there were many other actors involved (NGO, government and villagers) their roles and their tasks will also be highlighted in the accompanying diagram (see Table 4, p. 107; Table 8, p. 131; Table 12, p. 159). This approach will help to elucidate, first of all, how the various phases are interlinked, and how decisions taken in one phase of the project inevitably affected the other phases. Secondly, identifying the tasks and roles of the various stakeholders helps to examine who had the power to decide what should happen during the process, and who was excluded. Finally, it is hoped that approaching the subject in this way will help to illustrate the complexity and, most importantly, the sensitivity of operating in such an environment.

PART II:
THREE CASE STUDIES[1]

1 | To ensure the anonymity of the interviewees their names will not be identified. Even though most participants did not request anonymity, preserving the anonymity of all participants involved in the three case studies was considered to be paramount by the author.

Summary of the Three Case Studies

Table 1: Summary of the case studies

	Project Management Consultant Keezhakazakudy-Tsunami Nagar	**Draftswoman** Shanmuga Nagar	**Surveyor-Anthropologist** Tarangambadi-Tsunami Nagar
Type of the project	Relocation	In-situ	Relocation and in-situ
Number of houses	200	62	1,091
Size of the plot	1.85 cents ($74.25m^2$)	2.99 cents ($120m^2$)	3 cents ($120.10m^2$)
Size of the house (plinth area)	325 sq.ft. ($29.90m^2$)	375 sq.ft. ($34.50m^2$)	283 sq.ft. – 340 sq.ft. (26.0m2 – $31.28m^2$)
Construction technology	Reinforced Cement Concrete (RCC)	59 houses: Compressed Stabilised Earth Blocks (CSEB) 3 model houses: Reinforced Cement Concrete (RCC)	Reinforced Cement Concrete (RCC)
Cost per house (see also APPENDIX B)	2,25,000 Lakh	1,90,000 Lakh	2,56,000 Lakh (including land filling)
Rate of occupation	76%	100%	98.6%
Degree of satisfaction (new house)	13%	30%	90%
Degree of satisfaction (architect's performance)	25%	16.3%	62.5%

I: The Project Management Consultant

Programme Manager: 'For Caritas India the tsunami housing programme was not simply a technical matter of constructing houses [...] We wanted to ensure the implementation of people-centred projects, and [...] thus it was decided that in Tamil Nadu and in the Union Territory of Puducherry our implementing partners should appoint professional architecture firms. They should ensure the realisation of the goals formulated.'[1]

Fisherwoman: 'I don't know the architect who planned our village. I have never seen him. Only after construction was completed did I get to know which would be my house. I could not share my wishes [...] Who I would like to build the house with? I would call the mason as he plans and builds based on my wishes, and he does good quality work.'[2]

1 | Former programme manager of Caritas India. Interview on 15.12.2011 (Internet phone). In total, Caritas India and its local partners constructed approx. 7,300 houses in 37 villages in this region. Eight local architecture firms were assigned responsibility for the planning and the management of the projects.

2 | On 19.12.2011 in Keezhakazakudy-Tsunami Nagar.

Project Outline

Name of the revenue village:	Keezhakazakudy
Name of the old hamlet:	Keezhakazakudy-metu
Name of the new hamlet:	Keezhakazakudy-Tsunami Nagar
Community:	Fishers (Pattanavar)
District:	Karaikal (UToP)
Provider of the new houses:	NGO PMSSS
Architecture Firm:	'Project Management Consultant' (PMC) / Puducherry
Type of project:	Relocation
Number of houses constructed:	200
Type of construction:	Framed structure (RCC and brick in-fill)
Built by:	Contractor
Cost per house:	225,000 IRS[1]
Occupancy rate:	76%[2]
Duration of the project:	May 2005–December 2006
Occupation by the villagers:	January 2007
Field survey:	December 2011

1 | See APPENDIX B: Parameters affecting the Cost of the House.

2 | Out of 200 houses 50 houses were not inhabited regularly at the time of the field survey.

The Hamlet, Its Location and Inhabitants

Keezhakazakudy-metu is located in Karaikal, a district and municipality of the UToP. The hamlet lies on the shore of the Coromandel Coast, which stretches from Point Calimere in the south to the border with Andhra Pradesh in the north. Lying 130 km south of Puducherry and 4 km north of the city of Karaikal, the hamlet falls under Karaikal *taluk*[1]. As many fishers' villages in the Karaikal region are 'situated on huge dunes the names of the number of fishing villages end with a suffix *metu* (lit.: 'raised ground'), referring its location on a raised ground' (Bharathi 1999: 19). Keezhakazakudy-metu was hit by the tsunami of 2004, and a new hamlet, named Keezhakazakudy-Tsunami Nagar, was constructed approximately 500m inland. The latter was the subject of study for this research; it was there that the compiling of the household questionnaires, as well as the interaction with its inhabitants, took place.

In this region most coastal villages engage in artisanal fishing,[2] and most contemporary fishers trace their involvement in marine fishing back many generations. This long association with the profession manifests itself in the specialised castes which are concentrated in particular regions along the coast. The Pattanavar caste is dominant along the Coromandel Coast, the Paravar caste in the Palk Strait region, and the Mukkuvar caste in the southern-most parts of Tamil Nadu (Bavinck 2003: 636). The inhabitants of Keezhakazakudy-metu and Keezhakazakudy-Tsunami Nagar belong to the Pattanavar caste, and they work in the local fishing industry.

1 | Generally, a *taluk* (South India) or *tehsil* (North India) consists of a city or a town that serves as its headquarters, possibly additional towns, and a number of villages. As an entity of local government, it exercises certain fiscal and administrative power over the villages and municipalities within its jurisdiction. It is the ultimate executive agency for land records and related administrative matters. Its chief official is called the *tehsildar* or less officially the *talukdar* or *taluka muktiarkar*.

2 | Fishers who use beach-landing craft and passive fishing gear, and have a limited range of operation (Bavinck 2003: 636).

Figure 5: Location of Keezhakazakudy-metu and Keezhakazakudy-Tsunami Nagar

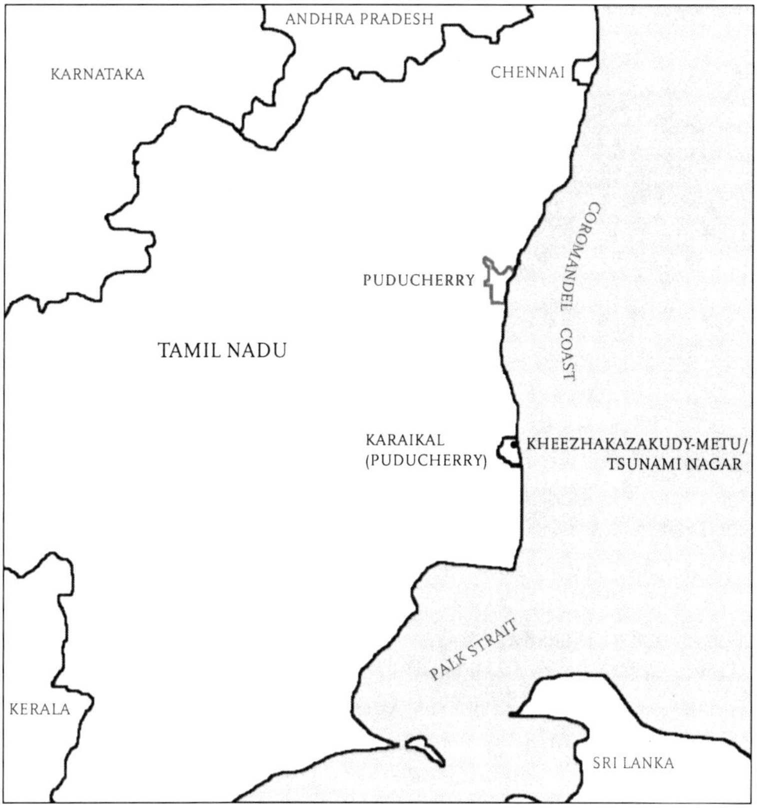

'Unlike other populations, for Pattanavars the basic economic region is the sea rather than the terrestrial region. Due to this specific attribution towards the sea their use of landscape is more social than economic alone. The terrestrial space around them is largely perceived in terms of coastline, village shore, village, living-clusters and homestead, depicting their multifaceted relationship with these categories of space' (Bharathi 1999: 14).

Picture 1: Location of the old hamlet, Keezhakazakudy-metu (red), and the new hamlet, Keezhakazakudy-Tsunami Nagar (orange)

Source: Based on Google maps 19.03.2012

The mental map below,[3] drawn by a fisherman of Keezhakazakudy-metu, shows the hamlet as a whole before the tsunami: its spaces, its temples and the different types of houses, its main roads and paths. At one point – as shown on this map – the road leads directly to the sea, and some of the houses almost touch the water. For the Pattanavars, the beach is an important space for the entire village. 'All fishing villages have a *kallāram* [beach] [...] in front of a village which is used for a variety of purposes such as auction place for fish, mending the nets, drying fire wood, fish and other commodities. Besides these uses, more importantly all the households will leave their logs, crafts, large meshes, anchors and other weighty accessories on the edge of the shore itself' (*ibid.*: 17). Moreover, the beach, more particularly the area where the surf lashes the shore, is used as lavatory. The residential areas of the Pattanavars have their own pattern. 'Within the settlement the residential clusters comprise haphazard conglomeration of houses, cut across by narrow and randomly curved lanes (however

3 | The map was drawn during a Participatory Rural Appraisal (hereafter PRA) carried out by the NGO PMSSS in Keezhakazakudy-metu in May 2005.

the settlement pattern leaves some order and meaning underlying it) giving them a fairly distinct entity' (*ibid.*: 21). The houses are of three kinds, as illustrated on the map: thatched houses (green), tiled houses (red) and concrete houses (blue).[4]

Figure 6: Mental map of Keezhakazakudy-metu

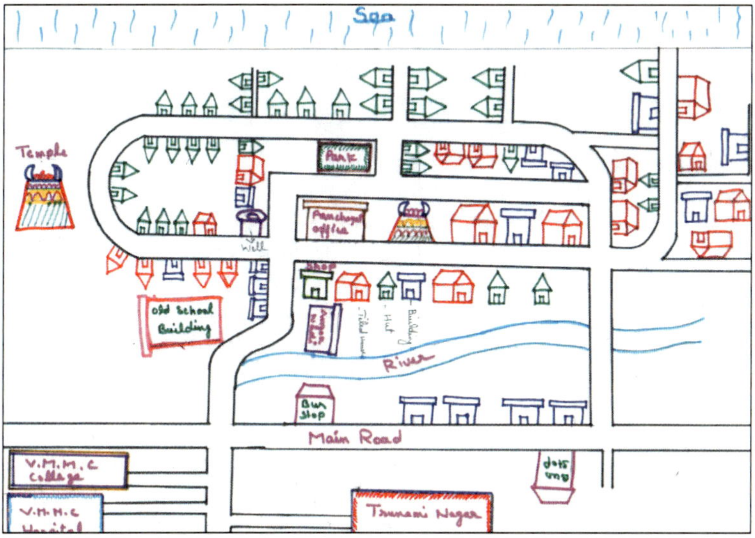

Source: Courtesy of PMSSS

The most predominant form of house constructed in Keezhakazakudy-metu (and in the fishers' villages in this region in general) is made of mud and thatch. The most traditional and uniform house pattern is a 'wall structure covered by a thatch using a kind of sedge and bulrush, plaited coconut fronds, palm fronds and locally available materials like sugarcane leaves, paddy and millet straws' (Bharathi 1999: 21).

The table below shows the percentage of the types of houses (according to the classification of the Government of India, see page 80) inhabited by the fishers before the tsunami. All the houses of Keezhakazakudy-metu were open to the Coromandel Coast, and some of them were located 10m or less from the sea.

4 | See APPENDIX C: 'Traditional' House Typologies in Pattanavar Villages.

Table 2: Types of houses inhabited before the tsunami[5]

Type of house	(%)
Kachcha (serviceable and unserviceable)	52.5
Semi-pucca (tiled house)	37.5
Pucca (Reinforced Cement Concrete / RCC with flat roof)	10

Before the tsunami, the socio-economic situation of the inhabitants was recorded by the NGO as follows: '60% are below poverty line, 30% do have a middle income, [and] 10% are financially sound' (PMSSS 2005: 1).

After the Tsunami of 2004

After the tsunami, government engineers inspected Keezhakazakudy-metu and noted that '8 in South Street, 35 in North Street, 102 in Kaliamman Koil Street and [...] 110 houses were completely destroyed and others partially damaged but not fit for dwelling' (PMSSS 2005: 1). Based on this survey it was decided that in total '200 houses are needed (new marriage, joint families separated etc)' (*ibid.*). Moreover, the fishers' housing situation (prior to the tsunami) was considered 'backward' by the government and the NGO. It was argued that the reconstruction of new houses at a new site would be, first of all, a matter of safety and, secondly, would help 'to improve the poor housing condition of the fisher families.'[6] On 24.08.2005 the NGO PMSSS signed a Memorandum of Understanding (hereafter MoU) with the government (Government of UToP 2006). It agreed to enter into a public-private-partnership for the housing project of Keezhakazakudy-metu, building 200 houses at a new site. The MoU contained detailed descriptions of the responsibilities to be undertaken by the two entities. The government was in charge of providing the new land and was responsible for finalising the exact number of houses (e.g. the

5 | For the definitions of the types of the houses see CHAPTER The Revised Policy.

6 | Former executive director of PMSSS. Interview on 12.12.2011 in Neyveli.

list of beneficiaries). The government was also in charge of providing the infrastructure, such as electricity, water, roads and the sewerage system. On the other hand, PMSSS was responsible for coming up with the new hamlet's master plan, the house plan and the construction of the houses (see CHAPTER The Reconstruction Policies).

Project Organisation

PMSSS is a partner of the international Caritas network and hence it was one of the recipients of financial and technical aid for its reconstruction projects. It was part of a local, national and international network carrying out reconstruction projects in Indonesia, in Sri Lanka and in all the states affected in India. In India alone 'approximately 10,000 houses were financed by the Caritas network and implemented by its local diocesan partners in Andhra Pradesh, Kerala, Tamil Nadu, the Union Territory of Puducherry and the Union Territory of the Andaman & Nicobar Islands. In Tamil Nadu and in the Union Territory of Puducherry – the most affected area – approximately 7,000 houses were constructed'.[7] The aim was the realisation of 'community-oriented projects and good quality houses' (Caritas India 2005a: 2). In addition, the scale of this programme had to meet the managerial, financial, and technical parameters formulated by the partners of the international network. As, however, most local partners had never carried out a post-disaster housing-project of this type and scale before, the partners of the international network, together with Caritas India, decided that an organisational structure (see figure below) should be set up in order to achieve their goals.

7 | Former programme manager of Caritas India. Interview on 07.02.2012 (Internet phone).

Figure 7: Organigram of Caritas India and its partners

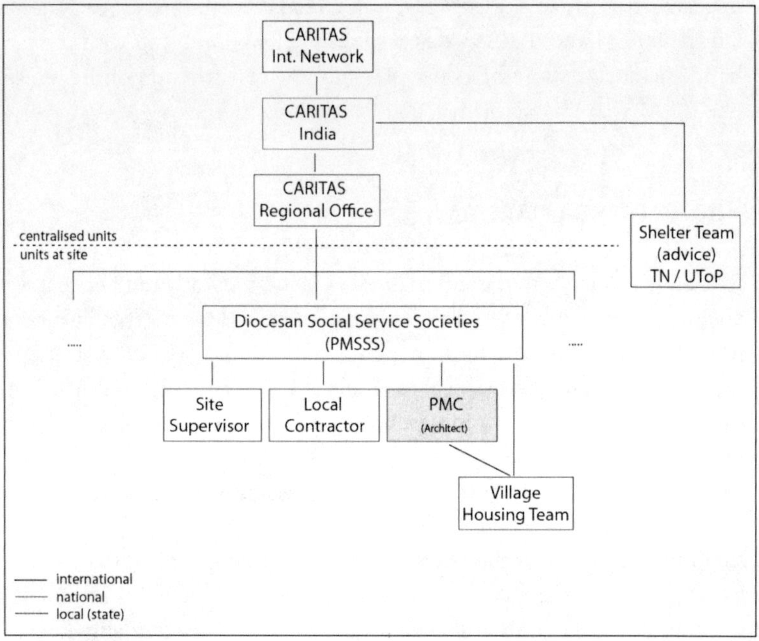

In this particular context, the NGO stressed the role of the architect as a project management consultant (hereafter PMC). The 'shelter rehabilitation programme is not simply a reconstruction project but a much more complex programme that ranges from mobilising the community to participate actively in the planning of the layout of the new habitat to the completion of the houses [In terms of] the complex shelter programme, each diocese has to appoint a project management consultant who will be responsible for handling the shelter programme throughout the various phases' (Caritas India 2005a: 2–3). In addition, a shelter team was appointed by Caritas India to help the local partners and their PMC with all issues related to the reconstruction projects.

The Role and Scope of Work of the Project Management Consultant

PMSSS appointed an architecture firm based in Puducherry with more than thirty years of experience in the construction business. The firm's professional record has ranged from small- to large-scale projects, from heritage conservation to low-income housing projects in India and La Réunion.[8] In this context it is important to ask the following questions. How were the scope and the role of the PMC defined in detail? How should the architect have ensured that the goals formulated by the NGO were realised? The contract signed between PMSSS and the architecture firm defined the scope of work, as illustrated in the grey-shaded column of the table below.

Table 3: Scope of work of the project management consultant

	PHASE I Programme formulation	PHASE II Project formulation	**PHASE III Planning**	**PHASE IV Construction**	PHASE V Post-Occupation
ARCHITECT / PMC	The reconstruction scheme(s) to be defined by the respective government alone or in cooperation with bi- and multilateral, international, national and local private agencies and NGOs	Finalisation of the beneficiaries' list, the location of the new village (relocation project); the size of the plot and the house; the infrastructure; the budget frame; and the mode of construction	Conceptual design Master plan House design Tender documents/ cost estimation Selection of contractors	Quality control Progress of work Certificate of completion	Follow-up on the project; repair of construction defects; modifications by the villagers

Apart from being responsible for all the technical aspects of the project, the 'PMC must ensure the participation of the community right from the beginning of the project start onwards in order to meet the villagers' needs. In order to achieve the goal of good quality houses the PMC must associate with specialists in the field of environmental planning, structural planning, sanitation and – eventually – with specialists on alternative technologies' (Caritas India 2005b: 7).

The PMC started working on Keezhakazakudy-Tsunami Nagar in phase III. At this time the new site had already been selected by government

8 | A husband (engineer) and wife (architect) firm. Their quotations will be labelled as PMC (eng.) and PMC (arch.).

officials along with *panchayat*[9] leaders, and the number of houses and the list of beneficiaries had already been finalised. A village-housing team was formed by PMSSS that should have, on behalf of the entire village, interacted with the PMC in the course of the planning stage. The PMC recalls the beginning as follows:

'We were under big time pressure. The government wanted houses to come up as quickly as possible. We were supposed to complete the planning process within a short time so that construction could take off. We started meeting and interacting with the fishermen randomly, and we tried to understand their needs. It was PMSSS staff who initiated the interaction with the villagers and discussed with them. We are not used to doing this kind of work. The idea of the new village layout is based on the creation of common spaces. We decided to develop a cluster plan on the 4.05 hectares of land provided by the government. We worked on several blueprints for the master plan, because the shelter team [of Caritas India], as you know, was strict and they also suggested to work out an alternative master plan. A cluster plan was finalised because we thought that it would meet the fishermen's daily life routines best. There are spacious open places were they can gather and repair their nets and boats, and dry the fish. These are crucial needs that we took into consideration. Moreover, trees can be planted on these open spaces to improve the micro-climate of the new hamlet. Also, space for a community hall, a school, an *anganwadi* and shops was provided in this plan. In fact, the community hall and the school were built, and they are in use. The cluster plan does have advantages when compared to a rigid row plan. It is not congested, and the breeze from the close by sea can pass easily. Finally, we had two meetings with the *panchayat* leaders before starting with the construction. There we presented the plans, and they said ok.'[10]

---

9 | Along the Coromandel Coast, almost every village has a *panchayat* of nominated members or elected members who represent the various lineages, headed by a man called *chettiyar* or *naddar*. This council, which consists wholly of adult males, is closely tied into a system of village membership and decision-making. Important matters are decided upon consensually in the context of the village meeting (Bavinck 2003: 650). The traditional (nominated) *panchayat* plays a crucial role in Pattanavar-dominated villages. Nothing can be done without their consent.

10 | PMC (arch.). Interview on 05.01.2012 in Puducherry.

Figure 8: Master plan of Keezhakazakudy-Tsunami Nagar (4.05 hectares), not to scale

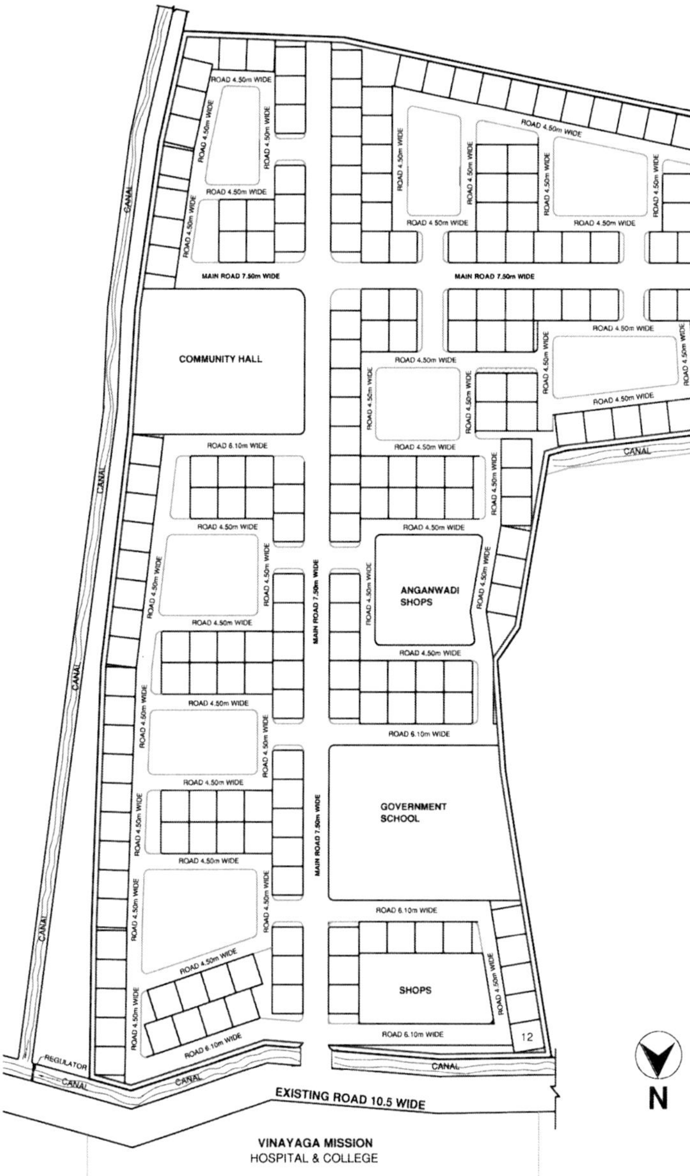

Source: Figures 8–11 courtesy of PMC

The house plan was developed 'providing 74.25m² per plot and 29.29m² per house. So within that given area we tried to accommodate all necessary features. The structure of the house was planned and constructed in such a way that the inhabitants can add, if needed, an additional floor, or they can, if wished, add a thatched roof. As the size of the plot is small, horizontal extension is not possible. Thus, we wanted to enable at least a vertical extension, and hence the structure was designed respectively. We also developed a colour scheme for the façade of the houses. Doing so, we wanted the village to look colourful, and not uniform. The house we planned is good, it is spacious and much better than the one most of the families had lived in before. They are now living in a *pucca* building, which the majority of the families could never have afforded in their lifetime.'[11]

Figure 9: Plot (74.25m²) and house plan (29.29m²), not to scale

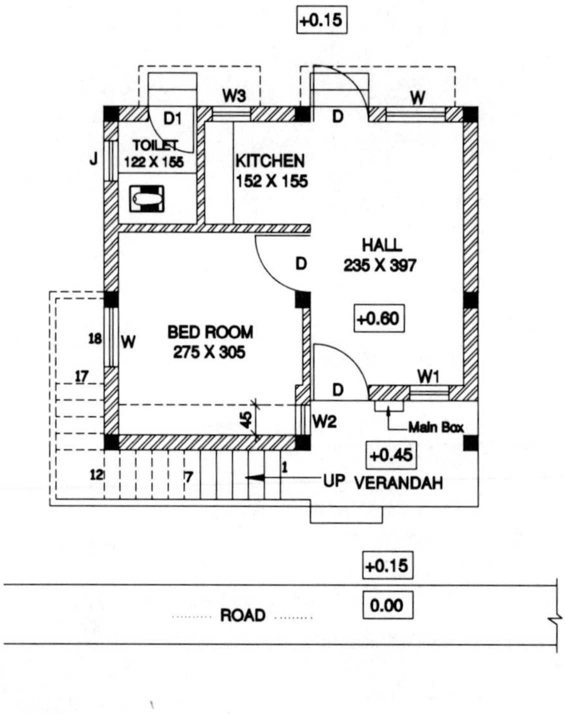

11 | PMC (arch.). Interview on 05.01.2012 in Puducherry.

Figure 10: Elevation, not to scale

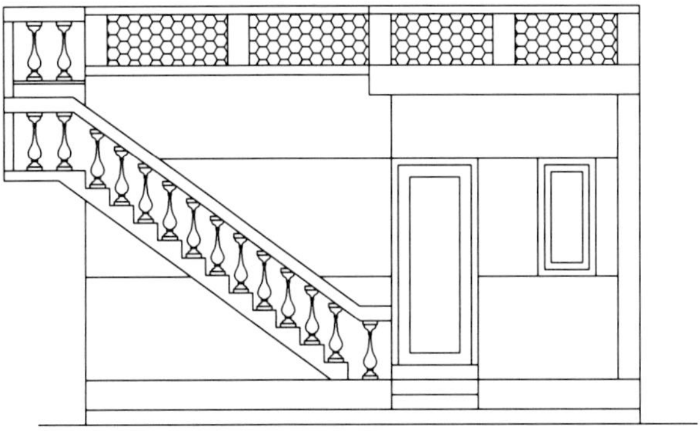

Figure 11: Section, not to scale

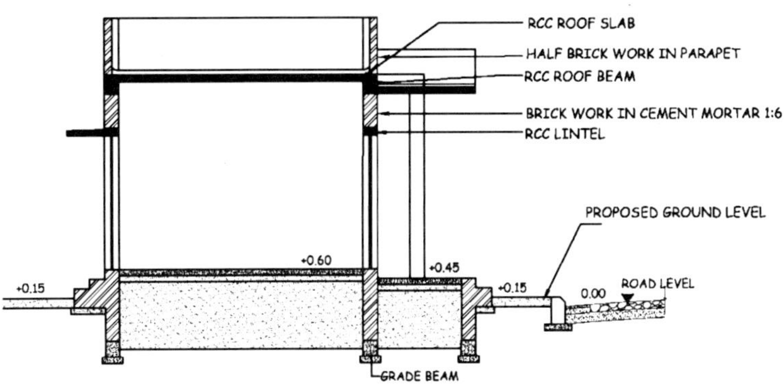

It was mandatory for NGOs to provide disaster-resistant houses, 'thus, we opted for deeper foundation with in-situ bored piles to a depth of 3.6m below the natural soil. Framed structure with RCC column and beam tied at ground level, roof level and at all free ends, and with burnt bricks in-fill.'[12] One type of house was developed for the entire village and the planning process was completed within two months. Construction began in September 2005. Two contractors were selected to ensure a smooth and quick construction of good-quality houses. The new houses were allocated to the

12 | PMC (eng.). Interview on 05.01.2012 in Puducherry.

fishers only after the completion of construction. Until then, the fishers did not know which, out of the 200 houses, would be theirs. 'We wanted to avoid the interference of the people in the construction process as this would lead to complications and further delays.'[13]

Picture 2: House close to completion

Source: Courtesy of PMC

The construction phase was, according to the PMC, a challenge, as by the middle of 2005 construction was in full swing all along the coastline. The availability of construction materials and of skilled and unskilled labour was scarce. Labour was unavailable and had to be imported from neighbouring states. Prices for bricks, cement, steel and wood, as well as for labour, 'went up exorbitantly and, in order to maintain good quality, extra money was allocated. Everyone struggled with this situation, all the NGOs and even the biggest and best contractors. Also, cooperation with government departments turned out to be very difficult. As they were in charge of the infrastructure works we had to coordinate closely with them. Housing and infrastructure need to be considered equally important. Co-

13 | Former executive director of PMSSS. Interview on 12.12.2011 in Neyveli.

operating with government engineers, however, was not at all a success.'[14] The project was completed in December 2006 and the houses were allocated to the fishers through lot, a guideline issued by the government. After having consulted their *svami* (priest) regarding the most auspicious date the fishers started moving into their new houses.

The Fishers' Voices Four Years Later

As has already been discussed the NGO's goal was the construction of people-centred houses of good quality. Further, it aimed to improve the housing situation of the fishers by providing *pucca,* disaster-resistant houses on a new and safer site. The field survey carried out for the purpose of this study revealed, however, that the housing situation had for only 45% of the households interviewed actually improved; another 27.5% said that their housing situation had not changed at all, and 25% answered that their housing situation had become worse. The findings suggest that the complex tasks of this reconstruction and resettlement project were addressed too simplistically (see Mathur 2006: 2). This feedback given by a fisherwoman reflects the overall atmosphere in the hamlet as found during the field survey:

> 'You can see, those who can afford it modified their house. People try to make best of the house they got. We struggle with many issues. The house is too small. We are eight people living in here: myself, my husband and our six children. And the plot is too small; we can not add any rooms. Some of us sleep outside. During the monsoon that is not possible. So we have to adjust, somehow. There is also not enough space for cooking and washing outside. We cook outside because of the smoke. All women cook outside [...] Now, you see, I have only a little space for cooking outside. The bathroom should not be in the house; it should be detached. They also forgot a *puja* room. We got a new house, but the quality is poor. They did not do quality work.'[15]

14 | PMC (eng.). Interview on 05.01.2012 in Puducherry.

15 | On 19.12.2011 in Keezhakazakudy-Tsunami Nagar.

She addresses several problems, namely the size of the plot, the size of the house, the layout of the house (location of the bathroom), the missing *puja* (prayer) room and the quality of construction. Who, in the course of the bu ilding process, was in charge of the issues mentioned by the fisherwoman? Which were the PMC's responsibilities and what do the results in the hamlet look like in detail?

The following table, 4, shows the breakdown of responsibilities in the course of the building process (who did what and when) and the results from Keezhakazakudy-Tsunami Nagar. The grey-shaded columns show the PMC's responsibilities, based on the scope of work as defined in the contract (see Table 3, p. 99). The household questionnaire identified eight aspects that were unsatisfactory (or a failure):

- the list of beneficiaries (unjust allocation of houses)
- the technology used (climatic condition inside the house)
- the sanitary facilities (the location and the technology)
- the size of the plot (too small compared to the old plot)
- the size of the house (too small compared to the old house)
- the house plan (the layout and the façade/design)
- the quality of construction materials
- the quality of construction

Out of the eight categories identified as unsatisfactory or a failure three, namely the house plan (the layout and the façade/design), the quality of construction materials, and the quality of construction, were among the PMC's responsibilities. How did the fishers view the PMC's performance?

Table 4 shows that the degree of satisfaction with regard to the house plan is very low. Only 13% of the interviewees were, according to the findings, satisfied with the new house, the arrangement of the rooms and the house as a whole. The majority, however, commented that their needs had not been incorporated into the design at all.

Moreover, it was found that the interviewees were not at all familiar with the architectural profession. In fact, the majority replied to the question, 'Do you know the architect who planned your new hamlet and your new house?' as follows: 'Architect? What is an architect? You mean engineer? I thought the village was planned by governmentengineers.'[16]

16 | Fisherwoman on 07.12.2011 in Keezhakazakudy-Tsunami Nagar.

Table 4: Breakdown of responsibilities and results for Keezhakazakudy-Tsunami Nagar (N=40)

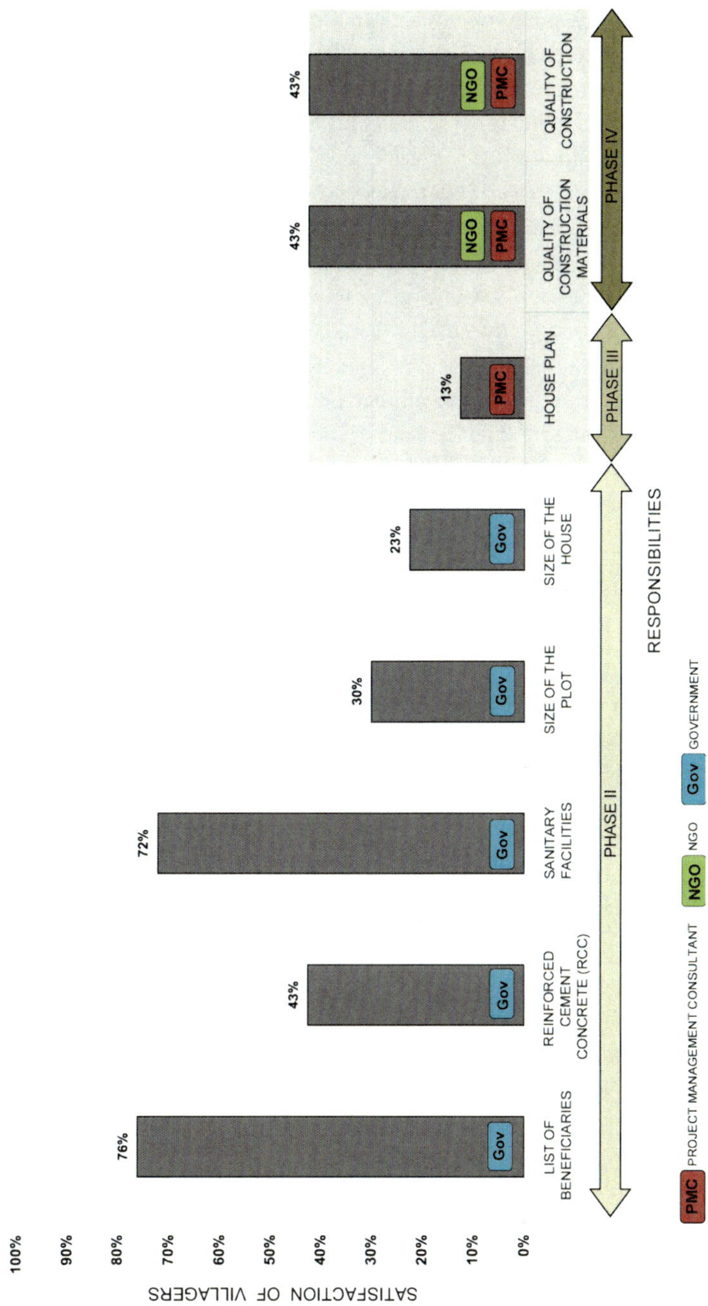

The field survey revealed that during the planning stage no interaction had taken place with the architect. In fact, 85% commented that they had never even seen the 'person' in charge of the project and that there had never been any opportunity to share their wishes and needs with him/her. Only, the '*panchayat* leaders were met prior to the start of construction, and they gave their consent to the plans presented.'[17] Furthermore, the fishers said that they were excluded from the entire construction phase. Hence, they could not carry out *pujas* at critical construction stages, and they did not have any influence with regard to the quality of construction. Even though they had observed the negligent work of the contractors, their complaints, as they expressed it, were not taken into consideration at all. The interviewees stated that 'no involvement of ourselves, the people, was permitted.'[18] The field survey further revealed that the villagers were disappointed as the promises given by the government and the NGO, namely the provision of a *pucca* house, did not correspond to the fishers' conception of a *pucca* house which, according to them, should 'meet our needs and be of good quality.'[19] Thus, many told us that they missed their old house. The table below shows the feedback given to the question: 'What are the positive and what are the negative features of the new house compared to the old house'.

Table 5: Positive features of the new house when compared to the old

Features	**(%)**
None	32.5
Sanitary facilities	5
Infrastructure facilities	50
Away from the sea (protection)	12.5

Interestingly, the features identified are mainly related to the provision of infrastructure facilities, namely the availability of electricity, and sanitary facilities. Moreover, the safety aspect (distance from the sea) is important. No feature was mentioned regarding the advantages of a *pucca* house. In-

17 | *Panchayat* leader on 17.12.2011 in Keezhakazakudy-Tsunami Nagar.

18 | Fisherman on 06.12.2011 in Keezhakazakudy-Tsunami Nagar.

19 | *Ibid.*

deed, the majority of the interviewees (82.5%) said that they missed their old house which was, in most cases, categorised by the government and NGO as *kachcha*. The overall evaluation of the PMC is shown in the table below. The answers given were diverse; however, a negative impression prevails.

Table 6: Impression of the architect

Impression	(%)
No answer	5
Bad (needs not included)	17.5
Did their job	10
Good	25
Not nice colour scheme	7.5
Not good/bad design and poor construction quality	5
Poor work	27.5
OK, they planned free of cost	2.5

The question, 'Would you like to work with this architect again?', was answered positively by 25% of the households interviewed. Nevertheless, they stressed, only provided that 'he sits with us, listens to what we need and plans accordingly.' Another 52.5% stated that they would, if they had a say, call the mason as 'he plans and builds according to our wishes, and he does good quality work.' Finally, 22.5% were undecided, however, they explained that the 'person doing this job should know us and understand what we need.'

Additional Factors Affecting the Degree of Satisfaction

During the field survey it was found that additional factors had a significant impact on the degree of success of the project, as 'complex problems inherent in the process [of resettlement were addressed] too simplistically' (Mathur 2006: 2). They were grouped into three main categories, namely social, technical and cultural factors.

- Social Factors

The finalisation of the beneficiaries' list and the allocation of the new houses carried out by government officials was, based on the fishers' feedback, unjust. According to the government's order a new house was provided only if the old one was relinquished (see CHAPTER The Reconstruction Policy). Out of the 200 houses built at the new site, however, only 150 households had to follow this policy. The other 50 houses are owned by fisher families who did not relinquish their old houses and, as they were in a powerful position, managed to get a new house at the new site as well. The former director of PMSSS commented that 'the finalisation of the beneficiaries' list was tricky and political. We did not interfere. It was the government's responsibility, as agreed in the MoU.'[20] The beneficiaries' list and the allocation of the houses were, as it turned out, a matter of power. Powerful fisher families managed to get a second house which 'they use in case of storms, for their guests and/or to store property.'[21]

- Technical Factors

It was found that the size of the land provided by the government for the new hamlet did not meet the requirements of a steadily-growing hamlet. The limited amount of land provided had a marked impact on the degree of satisfaction. 'By the end of 2006, when construction was completed, we had 46 new families in our village. We have had again 36 new families up until now, and they were all in need of a new house.'[22] However, there is no space available for the construction of new houses. Hence, young families 'are forced to settle elsewhere. The majority, however, return to the old hamlet; others migrate to neighbouring towns.'[23]

Furthermore, it was found that there was a striking difference between the houses with regard to the quality of construction. While some of the houses do not have any defects, others (approximately 25), located on the southeastern edge of the hamlet, have severe defects that range from cracks in the walls, to porous concrete (external staircase, veranda and flooring), leaking roofs, damp walls and crumbling plaster. The interviewees said that they had observed that the contractor in charge of this

---

20 | Former executive director of PMSSS. Interview on 12.12.2011 in Neyveli.

21 | Fisherman on 17.12.2011 in Keezhakazakudy-Tsunami Nagar.

22 | Traditional *panchayat* leader on 20.12.2012 in Keezhakazakudy-Tsunami Nagar.

23 | *Ibid.*

portion of houses did not care about quality at all. It became evident that the differences with regard to the quality of the house had a significant impact on the degree of satisfaction. Those living in the poorly-constructed buildings felt hard done by, as the NGO did not demand the contractors rectify the problems of all the houses. In addtion, it was found that the common open spaces which were, according to the PMC, planned based on the fishers' traditional lifestyle, are not in use.

Picture 3: A common space in Keezhakazakudy-Tsunami Nagar

Picture 4: Stagnating Water

- Cultural Factors

The degree of satisfaction was further influenced by the fact that the fishers were not involved at all when the houses were allocated. As they were allocated through lot only after the completion of construction, the fishers were excluded from shaping their own neighbourhood. In the Karaikal region the Pattanavar residential clusters are mainly based on lineage and kinship (see Bharathi 1999: 21). Thus, it is essential to consider and incorporate the complex and sensitive issue of neighbourhood when shaping a new habitat. However, this was not done in Keezhakazakudy-Tsunami Nagar, and it resulted, according to a fisherman, in neighbourhoods that are in conflict with each other. In addition, the absence of a temple lead to a high degree of dissatisfaction. 27.5% said that they missed having a temple and, as no temple had been constructed in the new hamlet, they continued worshipping in Keezhakazakudy-metu. Worshipping their gods in their temples, an essential religious habit and integral part of their daily routines, has become impossible at their new site. Thus, many interviewees said that they missed living in their old hamlet.

Picture 5: Temples in the old hamlet

The absence of big trees was another significant factor influencing the results. It mainly affected two categories, the construction technology used and the house (as a whole). In this hot climate trees are vital to create a micro-climate, providing shade from the strong sun (see also Naimi-Gasser 2012). Traditionally, coastal villages are immersed in thick and diverse vegetation. Likewise, Keezhakazakudy-metu was protected by thick vegetation, and thus, many fishers stated that 'the heat in the house during the summer time has become unbearable.' Trees are essential in rural habitations as they provide 'livelihood resources like fuel, fruits, vegetables, fodder,' (Duyne-Barenstein *et al.* 2010: 182), and they are used in construction (e.g. palm leaves for roofing).

Finally, it was found that the uniformity of the house design was a critical factor impacting on the degree of satisfaction. The diversity of houses found in the old hamlet was entirely neglected when developing the house design. As a consequence, those who could afford it started modifying the house immediately after having moved in. Some, it was found, added some extra room or an additional floor, others upgraded the house by laying tiles and by painting the interior and the façade with different colours. Those without financial resources, however, could not make any modifications, even if they had wanted. Many said that they wished that 'their house looked different from those of the rest of the village.'

Picture 6: A modified house

II: The Draftswoman

Director (Funding NGO Solidarité): 'We were ready to support a housing project using an alternative, a sustainable technology. We said no to mass housing in cement and steel. Also, we wanted the houses to be planned based on the Irulas' needs [...] Thus an architect was appointed, and we decided to implement an earthen, disaster-resistant technology, developed by the local Auroville Earth Institute.'[1]

Irula woman: 'Architect? I don't know the architect [...] We wanted to have normal houses like other villages. A house made out of bricks, plastered and nicely painted. This house looks like a police station. But we had no say. Who I would like to build the house with? With the mason; he plans and he builds based on my wishes, and he does good quality work.'[2]

---

1 | Interview with the co-founder and director of Solidarité on 15.12.2011 in Puducherry. This project was implemented by the local NGO BLESS and funded by the NGO Solidarité. In total, BLESS constructed 378 houses in this region (see http://bless.org.in/?page_id=26, accessed on 15.10.2011). This project was selected as a case study because the aim was to provide people-oriented housing using an alternative, more 'sustainable' construction technology, contrary to the NGO's other projects where the houses were constructed in RCC (reinforced cement concrete) (see CHAPTER Selection of the Case Studies).

2 | On 21.01.2012 in Shanmuga Nagar.

Project Outline

Name of revenue village:	Tirupanampakkam
Name of hamlet:	Shanmuga Nagar
Community:	Irula (Adivasi community)
District:	Cuddalore (TN)
Provider of the new houses:	NGO BLESS
Architecture Firm:	'Draftswoman' / Puducherry
Type of Project:	In-situ (reconstruction at the same site)
Number of houses constructed:	62 (semi-detached houses)
Type of construction:	Compressed Stabilised Earth Blocks (CSEB)
Built by:	Masons and villagers (unskilled labour)
Cost of house:	190,000 IRS[3]
Occupancy rate:	100%
Project duration:	May 2005–June 2007
Occupation by villagers:	June 2007
Field Research:	January 2012

3 | See APPENDIX B: Parameters affecting the Cost of the House.

The Hamlet, Its Location and Inhabitants

Shanmuga Nagar is situated on the north bank of the mouth of the Vellar river, approximately 30 km south of Cuddalore city. It is located in Cuddalore district, and it falls under the Cuddalore block[1]. Shanmuga Nagar is a small hamlet of an Adivasi community, the Irulas.

Figure 12: Location of Shanmuga Nagar

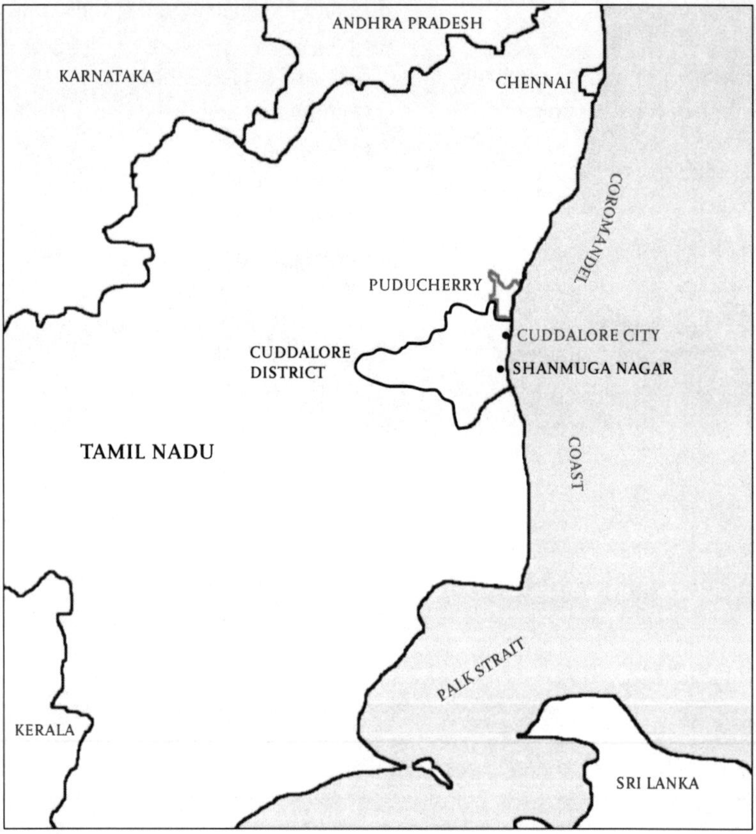

Irulas are mainly found in the states of Andhra Pradesh and TN. Predominantly they formed semi-nomadic groups of hunter-gatherers, mostly

1 | A block is a district sub-division which is below *taluk*-level administration.

living in forests (see Balaji 2007). However, the 'enactment of the Wildlife Protection Act in 1972 spelled a death blow to their lives in the forest' (UNTRS 2006a: 5). Intending to protect wildlife, this act prevented the Irulas from using forest resources. They were banished to non-forest areas and, in search of new occupations, they migrated to coastal regions. There, the Irulas settled in small villages, and since then they have mainly been engaged in subsidiary and allied activities. The government of India declared them 'one of many "Scheduled Tribes" which indicates the very low socio-economic statue that they occupy' (*ibid.*). The Constitution (Scheduled Tribes) Order of 1950 lists 744 tribes across 22 states in its First Schedule.[2] The Irulas of Shanmuga Nagar settled in Cuddalore district approximately 40 years ago. Since then, the families 'mainly subsist by labouring for fishermen and do backwater fishing for themselves. One alternative source of income is groping – using their hands beneath swamp backwaters for catching and collecting prawns. Some also work in mangrove forests along the coast' (*ibid.*: 6).

In total, 62 households are based at Shanmuga Nagar.[3] Traditionally, the Irulas' houses are built out of natural resources available in their vicinity. The materials they use are 'split bamboo, "*pompay*" grass or "*koyi*" grass, mud for the walls, wild creepers to tie the wood and bamboo' (Balaji 2007: 98). The ground level of the house is raised about a foot, protecting the family from floods during the monsoon. 'For the roofing they use bamboo poles over which they put the wild grass. This they tie with the locally available creepers' (*ibid.*). The Irulas plan their houses and their surroundings themselves. Houses are made individually, having open space around them. They also build their houses by themselves; there is no separate caste for this purpose. Each family builds a house of dimensions suited to their needs and capacity, and 'everyone knows how to build a house [...] Most of the houses consist of two rooms; one is a kitchen and the other one a bed room. They usually have small windows and doorways [...]' (*ibid.*). Before the tsunami of 2004, 100% of the housing stock in Shanmuga Nagar was classified as (serviceable) *kachcha*[4] by the government (see APPENDIX D: 'Traditional' House Typologies in Irula Villages).

2 | See http://lawmin.nic.in/ld/subord/rule9a.htm (accessed on 25.01.2013).

3 | Data based on the field survey of January 2012.

4 | For the definition see CHAPTER The Revised Policy.

Picture 7: Location of Shanmuga Nagar (red) and burning ground (red) (based on Google Maps 19.03.2012)

Source: Based on Google maps 19.03.2012

After the Tsunami of 2004

The locally registered NGO Bless had already been working with the Irulas living in Shanmuga Nagar for many years before the tsunami of 2004, and it came forward to provide new houses for them. A MoU was signed between Bless and the government. Even though the Irulas' houses were not as badly affected as most fishers' hamlets Bless decided to focus on the construction of *pucca* houses as the Irulas had been living in 'backward huts for generations.'[5] Unlike in other hamlets, however, the issue of relocation was not addressed. Shanmuga Nagar was located approximately 1km inland. Thus, it was decided that the new houses should be constructed at the same site (in-situ), adjacent to the Irulas' old houses.

First of all, however, before starting this housing project, the issue of land property had to be settled with the government. Even though the families had been living on this land for the past 40 years it was not theirs. Thus, BLESS demanded the government 'register the land in the name of the families [...] This, however, turned out to be a very tedious and time-consuming process. But we made it clear to the government that unless the land would be registered in the families' names we would not

5 | Executive director of Bless. Interview on 20.11.2011 in Reddychavadi.

construct houses.'[6] Furthermore, some more land had to be allocated to the hamlet for 'future expansion and also for the accommodation of some common utilities.'[7] It was agreed, finally, that BLESS would be responsible for 'the planning of the masterplan, the house plan and the construction of the 62 houses including sanitary facilities as well as a community hall, a *balwadi* (nursery school), a playground and some shops. The government, on the other hand, was in charge of providing infrastructure such as electricity and water which had not been – even before the tsunami – available in Shanmuga Nagar.'[8]

Project Organisation

BLESS was founded in 1989 in Cuddalore, and since then it has been working as a locally registered NGO with the financial support of local and international partners. Post-disaster reconstruction was a new experience for BLESS. Still, however, it took part in the reconstruction programme in various villages affected by the tsunami, constructing 378 houses in total.[9] The construction projects were funded by different partners. For Shanmuga Nagar the French NGO Solidarité, based at Puducherry, came forward to finance the construction project. However, as a precondition Solidarité made it mandatory that 'BLESS opted for an alternative approach [...] We said no to financing post-disaster mass housing in steel and concrete, and we wanted the community to participate right from the beginning [...] the Irulas should be convinced about the advantages of this alternative technology.'[10] In general, the implementation of alternative technologies was possible in TN. However, NGOs had to prove that this alternative technology met the parameters defined for disaster-resistant houses (see CHAPTER The Reconstruction Policy).

BLESS had no experience of implementing alternative housing technologies whatsoever. Hence, to achieve the aims defined by Solidarité and the parameters formulated by the government it was decided that, first of

6 | *Ibid.*

7 | *Ibid.*

8 | *Ibid.*

9 | http://www.bless.org.in/achievements.html (27.06.2012).

10 | *Ibid.*

all, an architect should be appointed. The architect should then, with the support of the local Auroville Earth Institute, design the new houses for the Irula families. Moreover, to meet the managerial challenges of this project an appropriate organisational structure had to be set up (see figure below).

Figure 13: Organigram of Bless

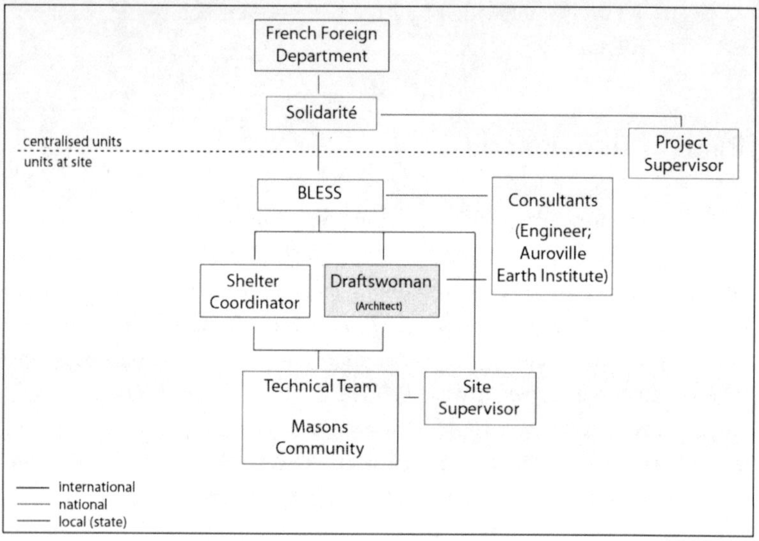

The Role and Scope of Work of the Draftswoman

BLESS appointed a locally well-established architect who, until that point in her career, had not been exposed to the planning and implementation of alternative construction technologies. Thus she had to, first of all, become familiar with the technology chosen for this project, namely Compressed Stabilised Earth Blocks (hereafter CSEB). CSEB were developed by the local Auroville Earth Institute. Since then they have been promoted as an alternative and sustainable technology, for the following reasons. 'Earth is a local material [...] Earth construction is a labour-intensive technology and it is an easily adaptable and transferable technology. It is a cost and energy effective material. It is much less energy consuming than country fired bricks (about 4 times less). It is much less polluting than country fired bricks (about 4 times less).'[11] The draftswoman attended a one-week course at the Auroville Earth Institute. This included, theory of the basics on earthen architecture, soil characteristics, designing with earthen blocks, calculation and the practice of block making and quality control. As BLESS had already decided what the new house plan should look like, the architect's scope of work (hereafter draftswoman) was defined as illustrated in the grey-shaded column of the table below.[12]

Table 7: Scope of work of the draftswoman

	PHASE I Programme formulation	PHASE II Project formulation	**PHASE III Planning**	PHASE IV Construction	PHASE V Post-Occupation
ARCHITECT / Draftswoman	The reconstruction scheme(s) to be defined by the respective government alone or in cooperation with bi- and multilateral, international, national and local private agencies and NGOs	Finalisation of the beneficiaries' list, the location of the new house (in-situ project); the size of the plot and house; the infrastructure; the budget frame; and the mode of construction	Master plan Adaptation of the house plan to CSEB Obtaining government approvals Cost estimation Demarcation of the new layout of the hamlet	Procurement of construction materials and skilled and unskilled labour; site coordination; supervision of the progress of work, and quality control	Follow-up on the project; the repair of construction defects; modifications by the villagers

The new master plan was based on the existing structure of the hamlet. However, 'the previous haphazard arrangement of the houses was changed slightly to bring more order. Also, the layout of the plot was changed from a single family house into a layout of semi-detached houses. The roads were straightened and widened, and the temple's space, which is located in the midst of the houses, has the shape of a semi-circle that opens out to the east.'[13] The reason for building semi-detached houses, instead of single-family houses was, according to the director of BLESS, threefold. 'First of all, it was a question of finance. When you build a semi-detached

11 | See: http://www.earth-auroville.com/compressed_stabilised_earth_block_en.php (accessed on 25.01.2013).

12 | Unfortunately, the architect was not available for an interview. All information gathered about the architect's role and scope of work was obtained during the interview with the executive director of BLESS.

13 | *Ibid.*

house you have one common wall for the two houses. So you don't need to construct two walls, and this reduces the cost. Secondly, by giving them a semi-detached house we wanted to prevent that the Irula families sell their house; and thirdly, we wanted to ensure that there is joint planning in the future.'[14]

Picture 8: Master plan drawn on the wall of the community building

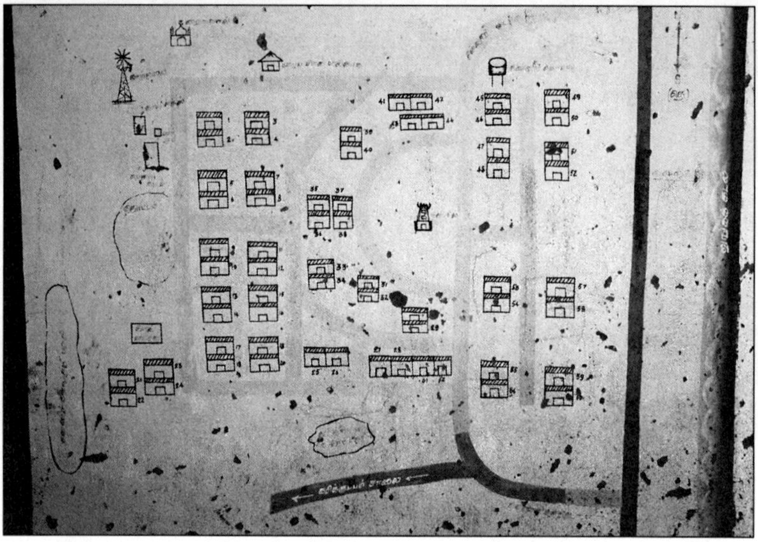

14 | Executive director of BLESS. Interview on 20.11.2011 in Reddichavady.

Figure 14: Master plan of Shanmuga Nagar, not to scale

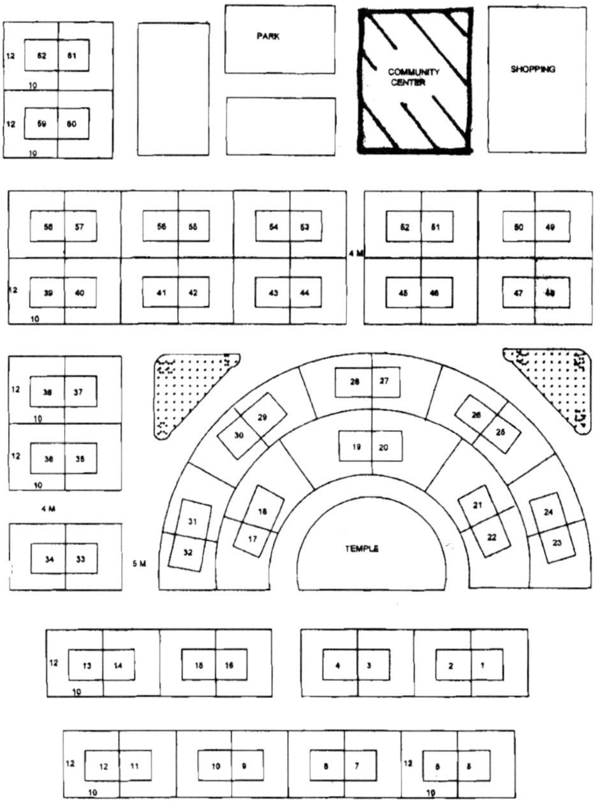

Source: Figures 14–17 courtesy of Bless

Figure 15: Layout of the plot (semi-detached houses with the toilet in the rear corner), not to scale

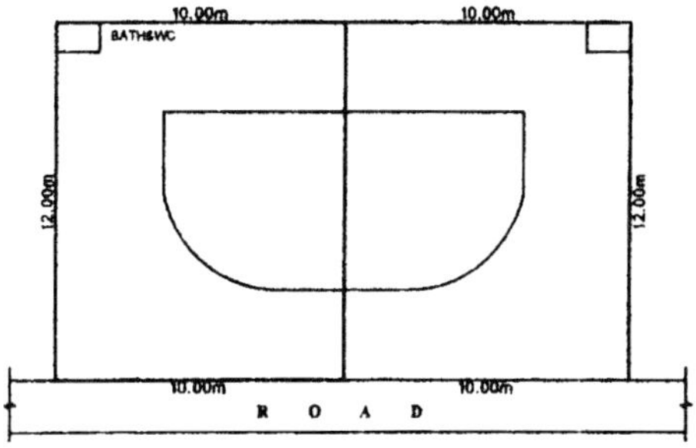

Figure 16: Semi-detached houses (base-plan which was adapted to CSEB), not to scale

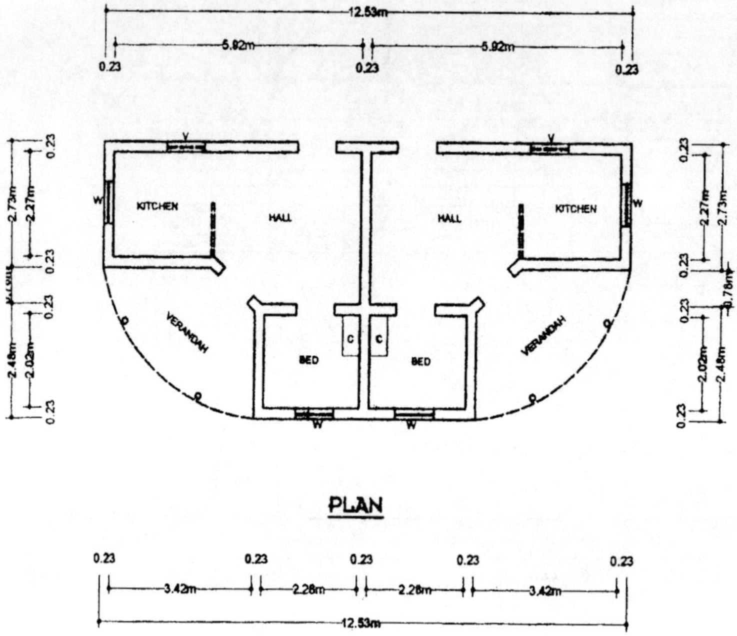

Figure 17: Elevation, not to scale

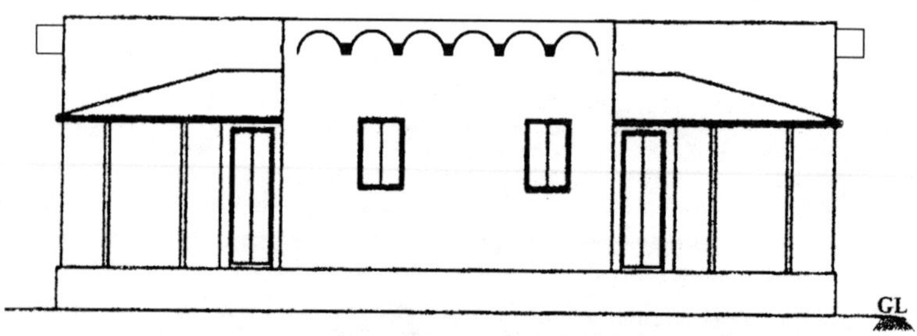

The house plan was adapted to the use of CSEB by the draftswoman after having attended the course at the Auroville Earth Institute. The plans were presented to the community, and the advantages of CSEB technology was explained by the draftswoman. However, as it turned out, the 'families were not at all convinced about this technology and about the twin house. They wanted their house to be built in RCC, and nicely plastered. They were not at all happy with this technology. Our office here in Reddichavady, as you can see, is also built with compressed blocks. To convince them, we invited them to our office. Only after seeing this building, they slowly, slowly got convinced.'[15]

Three model houses were constructed prior to finalising the plans as, according to the director of BLESS, 'the families should experience the future house in its third dimension.' However, the three model houses 'were built out of burnt bricks and plastered.'[16]

Planning and preparatory works were completed within eight months and construction began in December 2005. Before starting construction, however, the plans had to be approved by various public authorities. Though alternative technologies were allowed in Tamil Nadu 'obtaining the construction permit was a huge challenge. Convincing government engineers was not an easy task.'[17] Only after long negotiations, and the fact that CSEB technology had already been approved by other governments,[18] were the permits were obtained. Skilled masons were appointed for the construction work, and the Irulas (men and women alike) were engaged as unskilled labour, producing the bricks. They had to, 'first of all, be trained to get familiar with this technology [...] and then they were engaged as labour in this work until the completion of the houses.'[19] The soil for the blocks had to be transported from 'far away as the quality of soil available at the site was not good. It did not meet the technical specifications.'[20] The

15 | Executive director of Bless. Interview on 20.11.2011 in Reddichavady.

16 | *Ibid.*

17 | *Ibid.*

18 | So far, CSEB has been approved by three governments: the government of Gujarat for the rehabilitation of the zones affected by the earthquake of January 2001 in Kutch district; the government of Iran (Housing Research Centre) for the rehabilitation of the zones affected by the 2003 earthquake in Bam; the government of Tamil Nadu (Relief and Rehabilitation) for the rehabilitation of the zones affected by the tsunami of 2004. See: http://www.earth-auroville.com/disaster_resistance_introduction_en.php (accessed on 26.01.2013).

19 | Executive director of BLESS. Interview on 20.11.2011 in Reddichavady.

20 | *Ibid.*

production of the blocks at the site was organised as shown in the drawing below.

Figure 18: Typical block-yard layout, not to scale

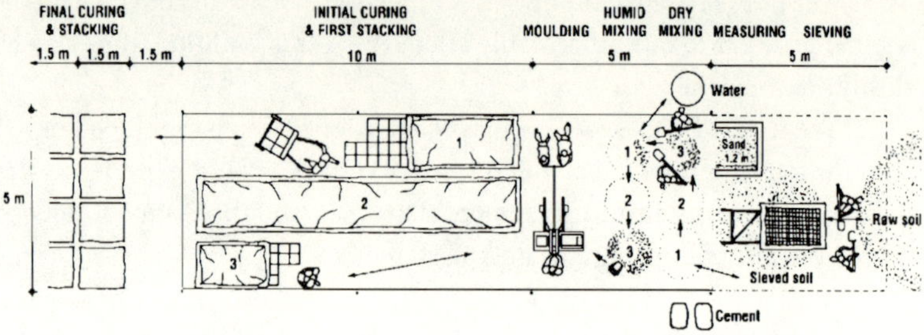

Source: Courtesy of Auroville Earth Institute[21]

During construction, the families lived in temporary huts right next to their new house. The project was completed and occupied by the families in June 2007.

Picture 9: CSEB semi-detached house with vaulted ferro-cement roofing

21 | http://www.earth-auroville.com/compressed_stabilised_earth_block_en.php (accessed on 26.01.2013).

The Irulas' Voices Four Years Later[22]

As has already been discussed, the NGO decided to use an alternative construction technology for the new houses to improve the Irulas' 'backward' housing condition. Moreover, they felt that the Irulas should actively participate during the construction stage actively as this would help to increase, according to the director of BLESS, 'the families' sense of ownership for the new house and the construction quality'.[23]

However, only 50% of the households interviewed stated that their housing situation had improved. Another 10% commented that their situation had remained the same and 33.3% said that their housing situation had become worse. 6.7% did not answer this question. The following comment given by an Irula man exemplifies the general atmosphere in the hamlet:

> 'We are not used to living in twin houses. Earlier each family had its own house; a small house with more land around it. Now the house is bigger but the land around it is less and we don't have enough space for gardening and for the goats [...] We asked for a normal house, made out of bricks and plastered. Whenever it rains, we cannot stay inside the house as water leaks through the roof and the walls. The quality is very poor. We would like to repair it but we can't do that as you need specific machinery and you need money. When cyclone Thane hit, our floors were flooded, water entered from the roof and the walls. We were evacuated. On coming back, the water was gone, however, the floors and walls were still damp [...] Also, we can't use the toilets; you need to put ash on them. But we need water [...] We never wanted such houses. However, we had no say.'[24]

This commentary notes that several problems have not been solved satisfactorily, namely the type of the house (semi-detached house), the quality of construction, the technology used which renders self-repair impossible, and the new sanitary system which they have still not become familiar with. Who, in the course of the building process, was responsible for the

22 | The project was completed in June 2007. Field research was carried out in January 2012.

23 | Executive director of Bless. Interview on 20.11.2011 in Reddichavady.

24 | On 22.01.2012 in Shanmuga Nagar.

issues listed by the Irula? What were the draftswoman's responsibilities and what does the feedback obtained in the hamlet look like in detail?

Table 8 (following page) shows the breakdown of responsibilities (who did what and when) during the course of the building process and the results obtained in Shanmuga Nagar. The grey-shaded column marks the draftswoman's responsibility based on the scope of work as defined by the NGO. In total seven categories were identified as unsatisfactory (or a failure):

- the technology of construction (CSEB)
- the sanitary facilities (unfamiliar with the technology)
- the size of the plot
- the size of the house
- the house plan (twin house, layout and design)
- the quality of construction materials
- the quality of construction

Out of the seven factors identified as unsatisfactory or a failure, one, the house plan, was among the draftswoman's responsibilities. How did the Irulas reflect on the draftswoman's overall performance?

83.3% of the interviewees stated that their needs were not incorporated into the new house. For example, they explained that they needed a roofed space outside for cooking. 'We women, we cook outside, always, because of the smoke.'[25] However, facilities for cooking were only provided inside the house. Constructing additional structures outside on their own was, as the field survey revealed, beyond the financial capacity of the families. Moreover, the interviewees said that they needed a flat roof which they could use, for example, for drying fish.

The answer to the question, 'Do you know the architect who planned your new hamlet and your new house?' shows that 76.7% did not know the architect at all. Moreover, it became evident that they are not familiar with the profession of being an architect, and they said that they had 'never seen him'.[26]

---

25 | On 22.01.2012 in Shanmuga Nagar.

26 | The interviewees referred to a man, assuming that the architect had been a man.

Table 8: Breakdown of responsibilities and results for Shanmuga Nagar (N=30)

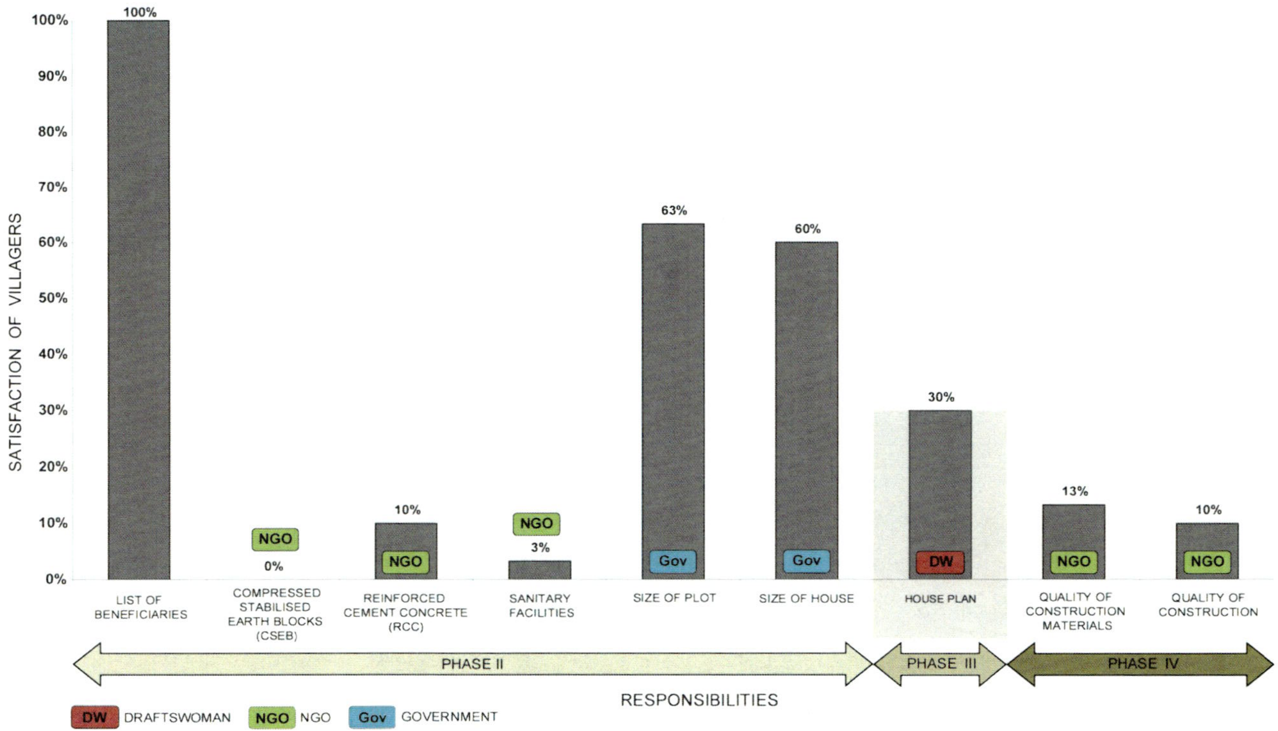

Furthermore, all interviewees (100%) pointed out that they did not play any role in the decision-making process. 'The final plans were shown to us, construction was started and we had to produce the blocks.'[27]

The field survey revealed that the concept of a 'sustainable house for the Irulas', as promoted by the NGO, could only be partially realised. 50% commented that their housing situation had improved. For 33.3% the housing situation had become worse, and another 10% stated that their housing situation had not changed at all. 6.7% did not want to comment on this question.

The table below illustrates in detail the feedback given to the question: 'What are the positive features of the new house compared to the old house?'

Table 9: Positive features of the new house when compared to the old

Features	(%)
None	33.3
Infrastructure facilities (electricity)	16.7
Permanent house	20
Permanent house and electricity	16.7

It was found that the majority of the interviewees were not satisfied with the draftswoman's performance. This was mainly in relation to two areas: the construction technology used and the poor quality of construction. The table below highlights how they evaluated the draftswoman's performance.

27 | Irula woman on 22.01.2012 in Shanmuga Nagar.

Table 10: Impression of the architect

Impression	(%)
Good	13.3
Bad	3.3
Good, well designed	3.3
Poor work	40
Well designed but poor construction quality	20
Not good, bad design and poor construction quality	13.5
No idea, I have never seen him	3.3
Did their job	3.3

Finally, the field survey revealed that only a minority (13%) would like to work with this architect again, provided that she cooperated with them, incorporated their needs and their wishes regarding construction materials, and the decoration of the façade. Another 10% replied with a clear yes. 53.5% responded with a no, and 16.7% explained that, due to the poor quality of construction, they would not work with this architect again. Another 6.7% did not want to comment on this question at all.

Additional Factors Affecting the Degree of Satisfaction

The survey was carried out three weeks after cyclone Thane had hit the region of Puducherry and Cuddalore district.[28] Shanmuga Nagar was, among many other hamlets, affected by this cyclone. 59 households (out of 62) had to be evacuated, as their houses were flooded. According to the villagers 'the water entered from everywhere: the roofs, the walls, the windows [...] The floors were full of water. In my house it came up to my knees.'[29] The families were brought to a nearby school where they had to stay for three days until the water was gone. However, after returning, 'the

28 | Cyclone Thane hit Puducherry and Cuddalore district on 30.12.2011.

29 | Irula woman on 23.01.2012 in Shanmuga Nagar.

floors, the walls and the ceiling were still damp. It took days to dry. Being inside was not at all comfortable.'[30]

During the course of the survey it became evident that the aftermath of this cyclone has had a clear impact on the degree of satisfaction. Disaster-resistant *pucca* houses had been promised to the Irulas. However, only three houses (i.e. the model houses built in RCC) out of 62 fulfilled this promise.

Picture 10: Model house in RCC (front) and CSEB (back)

Moreover, it was found that additional parameters influenced the degree of satisfaction. They were grouped into two main categories, technical and cultural factors.

- Technical Factors

Even though 36.7% said that they were satisfied with the fact that they were now living in a permanent house (see Table 9, p. 132), it was found that it was the poor quality of construction that influenced, above all, the degree of satisfaction. The roofs (vaulted ferro-cement roofing) of 59 hous-

30 | Irula man on 21.01.2012 in Shanmuga Nagar.

es leaked.[31] Ferro-cement is a form 'of reinforced concrete using closely spaced multiple layers of mesh and/or small diameter rods completely infiltrated with, or encapsulated, in mortar. The cement component of the mortar shall not be less than 1:3, cover over the mesh should not be less than 4mm' (Auroville 1997: 2). The construction work in Shanmuga Nagar, however, proved to be defective for two reasons. First of all, the roofing channels should incline '5cm per meter slope [as this] will drain the water off quickly and negate the effects of stagnating water' (*ibid.*: 5). However, it was found that the vaulted ferrocement channels of the houses in Shanmuga Nagar were not built to this specification. Hence, whenever there is a rainfall, heavy or light, the water stagnates on the roofs and can only, if at all, be removed manually. Secondly, the ferro-cement channels are porous as, most likely, the specifications of the mix ratio of 1:3 and the cover over the mesh of not less than 4mm were not carried out.

Picture 11: Vaulted ferro-cement roofing

31 | Out of the 62 houses the three model houses were constructed as flat roofed RCC (reinforced cement concrete) houses, and they are plastered. It was found that the quality of construction was far superior to the houses built with CSEB. Moreover, these houses were not affected by the cyclone.

The second major parameter influencing the degree of satisfaction was related to the fact that self-repair has become impossible. Repairing the defects described above requires specific machinery, know-how, construction materials and, above all, sufficient financial means. A interviewee states: 'We cannot do it, and we asked the NGO. They said they didn't have funds for this. Earlier, we used to repair our houses ourselves. We knew how to do it. We did not need anybody [...] The repair work to be done here is expensive and you need specific tools.'[32]

- Cultural Factors

The provision of semi-detached houses instead of single-family houses had a clear impact on the degree of satisfaction. Earlier, each family used to live in individual houses that differed in regard to size and shape, even though the construction materials were the same (mud walls with thatched roofs). They said that their old houses used to stand in the middle of the plot and were surrounded by land. Many said that the semi-detached houses were not in line with their traditions, and they were not used to this way of living.

Picture 12: Rear side of the semi-detached house (toilet, not in use, on the left)

32 | Irula man on 21.01.2012 in Shanmuga Nagar.

Furthermore, the provision of ecosan (ecological sanitation) toilets was another crucial factor affecting the degree of satisfaction. Ecosan solutions intend to solve sanitation problems more sustainably, recovering the resources contained in excreta and wastewater and using them, rather than discharging them into water bodies and the surrounding environment.[33] The ecosan latrine provided in Shanmuga Nagar is a dry-compost toilet with two chambers. Each of the chambers is to be used, alternately, every six months. The urine and the water for washing are let into a separate pipe, which is taken to a flowerbed or vegetable farmland. After defecation a handful of ash, kept by the toilet, is sprinkled over the excreta and it is closed with a lid. The chamber will fill up in about six months when it is sealed and the other chamber used. The excreta in the first chamber is transformed into compost in about six months and can be removed for use on agricultural fields.

Figure 19: Dry-compost double-pit latrine

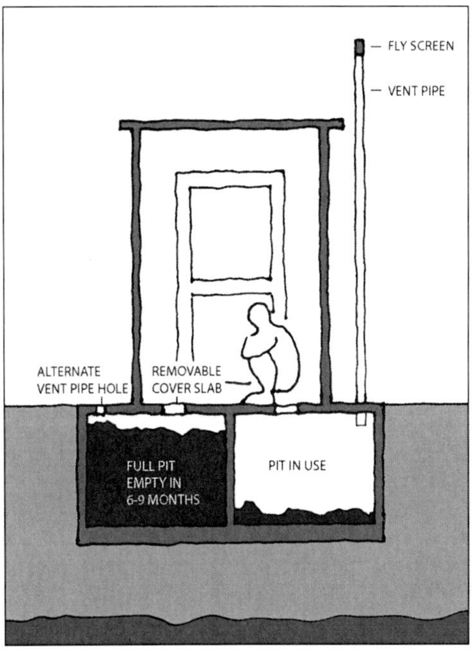

33 | See Ecosan Services Foundation: http://www.ecosanservices.org/esf/projects.html (accessed on 04.02.2013).

As the concept of ecosan toilets was new to the families, training courses were carried out intending 'to educate and to make them familiar with the technology.'[34] However, it was found that this technology was not accepted at all. The majority expressed a feeling of unease as 'we don't know how to handle the toilet. It is a specific technology. One needs to use ash, but we would need water. We don't use it.' 98% of the toilets, it was found, are not in use and already in ruins.

34 | Executive director of BLESS on 20.12.2011 in Reddichavady.

III: The Surveyor-Anthropologist

Project Manager, SIFFS: 'For SIFFS the questions to be answered were, what could be the right strategy and what type of architect would we need? We wanted an alternative that would overcome callousness towards community perception and lack of attention to individual needs. Thus, we were looking for an architect who could actually address these issues and put them into practice.'[1]

Fisherwoman: 'We were lucky with this architect. Many things are well done. But, there are some problems. For example: the orientation of the bathroom. It should not face the neighbour's house [...] Who I would like to build the house with? I would call this architect again, if he would like to plan a single small house. I would tell him about the toilet and the quality. But I think he goes for big projects in cities only. So, I would call the mason.'[2]

1 | Interview with the project manager of SIFFS on 31.01.2012 in Tarangambadi. In total, SIFFS constructed 1,380 houses in four hamlets in Nagapattinam districts (see also SIFFS 2009: 32).

2 | On 27.12.2011 in Tarangambadi-Tsunami Nagar.

Project Outline

Name of the revenue village:	Tarangambadi
Name of the old hamlet:	Tarangambadi
Name of the new hamlet:	Tarangambadi-Tsunami Nagar
Community:	Fishers (Pattanavar)
District:	Nagapattinam (TN)
Provider of the new houses:	NGO SIFFS (South Indian Federation of Fishermen Societies)
Architecture Firm:	'Surveyor-Anthropologist', Chennai[3]
Type of project:	In-situ and relocation
Number of houses constructed:	1,091 (278 in-situ and 813 relocated)
Type of construction:	Framed structure (RCC and brick filling)
Built by:	Labour contractor, NGO, community
Cost per house:	256,000 IRS (average cost per house)[4]
Occupancy rate:	98.63%[5]
Project completion:	Phase 1 (451 houses) May 2007; Phase 2 (170 houses) February and March 2008; Phase 3 (285 houses) May 2008, Jannuary and February 2009; Phase 4 (116 houses) February 2009; Phase 5 (69 houses) December 2009
Occupation by villagers:	Phase 1: May 2007 (The rest of the houses were occupied as soon as construction was completed)
Field survey:	December 2011

3 | The architect led a team of architects and students of architecture which was assigned responsibility for the village documentation, the conception of the master plan and the house plans. After the planning phase he left the project. However, the team members continued to work on the project until its completion. They were in charge of adapting the house typologies based on the villagers' feedback during the various construction stages.

4 | See APPENDIX B: Parameters Affecting the Cost of the House.

5 | Fifteen houses are not inhabited by families but they are used as storage (field survey December 2011).

The Hamlet, Its Location and Inhabitants

Tarangambadi (former Tranquebar) is a *panchayat* town in Nagapattinam district, located 15 km north of Karaikal near the mouth of the Kaveri River. Tarangambadi is the headquarters of Tarangambadi *taluk* and its name means 'place of the singing waves'. It was founded by the Danish East India Company and it was a Danish colony from 1620 to 1845. It was 'sold to the British East Indian Company and remained British until India's independence in 1947' (Grønseth 2007: 4).

Figure 20: Location of Tarangambadi and Tarangambadi-Tsunami Nagar

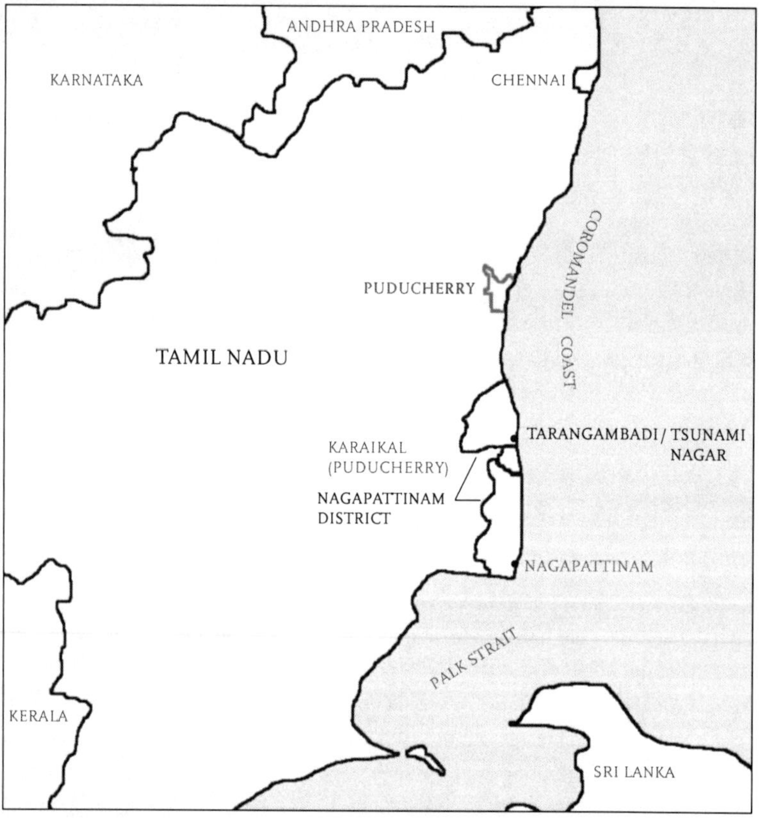

The historic part of Tarangambadi is elevated, and it is located in the southern area of the village. Here, the Danish, and later missionaries, constructed several buildings. The Danish fort, for example, used to be the governor's residence and headquarters. Today it is a museum hosting a collection of colonial artefacts. On the northern edge of Tarangambadi the fishers settled on a low lying land close to the shore. Earlier it used to be a busy harbour, however, since the construction of a road to Nagapattinam, it has lost its importance.

Picture 13: Location of the historic part (yellow) of Tarangambadi and the fishers' old hamlet (red)

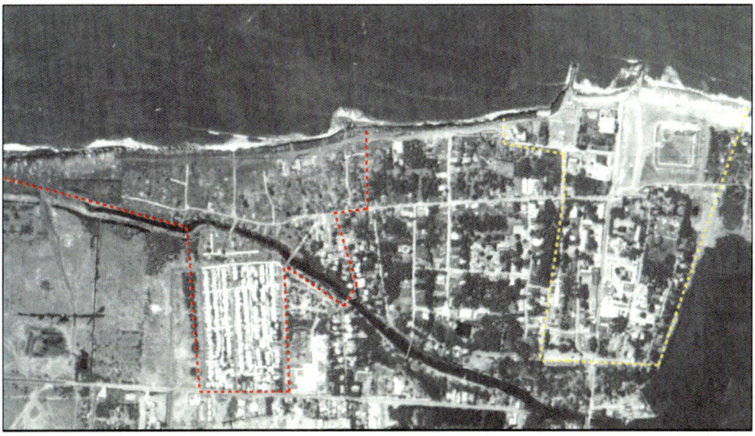

Source: Based on Google maps 15.04.2012

Tarangambadi is a relatively large village 'with 1,725 households. The village population of 6,991 comprises mainly [the] fishing community (1,112 households)' (SIFFS 2009: 1). Christian and Muslim families also live in Tarangambadi, but they are 'engaged in other occupations. Dalit populations inhabit Velli Palayam, Puthu Palayam, Kesavan Playam and Karantheru hamlets on the periphery of the village' (*ibid.*). The fishers of Tarangambadi belong to the Pattanavar caste and they work, like the fishers of Keezhakazakudy-metu and Keezhakazakudy-Tsunami Nagar, in the local artisanal fishing industry.

After the Tsunami of 2004

Tarangambadi was one of the worst-affected villages of the tsunami of 2004 in South India. The government of TN estimated that 'approximately 1,800 houses were destroyed.'[6] Based on this estimate Tarangambadi needed a total of '1,800 *pucca* and disaster-resistant houses to be reconstructed' (*ibid.*). Initially, the Kerala-based NGO SIFFS did not have any ambition to take on housing projects as, according to the project manager, 'we did not have any experience whatsoever with housing projects in general and post-disaster housing in particular.'[7] After long discussions, however, it was decided to join the reconstruction housing programme. SIFFS' response was, ultimately, conditioned by the fact that it had an 'ongoing relationship with many of the affected communities through its work with artisanal fishermen. The NGO was in a position of unique advantage because of its knowledge of fisheries and fishing communities' (SIFFS 2009: 2). Finally, four villages in Nagapattinam district were taken on by SIFFS. Tarangambadi was a natural choice as it was one of three villages in Nagapattinam district where SIFFS had founded fishermen's societies before the tsunami. A MoU was signed between the district administration and the NGO finalising the responsibilities of the two entities involved. The land was provided by the government, including infrastructure. The laying out of the master plan, the house plan and the construction of the houses had to be done by SIFFS.

Project Organisation

SIFFS habitat reconstruction projects were funded by various agencies, Swiss Solidarity (SwS) and the Swiss Red Cross (SRC), Terre des Hommes (Germany), Philips Electronics India Limited, and Christian Aid (CA), United Kingdom. 'Among the partners supporting the project, SKAT[8] had a major role in construction management and quality control.'[9]

6 | Project manager of SIFFS. Interview on 31.01.2012 in Tarangambadi.

7 | *Ibid.*

8 | Skat is an independent Swiss organisation working in the fields of development and humanitarian aid. See http://www.skat.ch/ (accessed on 25.01.2012).

9 | Project Manager of SIFFS. Interview on 31.01.2012 in Tarangambadi.

The starting point for planning the reconstruction was, according to the project manager of SIFFS, 'to study, first of all, past post-disaster experiences.'[10] A visit was organised for the SIFFS team and *panchayat* leaders of the proposed projects to Bhuj, Gujarat. They visited various housing projects that had been constructed in this region after the earthquake of 2001. 'The visit provided insights into typical examples of successes and failures in mass housing projects.'[11] This was 'facilitative for the formulation of the project approach. SIFFS understood that if the houses were not built based on the villagers' realities and needs, it would be another disaster involving colossal wastage of money and time.'[12] Hence, it was decided that the reconstruction approach for the post-tsunami projects in Nagapattinam district had to overcome the 'limitations caused by the three aspects of typical projects, callousness towards community perception, lack of attention to the individual needs, and contractor driven method which pre-empted the possibility of peoples' participation in the process' (SIFFS 2009: 6). The idea was to go beyond the mere provision of four walls and a roof; to see the houses as customised products, having cultural, economic, technical and political dimensions. Ensuring community participation was considered the core of the strategy. Thus, SIFFS formulated an ambitious plan to customise the houses for all house owners in a participatory manner. 'The maxim formulated was "2,000 houses in 2,000 designs"' (*ibid.*). However, to achieve this goal, two critical hurdles had to be overcome beforehand: the order issued by the government, and the definition of the architect's scope of work during the building process.

SIFFS expressed its concerns regarding the government's order for various reasons. First of all, many of the houses on the beach were 'valued [at] more than what the government was promising to give [...] The government guidelines were silent on the requirement of joint families, a common occurrence among fishing communities. There would be a need for ensuring the possibility of extension in the houses constructed. The differences in cost of land across villages for the future expansion had not been taken into consideration by the government. In Tarangambadi, for instance, the cost of land was higher than in Chinnangudi. As a consequence, house owners might not be able to purchase plots in Tarangamba-

10 | *Ibid.*

11 | *Ibid.*

12 | *Ibid.*

di for the purpose of future extension [...] The government acquired land at the rate of one acre per 25 houses, which left little space for recreational use and for public buildings [...]' (SIFFS 2009: 7-8).

According to SIFFS, the government's order violated many of the basic principles of housing in fishing communities. Thus, 'in order to achieve the goals formulated we had to adapt this order. However, confronting the government with adaptations would only be possible with precise data. Thus, for this purpose, we carried out, first of all, a comprehensive survey and documentation, a habitat mapping, in all the project villages.'[13] For this particular reconstruction programme a specific organisational structure was set up (see table below).

Figure 21: Organigram of SIFFS

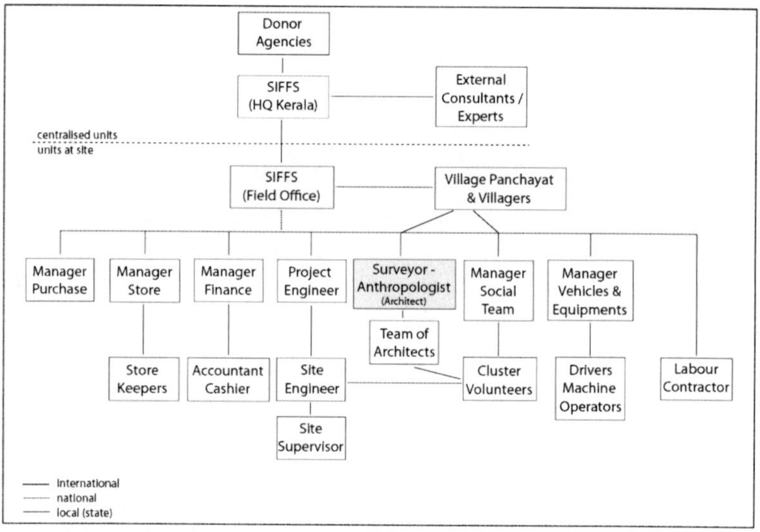

Source: Adapted from SIFFS 2009: 60

SIFFS emphasised the importance of the role of the architect for the entire project cycle. 'He should be the link between the village level and the decision making level. He should, based on the results of his documentation and survey in the villages, direct us in the course of the reconstruction

13 | *Ibid.*

project. We wanted that critical parameters should be defined based on the outcomes of his interaction at village level.'[14]

The Role and Scope of Work of the Surveyor-Anthropologist

SIFFS appointed an architect based in Chennai with more than twenty years experience in the construction business. The architect's professional record ranged from low-cost and cost-effective housing to conservation projects and post-disaster reconstruction in various Indian regions. How was the scope of work of the architect (hereafter surveyor-anthropologist) defined in detail? A contract was signed defining his responsibilities highlighted in the grey-shaded column of the table below.

Table 11: Scope of work of the surveyor-anthropologist

	PHASE I Programme formulation	**PHASE II Project formulation**	**PHASE III Planning**	PHASE IV Construction	PHASE V Post-Occupation
ARCHITECT / Surveyor-Anthropologist	The reconstruction scheme(s) to be defined by the respective government alone or in cooperation with bi- and multilateral, international, national and local private agencies and NGOs	Habitat mapping: survey and documentation of the damage, socio-economic conditions, topography, and risk zones of the old hamlet and the site suggested for relocation; assessment of local skills, resources, know-how and construction technologies; architectural data; size and use of private spaces; type of use of common spaces; preferences with regard to reconstruction in-situ and relocation	Comprehensive master plan for 'old' and 'new' village (insitu and relocation) Customised house plans Construction technology Cost estimation	Procurement of construction materials and skilled and unskilled labour; site coordination; supervision of the progress of work; and quality control	Follow-up on the project; repair of construction defects; modifications by the villagers

The surveyor-anthropologist started working on Tarangambadi in phase II. During this time essential parameters (the list of beneficiaries, the new land, the size of the land, the size of the plot, and the size of the house) had to be finalised at project level. Before doing so, however, detailed damage assessment and habitat mapping were carried out in the village. A

14 | *Ibid.*

team was formed under the leadership of the surveyor-anthropologist of graduate architects and students of architecture. This team was based at village-level for a 'total of six months, collecting data, interacting with the villagers, preparing thematic maps, developing concepts for a comprehensive master plan and customised house plans. It closely cooperated with the villagers, so to identify critical parameters for the reconstruction project as a whole.'[15] However, to facilitate this work, a 'social team had to join the architects [...] Without them the work would have been much more difficult, if not impossible, sometimes. The social team mediated whenever needed. Now and then for example I did not even understand the fishers' language, even though we are all Tamilians.'[16] Based on thematic maps drawn up by the surveyor-anthropologist and his team, SIFFS adapted the government order and decided on the most critical parameters for the project.

First of all, the benficiaries' list was finalised by SIFFS (not by the government) based on the damage assessment which identified that '904 houses were fully damaged and another 266 had partial damages [...] The low lying northern part of the village where most of the fisher people lived suffered near total damage. Houses in the southern part, which was more elevated with good vegetation and less density suffered much less' (SIFFS 2009: 1).

Secondly, the villagers were free to decide if their house should be reconstructed in-situ or if they wished to be relocated. The socio-economic survey had a question on the family's preference 'to move or not to move'. The decision of whether to move or not to move was conditioned by two facts, namely the size and the quality of the old plot and house and the results obtained from the hazard mapping. For many house owners, who had enough land in the old hamlet and a good-quality house with minor damage, 'the incentive of getting three cents [121.4m²] of land and a house worth Rs 150,000 was unattractive. Those who owned more than three cents of land did not want to vacate the plots, because they could get a new house in the existing location itself' (*ibid.*: 9). The hazard mapping showed the extent of inundation caused by incoming waves of different heights. It showed that the 'issue of safety was not related to the distance

15 | Surveyor-anthropologist. Interview on 11.01.2012 in Chennai.

16 | Architect and team-member. Interview on 10.12.2011 in Puducherry.

to the sea but to the fact whether the land was elevated or low lying.'[17] The survey found that '24.8% of the people wanted to stay in their existing plots' (*ibid.*: 13). In both cases – reconstruction in-situ or relocation – the NGO fully supported the villagers' decisions. As a result, many houses were repaired and not demolished. Furthermore, the government order relating to the selection of the beneficiaries was changed. SIFFS decided to apply the following criteria for the finalisation of the beneficiaries' list. One was 'a house for a house but based on where you lived'; two was 'each family within a joint family to get a new house'; and three was 'criteria for special cases' (*ibid.*: 16). With this comprehensive database of information the number of houses to be constructed was brought down from 'initially 1,800 – as estimated by the government – to 1,091 houses.'[18]

Thirdly, the results of the habitat mapping had shown that the area of land for the new hamlet was much higher than defined by the government. 'The government had stipulated a house density of 25 per acre. Each house was to be built on three cents and the balance 25 cents were to be assigned for common space. Initial studies had shown that the requirement of common space was much higher and hence, in Tarangambadi the house density was fixed at 20 per acre' (SIFFS 2009: 14).

Fourthly, the habitat mapping revealed that '77% of the families [...] would like to have the same neighbours in the new settlement as well' (*ibid.*: 13). Moreover, the families preferred 'the cooking space outside the house. A majority of households pointed out the importance of a *puja* room, or a space earmarked for that' (*ibid.*). The parameters defined in phase II provided, first of all, the base for a comprehensive master plan aimed at integrating the old and the new. Yet, two concepts were formulated for the new site. 'One was based on a grid layout and the second one on a cluster layout. The density was less in the cluster layout due to additional common spaces provided there. After long discussions, the *panchayat* leaders found the grid layout more appropriate. Unauthorised encroachment of open spaces, they said, could be handled much better [...] The concept for the old hamlet was based on two main criteria. First of all, the low lying land where no new construction would be taken up anymore should be planted with trees and bushes. This area should become a garden. Behind that, the newly planted trees of different varieties should provide the

17 | Surveyor-anthropologist. Interview on 11.01.2012 in Chennai.

18 | Project manager of SIFFS. Interview on 31.01.2012 in Tarangambadi.

inhabitants with fruits etc. in the future. Secondly, those plots that were relinquished by the fishers, as they had decided to move to the new site, were allocated as common and public spaces.'[19]

Figure 22: Master plan for old Tarangambadi and new Tarangambadi-Tsunami Nagar, not to scale

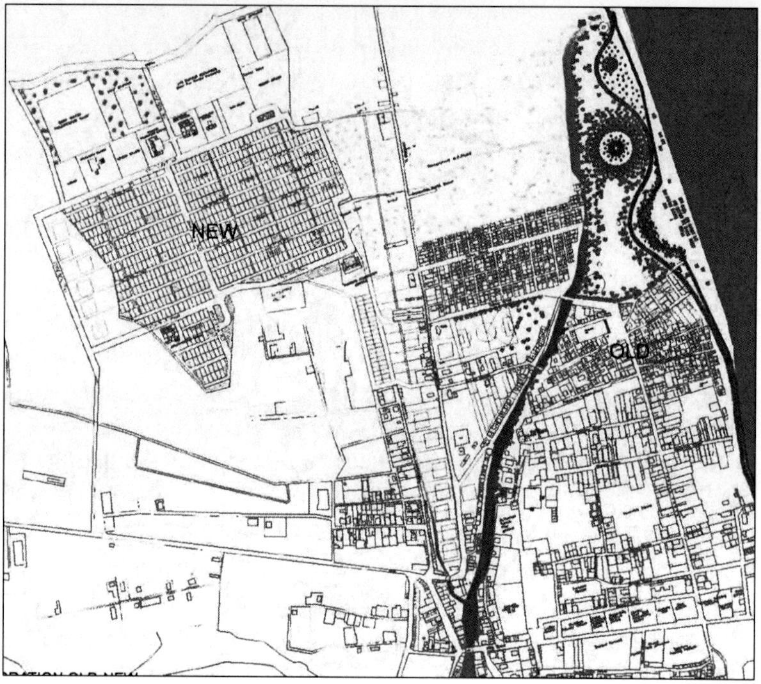

Source: Figures 22–29 courtesy of the surveyor-anthropologist

19 | Surveyor-anthropologist. Interview on 11.01.2012 in Chennai.

Figure 23: Master plan for Tarangambadi-Tsunami Nagar, not to scale

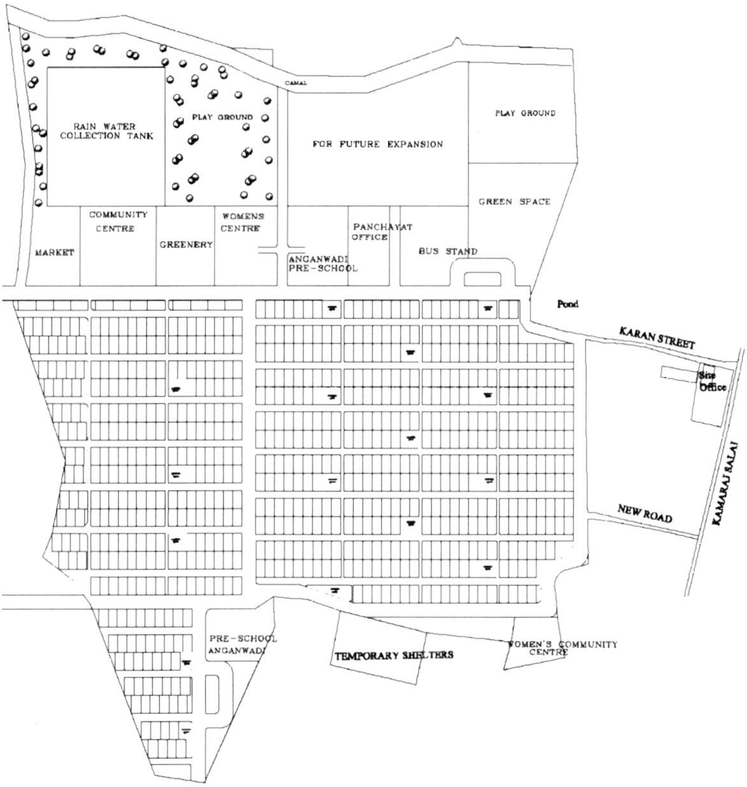

Based on the parameters highlighted by the villagers during the course of the habitat mapping 'we developed six types of houses. They were then constructed in actual dimension. The model houses provided the very important aspect of to see, to feel and to touch. Yet, we wanted to encourage the families to picture their future house. At that stage, however, we did not visualise the full impact of this procedure, as we did not know to which extent the families would ultimately customise the model houses presented.'[20] After having inspected the model houses the families were invited to 'face to face' meetings (SIFFS 2009: 21). During these meetings

---

20 | Architect and team-member. Interview on 10.12.2011 in Puducherry.

each house for each family was, based on the house owners' feedback, customised and finalised. The 'process of customisation became so elaborate that some of the models constructed hold only distant similarities to the model houses presented at the concept stage.'[21] Three types of construction technologies were suggested: load bearing walls, reinforced cement concrete framed structure, and, as an alternative technology, CSEB (Compressed Stabilised Earth Blocks). The latter, however, had to be dropped as, according to the surveyor-anthropologist, 'it was too expensive.'[22] Finally, the traditional *panchayat* leaders opted for reinforced cement concrete framed structure instead of load bearing walls for safety reasons[23] (see also SIFFS 2009: 20).

Model house 1 (see below) is the only option with an attached toilet, and it was chosen by some families, however, on condition that the entrance of the toilet was moved to outside of the house.

Figure 24: Model House 1, not to scale

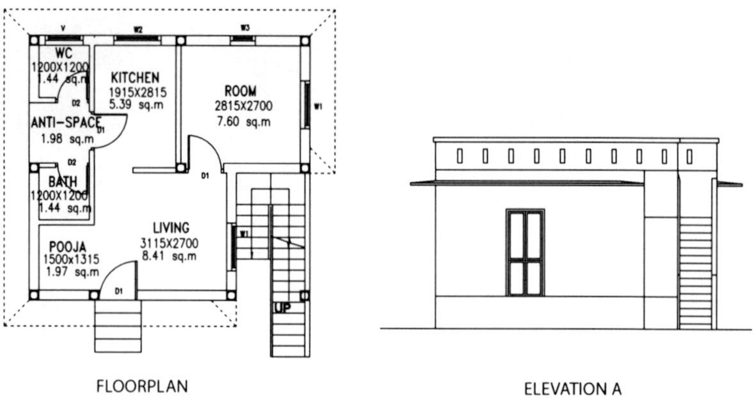

Model house 2, was, according to SIFFS' site manager, the preferred option as it perhaps came closest to the needs of large families. It had no veranda, though the house owners could add one, if they wished, at a later stage.

21 | *Ibid.*

22 | Surveyor-anthropologist. Interview on 11.01.2012 in Chennai.

23 | Site manager of SIFFS. Interview on 31.01.2012 in Tarangambadi.

Figure 25: Model House 2, not to scale

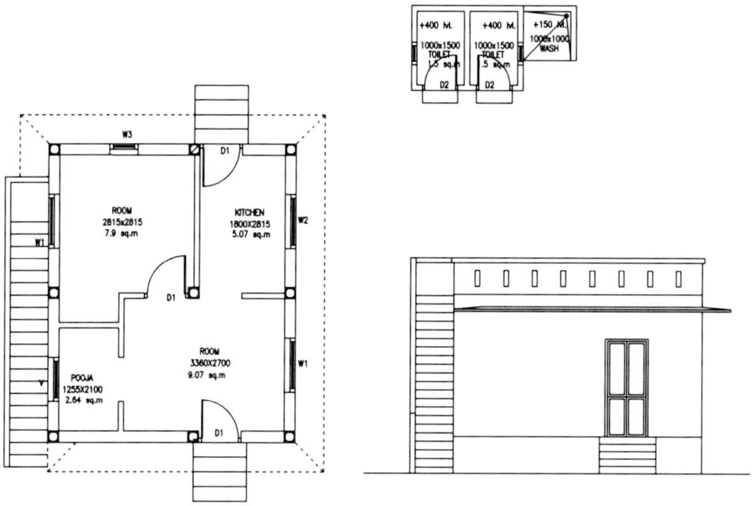

FLOORPLAN

ELEVATION A

Model house 3 (see below) was mainly chosen by families who wanted to stay on the site of their original homesteads but who had serious space constraints. It was also chosen by families at the new site who preferred to have a more spacious garden.

Figure 26: Model House 3, not to scale

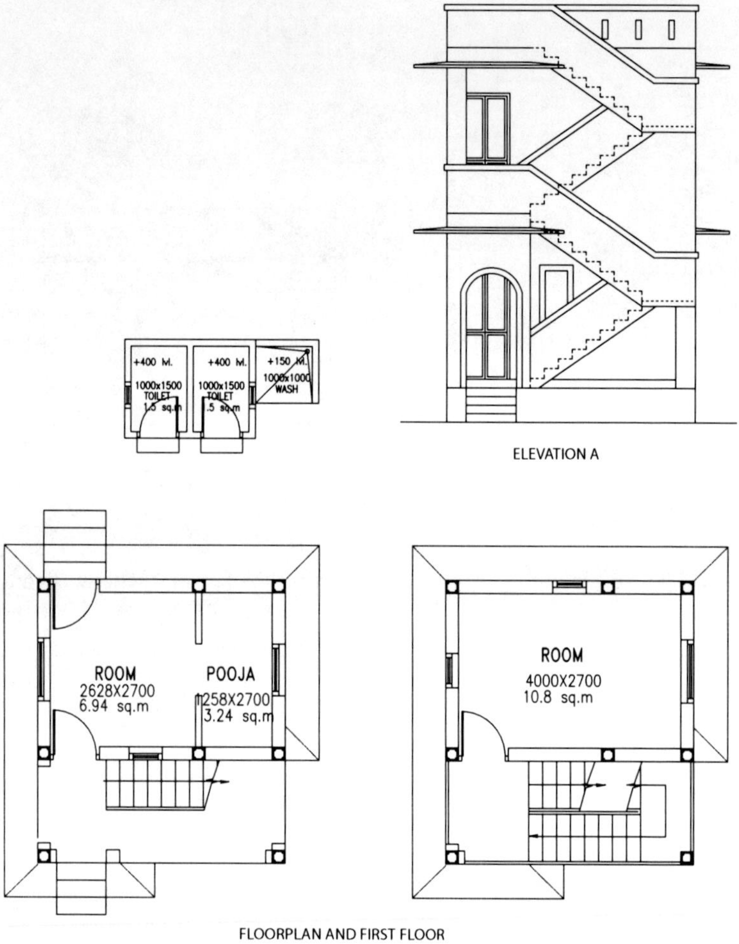

Model houses 4 and 5 (see below) were chosen because of their verandas with arches which, as the field survey revealed, the families liked. Even though the house did not have a *puja* room, the families who opted for this model decided to add one at the rear of the house.

Figure 27: Model House 4, not to scale

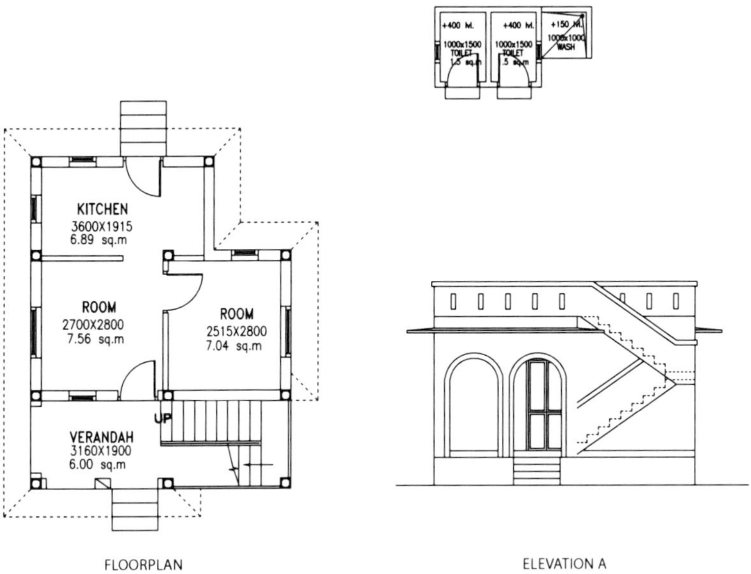

Figure 28: Model House 5, not to scale

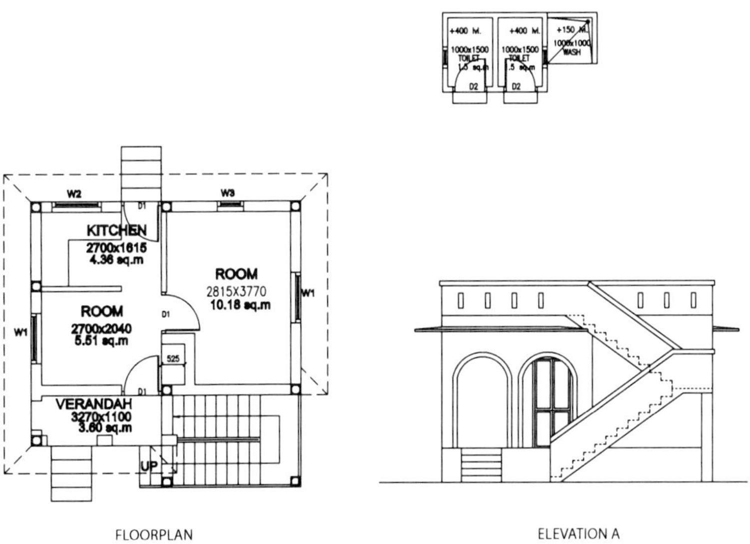

Model house 6 was mainly selected by smaller families who preferred to have a big room (in the plan below defined as 'Bed').

Figure 29: Model House 6, not to scale

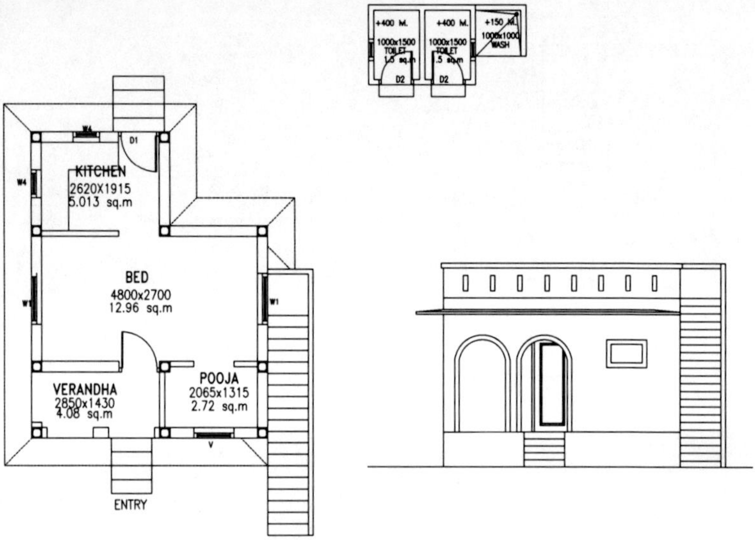

FLOORPLAN ELEVATION A

The habitat mapping carried out by the surveyor-anthropologist found that the fishers' building tradition requires a number of *pujas* to be carried out when constructing a house. Hence, the plots at the new site were allocated to each family before starting construction. In doing so, SIFFS wanted to enable, first of all, each family to carry out *pujas* according to their customs. Secondly, they wanted the families to play a crucial role during construction. For example, curing was done by the owners themselves, and they were encouraged to report issues related to the quality of construction.

SIFFS had already decided to avoid employing contractors during construction at an early stage. Contractors were to be used only to provide labour for the project. Construction materials were purchased by the NGO and a team of engineers was appointed to monitor the quality of construction. However, at the peak of post-tsunami reconstruction in 2006, this strategy had to be revised as it became increasingly difficult to procure materials and labour. The site manager recalls: 'Work was delayed quite often and interrupted. Even repeated hikes in labour rates did not help in breaking the stalemate. At this stage the government wanted to take over the project in order to bring the project back on track. Even though the villagers were all living in temporary houses and yearning for the completion of the houses, they objected the government's plan, demonstrating in front of the collector's office. By all means they wanted SIFFS to continue with the construction and complete this project [...] So we devised a new strategy, namely the "piece rate system". This system involved breaking up the construction process of an individual house into several stand-alone components such as excavation, foundation, wall masonry, pillars, roofing, plastering etc. The smallest component of work was arrived at in such a way that a small group of people could finish it in a day's time. Once a group completed a component, the payment was done the same day at the site office. This system proved to be highly effective, however, at the same time, the administration was fairly complex as a typical house was divided into approximately 40 components.'[24]

The reconstruction project in Tarangambadi ended up as the largest tsunami reconstruction project at a single location in Tamil Nadu. Due to its size and the strategy adopted for its construction, the project was completed in several phases. Phase one (451 houses) was completed in May 2007; phase 2 (170 houses) in February and March 2008; phase 3 (285 houses) in May 2008; phase 4 (116 houses) in February 2009; and phase 5 (69 houses) in December 2009.

The Fishers' Voices Four Years Later

As has already been discussed, SIFFS' maxim for post-tsunami reconstruction was to try and overcome the typical limitations faced by the provision of mass housing. The new houses for the fisher families in Tarangambadi were intended, in addition to providing enhanced safety and quality, to be in line with the villagers' housing customs. It was found that 75% of the households interviewed stated that their housing situation had actually improved, 20% commented that their housing situation had re-

24 | Site manager of SIFFS. Interview on 31.01.2012 in Tarangambadi.

mained the same, and 5% stated that their housing situation had become worse.[25]

The last day of my field survey in Tarangambadi-Tsunami Nagar was on the 29th December 2011, the day before cyclone Thane hit the region of Puducherry and Cuddalore district. The cyclone warning had been announced on TV and in the newspapers. Precautions were taken in all the villages along the coastal belt. For that day I had organised a meeting with the traditional *panchayat* leaders. We met on the shore of Tarangambadi as they were, along with a number of fishermen, busy bringing the boats, the nets and the engines to safer places. Despite their worries due to an imminent cyclone, they took their time to reflect on and to answer my questions. My question: 'Are you satisfied with your new hamlet and your new houses?' was answered by one of the leaders as follows:

> 'We are satisfied, yes. The houses are good. The new site is good. The village plan is good. But the bathroom and the toilet should not face the neighbour's house or be adjacent to the neighbour's plot, and the quality of construction is, in some cases, very poor. The roofing and the flooring, especially, are not done well in some houses. We are not sure about the quality of sand which was used. And they also used blue metal which was too big. That is why there is leakage in some of the houses.'

The answer reflects the overall atmosphere in Tarangambadi-Tsunami Nagar: the *panchayat* leader brought up several areas that were not satisfactory, namely the orientation of the bathroom and the toilet, the quality of construction materials and the quality of construction. However, what do the results from Tarangambadi-Tsunami Nagar look like in detail?

Table 12 on the following page shows the breakdown of responsibilities (who did what and when) during the course of the project process and the villagers' degree of satisfaction. The grey-shaded columns give the surveyor-anthropologist's responsibilities, based on the scope of work as defined by the NGO.

25 | Results of the field survey in December 2012 in Tarangambadi-Tsunami Nagar.

Table 12: Breakdown of responsibilities and results for Tarangambadi-Tsunami Nagar (N=40)

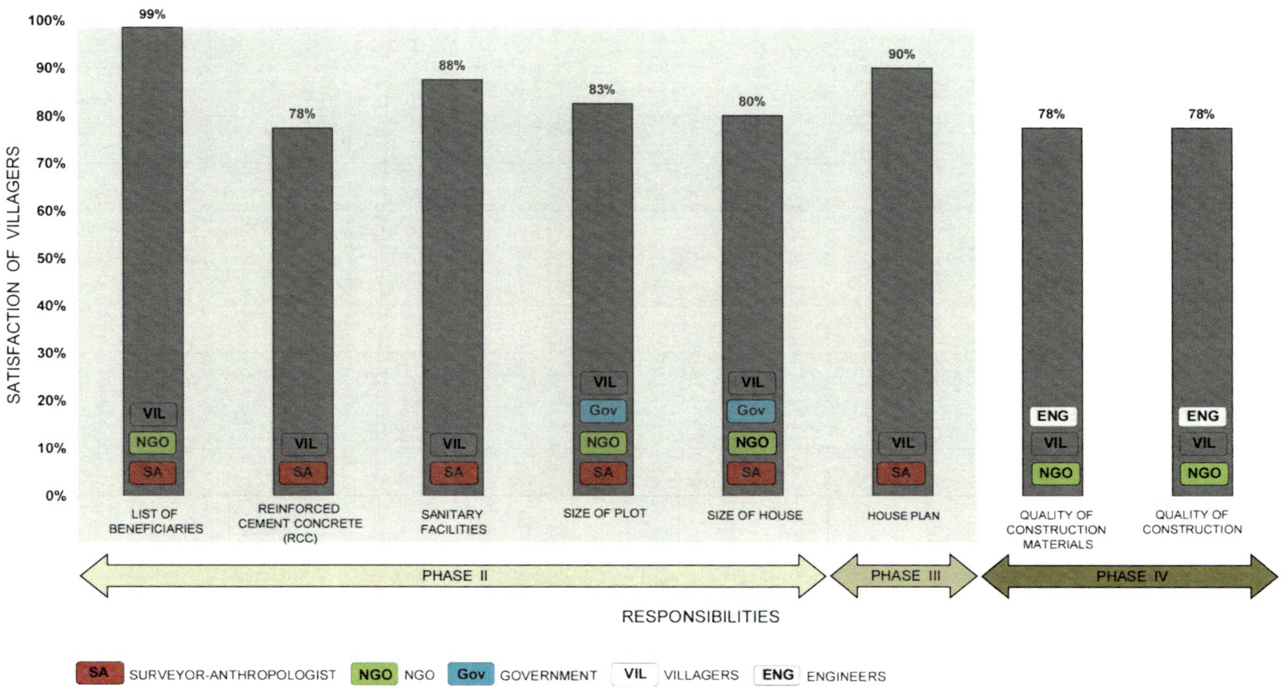

According to the fishers, three aspects were identified as unsatisfactory:

- the RCC technology (the climate inside the house)
- the quality of construction materials
- the quality of construction

Out of the three categories identified as unsatisfactory one, the RCC technology, was among the surveyor-anthropologist's responsibilities. How did the inhabitants of Tarangambadi-Tsunami Nagar reflect on the surveyor-anthropologist's performance in detail?

The question, 'Do you know the architect who planned your new village and your new house?', was answered positively by 50% of the interviewees. They commented further: 'We were lucky with this architect, he planned well.' 90% of the interviewees said that they were satisfied with the location of the new house and the house as a whole. Their needs had been incorporated into the design. It turned out that there had been intensive interaction with the surveyor-anthropologist and his team. The fishers said that a thorough survey had been carried out with each family in their old hamlet. Also, they stated that they liked the model houses that were constructed at the concept stage. However, they stressed that the orientation of the bathroom and the toilet turned out to be a failure as they were not hidden and faced the neighbouring house. They explained further that they could not have visualised these issues at the concept stage as the model houses were built on plain terrain, not demonstrating and contextualising (with regard to the neighbouring houses) their future orientation at the new site. This issue was, according to the *panchayat* leaders, critical as the families did not at all feel comfortable and women especially were uneasy when using the bath. The problem was solved by constructing compound walls. However, as some said, this was beyond their financial means. The field survey revealed that the promises given by the NGO and the surveyor-anthropologist were realised. They were in line with a new and *pucca* house, as by the villagers visualised. The table below highlights the aspects identified as positive with regard to the new house.

Table 13: Positive features of the new house when compared to the old

Features	(%)
None	15
Infrastructure facilities	15
Pucca house	5
Pucca house and bathroom/toilet	17.5
Pucca house and infrastructure	12.5
Sanitary facilities	35

It was found, moreover, that the majority of the villagers were satisfied with the overall performance of the surveyor-anthropologist, as the following table illustrates.

Table 14: Impression of the architect

Impression	(%)
No answer	2.5
Bad	17.5
Good	42.5
Good, well designed	20
No idea, I have never seen him	5
Poor work	2.5
Did their job	10

Finally, 58% of the interviewees said that they would like to work with this architect again provided, they stressed, that the orientation of the bathroom/toilet and the quality of construction was handled much better. Another 27.5% commented that they would call the mason, as 'he does good quality work'. 14.5% of the households interviewed were undecided. They explained, though, that whoever was appointed to build their new house should 'listen to what is needed and suggested and do good quality work'.

Picture 14: (Modified) houses in Tarangambadi-Tsunami Nagar

Additional Factors Affecting the Degree of Satisfaction

The field survey revealed that additional factors affected the results in Tarangambadi-Tsunami Nagar. The parameters identified are listed below under two categories: cultural and technical.

- Cultural Factors

The majority of the households interviewed like their new hamlet and their new house. At the same time, many said that they missed the beach. Their daily routines have changed since moving into the new houses. Previously, living and working used to take place within the same hamlet. Unloading the fish, mending the nets, repairing the boats and the engines, watching the sea as well as social gatherings took place on the beach. Now, however, it is far [up to 1 km] from their houses. 'Children and women are back home at the latest by dusk; they do not spend evenings on the beach anymore and going to work now feels like going to the office.'[26]

26 | *Panchayat* leader on 29.12.2011 in Tarangambadi-Tsunami Nagar.

Picture 15: On the beach in Tarangambadi (behind the temple on the left is the silhouette of Tarangambadi-Tsunami Nagar)

Furthermore, it was found that many of the interviewees missed the 'comfortable climate of their old place and the cooling breeze of the sea.' The field survey also revealed that the lack of thick and protective vegetation in the form of bushes and trees in this hot climate had a critical impact on the degree of satisfaction with regard to the construction technology.

Even though many trees and bushes had been planted already, and had reached a satisfactory height, the results illustrate that only 78% are satisfied with the fact that their house was built in RCC. The other 22% commented that the climate inside the new house was unbearable, especially during summer. However, these houses were, much more than others, particularly exposed to the sun as no trees provided any shade. This factor became conflated in the villagers' minds with the houses being built in RCC. Further enquiries revealed that 6% (out of the 22%) had lived in RCC houses in their old hamlet. The other 16%, on the contrary, used to live in thatched houses.

Picture 16: Vegetation not yet providing sufficient shadow in some areas of the new hamlet

- Technical Factors

It was found that the quality of construction varied within Tarangambadi-Tsunami Nagar. While in some of the houses leakage is not a problem at all, it was found that a number of houses had serious problems with the poor quality of construction. The roofs leak and the walls are damp. During the monsoon especially they hardly ever get dry. Further investigations revealed that, despite the use of the same construction strategy, the houses that were of poor quality had had serious trouble with the labourers involved in the construction.

A fisherwoman recalls: 'We were struggling with the labourers working on our house. They were from Andhra Pradesh, and we spoke different languages. They did not understand us, and we did not understand them. So, when we pointed out mistakes, it was useless and they carried on with their work as usual.'

Finally, the field survey reveald that even though additional land was provided for future expansion (see Figure 23: Master plan, p. 151) the limited size of the land had an impact on the results. 'Since the tsunami,' a *panchayat* leader said, 'we have had 250 marriages. But we do not know where to accommodate all the young families. The land is too small and purchasing additional land is too expensive. Earlier, our village used to grow along the beach, towards the north. So now many have moved back to the old hamlet; others, the majority, moved to neighbouring towns.'[27]

27 | *Panchayat* leader on 29.12.2011 in Tarangambadi-Tsunami Nagar.

PART III: NEGOTIATING THE ROLE OF THE ARCHITECT

Understanding the Results

> Though the project was built and occupied as planned, there remained in it, a certain sense of incompleteness [...] This is perhaps [due to] the inability of a professional to comprehend the underlying patterns of a tribal group and to respond to its private needs.
> Laurie Baker (quoted in: Bhatia 1991: 204)[1]

> In any design process [...], the issue is not of a rapport between design and residence but at a profound level between designer and resident.
> Paul Oliver (quoted in: Asquith 2006: 143)

Comparison of the Three Case Studies

The reasons for portraying the three case studies individually were twofold. First, I aimed to show the distinctive nature and complexity of this working environment, which derives from the fact that many stakeholders are involved, which, in turn, are not homogenous entities (see Sökefeld 2012: 187). Second, I sought to demonstrate, that it is, amongst other reasons, the skilful interplay of the various actors and their responsibilities that leads to the realisation of people-oriented housing and not necessarily the appointment of formally trained architects, as assumed by the NGOs. While the surveyor-anthropologist received the highest level of approval

1 | The British-Indian architect Laurie Baker, renowned for his initiatives in cost-effective and sustainable architecture using 'traditional' construction materials and techniques, after the completion of the reconstruction project for fisher families affected by floods in 1974 in Thiruvananthapuram (Kerala, India).

at village level, the draftswoman and the project management consultant failed to meet the villagers' needs with regard to fundamental areas of the projects. What are the reasons? This chapter seeks to explore this question in more detail by comparing the findings of the three case studies.

Table 15 (following page) highlights the degree of success of each of the projects, and, at the same time, the table documents the responsibilities of the various actors involved during the project. It gives an answer to the questions: who did what and when during the project, and what are the results? Moreover, it shows that the degree of satisfaction of the villagers about the house (and the new habitat) cannot be assessed in isolation from the entire building process, its actors and its multilayered components.

The three case studies vary in many respects. They differ with regard to the role and scope of their architects during the project, the process design and the responsibilities of the different stakeholders (NGO, government, and villagers), the degree of adherence to the reconstruction policy issued by the government and, finally, the attitude towards the building culture in place in each village. In other words, they differ in regard to the entire process. Below, I will reiterate the core features of each project.

- The Project Management Consultant (see also CHAPTER The Role and Scope of Work of the Project Management Consultant)

The project brief for Keezhakazakudy-Tsunami Nagar was defined in phase II, and its core parameters (the size of the plot, the size of the house, the sanitary facilities and the construction technology) were adopted wholesale from the government's policy (see CHAPTER The Reconstruction Policies). The list of beneficiaries was finalised by the government, without any interference from the NGO. The PMC was assigned responsibility for the project in phase III, after the brief had been defined. Thereafter, he took on the 'classical' role of a planner-designer-manager. His scope of work was the planning and designing of the new settlement and the new house, based on the parameters defined in phase II. One type of house was developed for the entire village. Furthermore, he was in charge of managing the project as a whole (preparing the tender documents and co-

Table 15: Comparison of the three case studies

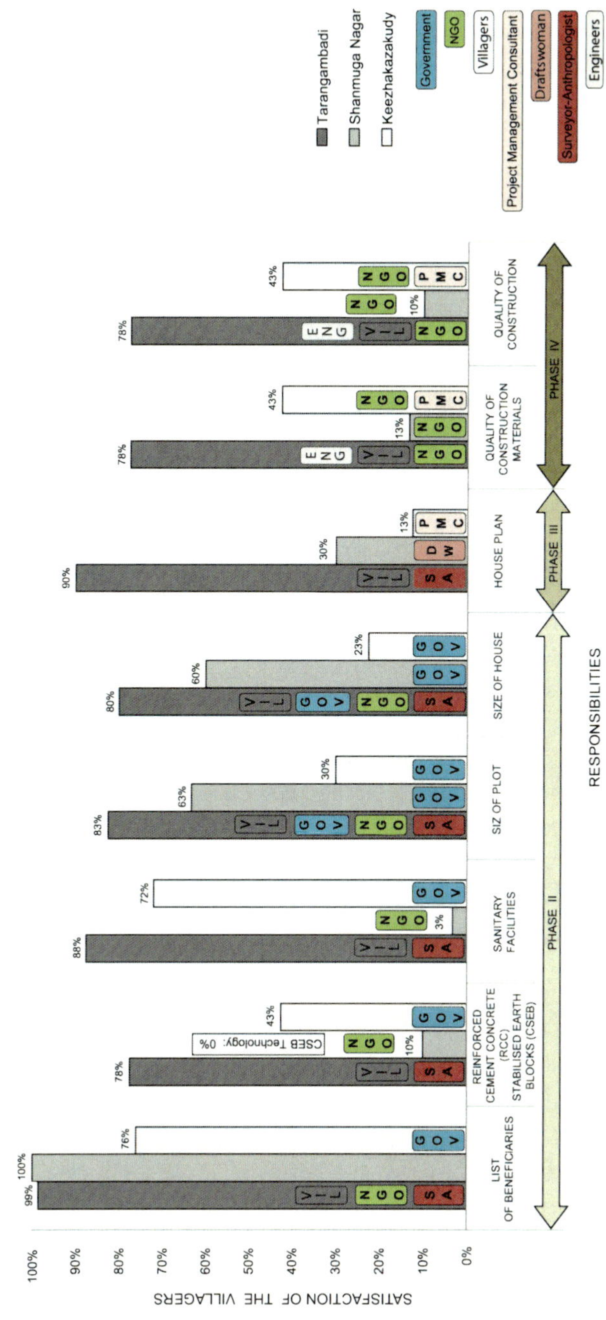

st estimates, identifying contractors with a suitable capacity, supervising the quality of construction, controlling the progress of the work and issuing the certificate of completion). Construction was outsourced to professional construction companies, and the houses were allocated to the villagers through lot by the government after the completion of construction. All the interviewees commented that their building customs *had not been* taken into consideration during the project. The building process was dominated by the local government, the NGO and the PMC. The *panchayat* leaders were informed about major decisions that had been made, however, rural professionals and the villagers were not assigned any responsibility during the project.

- The Draftswoman (see also CHAPTER The Role and Scope of Work of the Draftswoman)

In a similar way to the PMC, the draftswoman was assigned responsibility in phase III, after the project brief had already been defined by the NGO and government (at district level). At the same time, however, the project differed from that above in several respects. First, reconstruction was done in-situ, and second, NGO representatives had decided that the new houses should be constructed using an alternative technology (CSEB). The architect appointed for this project, however, had no experience with this technology, and thus she had to attend a training course at the Auroville Earth Institute, where this construction technology had been developed.[2] Thereafter, she took on the 'classical' role of a planner-designer, adopting the technology for the new houses to be constructed. The master plan of the village, the house plan, the cost estimates and the demarcation of the new village layout were within her scope of work. One type of house was designed for the entire village. Skilled (mason) and unskilled (village) labour was employed for construction. However, the villagers had to be trained how to produce the bricks as their traditional source of livelihood is fishing and not the construction industry. 64.5% of the interviewees said that their building customs *had been* incorporated into the process during the construction phase. 34.5% of the villagers commented, however, that while they could carry out *pujas* during construction, their building customs had not been taken into consideration during the other phases of the project. Even though the NGO had attempted to follow an alternative and

2 | For further information on this institute see: http://www.earth-auroville.com/ (accessed on: 15.11.2011).

more 'sustainable' path by introducing an alternative construction technology, this project too has been, at its core, top-down and exclusionary. It was dominated by the NGO and the draftswoman. The villagers did not have a voice. In the best case, they were informed about decisions that had already been taken.

- The Surveyor-Anthropologist (see also CHAPTER The Role and Scope of Work of the Surveyor-Anthropologist)

Contrary to the first two cases, the surveyor-anthropologist took on an entirely different role. His role could be described as that of a 'searcher' (see Easterly 2006: 5), looking for an alternative approach to the tasks at hand by attempting to become an 'insider' (see Desai 2011) of the villagers' building culture. The surveyor-anthropologist was assigned responsibility during phase II, at a stage where the project brief had yet to be defined. As has already been mentioned, the NGO was concerned about some of the parameters defined by the government (see SIFFS 2009: 7–8), such as the size of the plot, the area of land for the new hamlet in the case of relocation, disregarding the needs of joint families (a common kinship pattern among fishers), and ambiguous legal claims to the vacated land in the case of relocation. Knowing that all these would ultimately have a significant impact on the degree of success of the project, the NGO challenged the government over them, with the support of the surveyor-anthropologist. The brief was defined only after a thorough habitat assessment had been completed, during which the surveyor-anthropologist, his team and a team of social workers worked closely together in order to identify the core parameters of the size of the plot, the size of the house, the use of public and private spaces, the arrangements of private rooms, the location of open spaces within the habitat and neighbourhoods, the list of beneficiaries, and the preferences of the villagers for relocation or reconstruction in-situ. After the habitat assessment had been completed and the most significant parameters discussed with the villagers, the project brief was finalised and presented to the government. The conception of the master plan and house plans followed. The latter were finalised in accordance with the villagers' wishes in 'face to face' interviews (SIFFS 2009: 21). As a result, a variety of houses (see pages 152–156) were designed and built. The surveyor-anthropologist did not play any role during construction. Some of the architect's team members, however, continued to stay on in the field, as the project was implemented in a stage-by-stage fashion (see page 141). A team of engineers, NGO staff and the villagers were assigned responsibility for surveying the quality of construction. The houses had been allotted to the villagers before starting construction so that they could carry out their rituals according to their building culture. Contrary to the first two case studies, 100% of the interviewees stated that their building customs *had been* an integral part of the project. The process was bottom-up and shaped by many different stakeholders (see Figure 21: Organigram, p. 146), and expertise from within the village was also incorporated throughout the duration of the project. The role of the surveyor-anthropologist was not top-down, a significant difference from the other two cases. At this point, it is important to point out here that the conception of this project was not the result of a process design that had been laid out in detail well in advance. During a conversation with the NGO's project manager it became clear that, due to the NGO's inexperience in this field (they had not previously built post-disaster housing), 'many tasks had to be handled ad-hoc, as certain issues were unpredictable, a peculiarity of course of this working context, and hence they could not be planned well in advance. For example, the project was lacking a "planner" at the top of the project who would have a total view of the project, with all the facets of the project and, most important, its pace and cost. We are accountable to so many actors: the government, the people, the donors, and to our boards. The architect moved out, after having completed the planning stage. We were still able to manage the project because various people contributed. We got support from the Swiss organisation SKAT [an organisation that provides technical expertise, management support and training to bi- and multilateral organisations and NGOs] and from people who had been involved in Kutch [Gujarat earthquake in 2001]. We had workshops during the project were we got crucial inputs. Right from the onset of the project, however, the inclusion of the villagers' culture throughout was beyond question.'[3]

So far, the three projects have been examined as a whole, their many participants and their responsibilities, and, in doing so, it has been found that the architect is one among many players in an intricate net of actors. The findings show that the degree of satisfaction of the villagers is related to much more than to the material features of a house and a habitat. The projects highlight, among other things, the relationships that matter between the people and activities across various phases of a project (see Davis 1999, Oliver 2003, Turner 2009 [1976], Davidson 2010).

3 | Project Manager of SIFFS. Interview on 31.01.2012 in Tarangambadi.

At this point, therefore, it becomes important to examine the planning phase (phase III) in detail, and here in particular the quality and nature of the relationship between the architect and the villagers. In doing so, I aim to identify the peculiarities of the planning process in this particular working context. Planning and designing fall within the architect's domain. However, this may reveal if formally trained architects have adequate skills to take on this task in this particular environment. Therefore, the following questions will be explored: what are the challenges and the limitations facing the architect at project level; which skills and attitude(s) are required; and, what do the villagers expect from 'their architect' in terms of services and skills? The following chapter seeks to investigate these questions in more detail, by scrutinising the villagers' voices, first, and by complementing them with the experiences of architects who have worked as project architects in both the context portrayed in this study and in other (rural)post-disaster environments across the world.

The Key-Qualities of 'Their Architect'

In order to identify the challenges and limitations of formally trained architects, and the skills and attitudes they require, it will be critical to consider the quality of the relationship between the villagers and the architect during the project in more detail, and, in doing so, to find out what the villagers expect from 'their architect' in terms of services and skills. More precisely, this chapter seeks to identify what this relationship lacked.

I will outline, first of all, the results from the villages. One part of the household questionnaire focused exclusively on the interaction between the villagers and the architect. I will, however, draw upon both the answers to these questions and the notes taken during informal interaction.

Secondly, I aim to complement the villagers' voices with the reflections of architects who have worked extensively in rural post-disaster reconstruction, and whom I interviewed for the purpose of this study (see CHAPTER Semi-structured Interviews). It was striking (for me and the team) to find out that many villagers were not at all familiar with the idea of the architect as a profession (see CHAPTER The Household Interviews). Their first reaction to the question, 'Do you know the architect who planned your hamlet and your house' was as follows: 'Architect? What is an architect?' In Keezhakazakudy-Tsunami Nagar, for example, the majority of the interviewees (80%) did not know what an architect was, and they assumed that the project had been planned by government engineers. In Shanmuga Nagar it was found that 77.4% were not familiar with this profession and in Tarangambadi-Tsunami Nagar 15% of the interviewees had no knowledge of this profession. Interestingly, these percentages directly correlate to the intensity of interaction between the architect and the villagers during the project, and, moreover, to his/her physical presence in the field. While in the first two cases the PMC and the draftswoman did not interact with the villagers (only with the *panchayat* leaders, who are only adult men) and their physical presence in the field was almost nil (only two times during the planning stage), in the third case the surveyor-anthropologist and his team had interacted intensively with the villagers throughout the planning stage, and, moreover, they were based in the village for almost eight months. The villagers of Keezhakazakudy-Tsunami Nagar and Shanmuga Nagar stated, that 'there was nobody who would listen to what we need'. As a consequence, 88% of the interviewees in Keezhakazakudy-Tsunami Nagar, and 83% in Shanmuga Nagar commented that their most important needs were not incorporated into the project, compared to 21% in Tarangambadi-Tsunami Nagar. Below are some of the villagers' comments that show their experience of the 'person who planned the house'.

- Keezhakazakudy-Tsunami Nagar

Fisherwoman: 'The one who planned this house does not know us and our culture. Otherwise, the hamlet and the house would be different. He should have sat with each of us first, listened carefully, and only then planned.'

Fisherwoman: 'There is no space for cooking outside. We do not cook inside the house because of the smoke. But the space for cooking they provided is inside. They don't know, they should have asked.'

Fisherman: 'The house was handed over to us only after construction was completed. So, I did not know what the house would be like in the end. There was nobody to tell or show me in detail what it would look like, and where it would be located. They had posted some papers, but I did not understand.'
Fisherwoman: 'The mason could have done this work much better. He knows best how to do this work.'

- Shanmuga Nagar

Irula man: 'I have never seen the person who planned the house. He was from outside, I think, from a distant city. He did what he wanted. He has never spoken with us, maybe because he speaks a different language.'

Irula woman: 'I have never seen the person who planned the house in our village. I have always wished I could have told him what I needed, so that he could have built the house accordingly.'[4]

- Tarangambadi-Tsunami Nagar

Fisherman (*panchayat* leader): 'Different types of houses were built as model houses. We could see and give suggestions on how to improve the house. That was well done. But there is one thing which does not work: the orientation of the bathroom. It faces the neighbouring house, and this is a problem. But we could not anticipate that this would be a problem when we saw the model house, because the model house was built in isolation, without any reference to the orientation of the other houses in the new village.'

Fisherwoman: 'They asked so many questions, and we had to explain many things to them about our village and about the houses we had lived in. They came from the city, they told me. Sometimes we did not understand each other. They speak differently.'

Fisherwoman: 'We were lucky with this architect, compared to other villages. But still, I would have preferred working with the local mason, because we know each other.'

The villagers' comments highlight that they had no voice in choosing 'their architect'. Nevertheless, they were asked during the field survey if they would like to work with this architect again and the results to this question are outlined in the table below.

---

4 | It is interesting to observe here that they speak of a male person. The architect appointed for this project is a woman.

Table 16: Answers to the question: Would you like to work with this architect again?

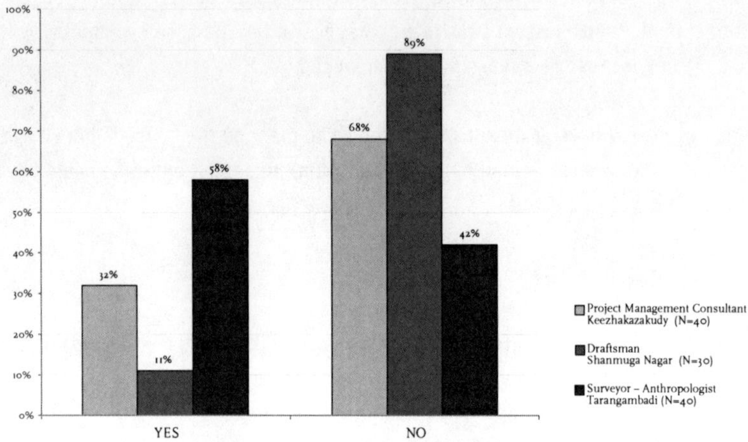

These results further emphasise the complexity of the subject of this study. Even though the 'surveyor-anthropologist' received the highest level of approval, it becomes evident that there must be additional, and significant, factors that need to be taken into consideration when designing the building process, particularly with regard to the personnel in charge of planning and designing. Therefore, it is critical to identify, first of all, what the villagers would expect from this person.

They were also asked whose support they would seek if they could choose with whom to build their house. The table below shows that the majority of the interviewees would prefer to work with the mason.

Table 17: Answers to the question: If you could choose with whom to build your house whose support would you seek?

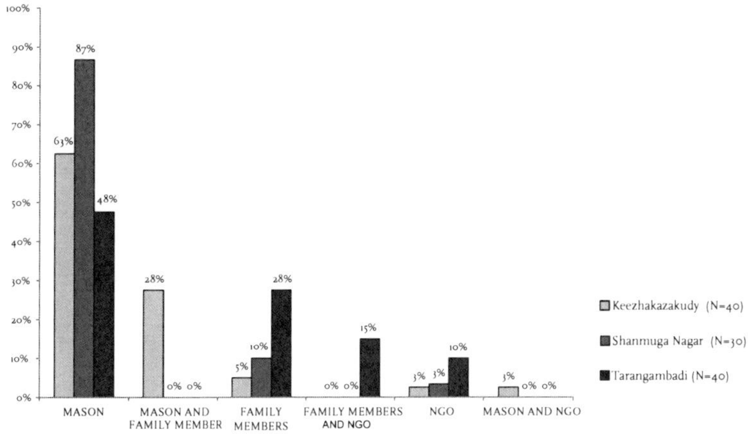

What are the reasons for their answers? Which particular services and abilities does the mason provide? They were asked therefore: 'What kind of support do you expect from your chosen option?'

Table 18: Answers to the question: What kind of support do you expect from your chosen option?

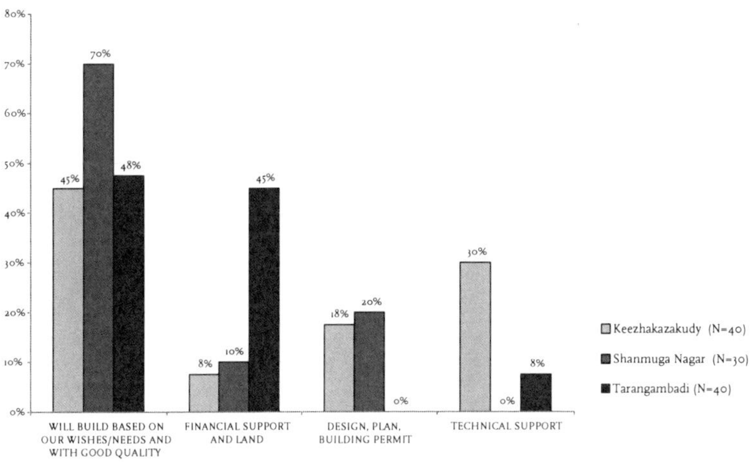

Interestingly, the support expected by the villagers falls within an architect's classical scope of duties (except financial support and land). However, as the villagers' feedback indicates (see pages 176–177), there are subtle distinctions between the mason and the architect. This is for various reasons.

First, as has been discussed already, the architect does not play any role whatsoever in a rural housing project in normal times (see CHAPTER The 'Modern' and the 'Traditional'). Moreover, the villagers have not found (particularly in the first two case studies) that the involvement of the architect resulted in an appreciable improvement to their new house and habitat.[5] So, why should they approach an architect instead of their mason when building a new house?

Second, the villagers' responses emphasise the many advantages of working with the mason. While the mason 'knows best how to do this work', the 'person who planned the house' did not 'listen carefully', did not 'tell or show me in detail what it [the house] would look like', spoke a 'different language', 'has never been in our village', 'did what he wanted', 'asked so many questions', and built the model houses 'in isolation, without any reference to the orientation of the other houses in the new village.'

Their responses are expressions of a variety of experiences, emotions and unfulfilled hopes. At the same time, however, all of them imply a critical message, namely, that the 'person who planned the house' was an 'outsider', who came from a 'distant city' and was not acquainted with their culture in general, and with their building culture in particular. Their feedback accentuates once more the importance of an intimate relationship between the one who plans and designs the new house (and habitat) and the user (see Davis 1999, Oliver 2003).

How did architects experience their relationships with the villagers during the planning stage? What was specific to the situation, insolvable, and/or repeatedly challenging for them?

I will now turn to the 'trivial' matters that architects (and engineers) were faced with at project level. Some of them have worked extensively as

---

5 | I would like to thank the architect Antje Wemhöner for drawing my attention to the issue of the architect as 'added value'. According to Wemhöner a target group will perceive professionals who are usually not involved during the building process only as positive if he/she has added noticeable value to the project. I will resume this discussion in CHAPTER Conclusion and Recommendations.

project architects in rural post-disaster environments, mostly in different contexts on the Indian subcontinent, but also in different countries across the world (see APPENDIX A). Others were new to this working environment. I show here some of their reflections on various subjects relevant to this chapter, and have placed them into five categories: 1) language/communication, 2) expertise/know-how, 3) outsider/insider, 4) presentation of the project, and 5) 'small things'.[6]

I quote the different voices without further commenting or summarising their content due to the deep insights and strong messages they provide. However, I will come back to their arguments again in the final part of this book (see CHAPTER Conclusion and Recommendations).

Language/Communication[7]

Purnima McCutcheon (architect, worked for different NGOs): 'There were many things that were not clear to me, pure communication things. I am Indian, I was born in Bombay. But I don't speak the language, Tamil. I can speak other Indian languages but not Tamil. Tamil language has a different base, it is not Sanskrit. So, I always had to have somebody to translate, which also dilutes. I realised that it would probably have been better if I had lived there 24/7, and spoken the language well enough to catch all the nuances.'

Rupal Desai (architect, NCPADP[8], Ahmedabad): 'We are a wife and husband, an architect and an engineer, team. This is important, because we work also in societies where it is critical to communicate with women se-

6 | I have borrowed 'small things' from Regan Potangaroa, associate professor at the School of Architecture at Unitec Auckland, who discussed the importance of incorporating 'small things' during the reconstruction process at the 6th International i-Rec Conference on 'Sustainable Post-Disaster reconstruction: From Recovery to Risk Reduction', in Ascona/Switzerland, May 2013. The paper presented by Regan Potangaroa was: 'Community Engagement: Rebuilding Samoan Fale post 2009 Tsunami', see: Waqabaca *et al.* 2013.

7 | Anonymity will be preserved for the interviewees involved in the three case studies throughout (see also page 85).

8 | NCPADP: National Centre for Peoples' Action in Disaster Preparedness, Ahmedabad, India.

parately. It is important to provide a space that is not dominated by men. For example, during the planning after the Kashmir earthquake [in 2005], I sat with the women separately. We were only women, having intensive discussions about their wishes and needs.'

Rajendra Desai (engineer, NCPADP): 'You must speak their language. At least, you need to have someone in your team that knows the local language well. Being dependent on translation is very tricky. It can be dangerous and hilarious at the same time. You need to be in a position to catch sensitive and subtle information. Otherwise, you may make irreversible mistakes.'

Architect (team member, SIFFS): 'You know I worked with villagers who live approximately 40km south of my home town. We all speak Tamil. But, communication was a challenge. Their language is different. They use words I am not at all familiar with. Without the social workers who mediated between us, and explained the meaning of their words to me, I think, we as architects would, most probably, not have succeeded.'

Expertise/Know-how

Rajendra Desai: 'In September 2011, the Indian state Sikkim was hit by an earthquake. We went there as a team [architects and engineers]. And we were surprised to be confronted with a timber construction that we had never seen before. We were not at all familiar with it. However, this technology had withstood, largely, the earthquake. In this project we learned many things from the local carpenters [...] A similar experience we had in Kashmir, after the earthquake in 2005. There the houses were built in stone masonry, and we worked together with excellent local masons.'

Satprem Maini (architect, director of the Auroville Earth Institute): 'When entering a rural environment as an architect, you should assess and learn first, about their way of living and building. Each context is different. Each context has its own experts. You need to identify those people first, as they can teach you many things, and together with them the project should be developed.'

J. S. Rajasingh (architect, Kingsway Consultants, Chennai): 'The architect's way of thinking is different. When you work in this context, when you engage with villagers, you need to "de-professionalise". You need to come down to their level, in order to learn. Very often, they give practical ideas we may not even have thought about. If you do the work the way you think it is to be done, you have already failed.'

Outsider/Insider

Rajendra Desai: 'When you enter a new village, one of the main challenges is that you are confronted with the villagers' lingering anxieties and their distrust of outside experts. So, the first thing you need to do is to build up confidence and trust. You need to become an insider.'

S. Vasanth (Quadrant Architects, Chennai): 'I was an outsider, you know. I am from Chennai, and I worked in remote villages. The people were foreign to me, and I for them. The first thing I had to do was to build up their confidence. It was not easy. I spent time with them in their old village. I had tea and coffee with them. I tried to become "one of them" which is not possible, of course, but I tried to become their comrade, who would eventually enjoy their trust. This was critical because the project went on for more than two years. So, I put many efforts in building up this relationship.'

Presentation of the Project

Surveyor-anthropologist (architect, SIFFS): 'There are many different ways you can present a project. You need to find out what is effective and what not. This is actually a crucial stage during a project because it is about sharing critical information. So, posters, for example, may have a limited utility in one context. Finding out, which way is the best to present may also be a process. The 1:1 model house has proven to be very useful. The people can experience it. It becomes real, what you have been talking about. You know, we architects are trained in a particular way how a project should be presented. But in a rural context this may not work.'

'Small Things'

Architect (team member, SIFFS): 'The planning of the master plan in Chinnangudi village [another village reconstructed by SIFFS after the tsunami of 2004], for example, turned out to be a challenge because of "minor" issues. I will give you two examples: the additional land allocated by the government for those who wanted to be shifted was located in such a way that certain houses where located too close to the burial ground. So, we had to revise and rearrange again and again, in order to arrive at a distance and an orientation which was accepted by the people. And, another thing, which had not been given any importance initially, really, was the location of the toilet and its orientation. It was a cluster layout and the problem was that some of the houses' toilets were facing the other houses' entrance. This was a major problem. This, I found out during a coffee break, gathering with the women under the shadows of the trees, and we had to rework on it.'

J. S. Rajasingh: 'I was born in a village, and my father was into social work. I am very much familiar with rural environments. However, I have learned in the many projects I have worked on so far, that each and every village is unique. The peculiarities you will find out only, however, when engaging closely with the people. You need to be sensitive, however, how to engage, and with whom best. This is particularly important at the beginning.'

Purnima McCutcheon: 'I realised that the familiarity with that specific work culture is quite important. Tamil Nadu's work culture is very different from that of Maharashtra in the same country. Chennai [capital of TN] has a different work culture. Rural Tamil Nadu has a different work culture. It is so contextual. There are just so many aspects one needs to be familiar with. It is not a "minor" thing. It is fundamental in order to work effectively.'

In addition to the intricacies of this context as a whole are the many practical aspects, unexpected incidences and subtle themes, as the reflections above illustrate, at project level, which are, probably, far beyond the skills and experience of formally trained architects. Therefore, the following questions arise: can formally trained architects ever become 'insiders', versed in handling the many aspects, subtle themes and 'small things', critical for the degree of success of a project; and, which essential factors do NGOs and architects need to consider in order to chose appropriate staff? Or, to put it differently, what if, for example, the villagers chose 'their architect' themselves as a first step in the reconstruction process?

This chapter has highlighted that, in addition to the importance of handling the many 'hard facts' (technical and managerial issues) skilfully during the project, there are a number of 'soft facts' that are of the utmost importance for the degree of success of a project. In many cases, however, decision makers and architects attach low (or no) priority to them. While I will resume this discussion again later on (see CHAPTER Conclusion and Recommendations) I will now focus on the construction phase and its challenges in more detail, as the quality of construction had, as has been touched upon already, a significant impact on the degree of satisfaction in all the three villages (see CHAPTER Additional Factors Affecting the Degree of Satisfaction, p. 109; 133; 162).

An Unsettled Concern: The Quality of Construction

The field survey has revealed that construction quality has continued to be of concern for the people in all the three villages, if to varying degrees. While in Shanmuga Nagar the defects of 90% of the houses can be classified as serious, the deficiencies in Keezhakazakudy-Tsunami Nagar and in Tarangambadi-Tsunami Nagar range from minor to severe. It has already been shown that in Shanmuga Nagar the villagers are repeatedly confronted with leaking roofs and walls, and that they have had to be evacuated already as their new houses were completely flooded because of severe construction defects (see CHAPTER Additional Factors Affecting the Degree of Satisfaction, p. 133).

In Keezhakazakudy-Tsunami Nagar the problems with the quality of construction range from minor problems such as small cracks on the floors and staircases, to severe defects such as repeatedly inundated walls and leaking roofs. Interestingly, the quality differed not so much from house to house, but from area to area within the hamlet. This was because construction was allocated in packages to different contractors, and it has to be assumed that their skills varied significantly. Most importantly, the findings suggest that strict quality control, hamlet-wide, was lacking.

In Tarangambadi-Tsunami Nagar, it was seen that overall the construction work was of better quality. However, in this hamlet several houses could also be found where the walls remained damp for days after rainfall, and that roofs leaked. As in Keezhakazakudy-Tsunami Nagar, it was found that the quality differed from area to area, and not between houses. This, most likely, was because the hamlet was constructed in phases (see CHAPTER Project Outline, p. 141). It seems that the houses built during the first phase are of better quality than those constructed in phase four.[9]

The findings suggest that the construction phase poses particular challenges, regardless of the mode adopted. Thus, the following questions need to be addressed: what are the realities, the peculiarities, and the constraints of the construction phase; and what role can an architect play in this phase, and why? Before examining these questions in detail I will summarise the three different modes of construction adopted in the three hamlets. As in the previous chapter, I will then aim to identify the critical factors related to this topic by depicting different voices, namely those of the villagers, NGO personnel, architects, engineers and site managers.

- Keezhakazakudy-Tsunami Nagar

Professional contractors were appointed for the construction of the houses (see Figure 7: Organigramm, p. 98). As the number of houses (200) was too large for one contractor, the project was split into packages and allocated to three different companies. The procurement of construction materials and the assignment of skilled and unskilled labour were within the contractor's scope of work, as well as the management of the various construction stages. The architect and a site supervisor appointed by the NGO were assigned responsibility for the supervision of the quality. Moreover, the architect was in charge of overseeing the pace of the construction works, and of issuing the certificate of completion. The villagers did not play any role during this phase; more precisely they were not allowed to enter the construction site at all.

- Shanmuga Nagar

In this case, construction was carried out by a technical team (see Figure

9 | These findings are related to the number of households interviewed only and not to the hamlets as a whole. They make no claim to be representative/complete. Also, how far the quality of construction was related to the phase of construction (and the respective strategy devised for it) has not been investigated further.

13: Organigram, p. 122) which was composed as follows. A technician was appointed as site supervisor (appointed by the NGO), and he was in charge of coordinating and supervising the construction works. Skilled masons were assigned as site foremen, and the villagers were deployed as unskilled labour in charge of producing the earth blocks. For that purpose, special machinery (an Auram Press 3000) had to be purchased and installed at the site. The villagers were trained specifically for this purpose. The procurement of the construction materials was managed by the NGO staff, specifically the shelter coordinator and the site supervisor. The architect was not assigned any role at this stage of the project. During construction, the villagers were living on the plot where the new house was being built, and they could carry out their rituals at this stage of the project.

- Tarangambadi-Tsunami Nagar

The management of the construction of this project turned out to be fairly complex. This is for two reasons. First, the NGO did not outsource the entire responsibility for construction to a professional contractor. Second, due to the size of the project, construction had to be split into packages, and the houses were constructed in several phases. In total, the project was subdivided into five phases, and the final one was completed in December 2009 (see CHAPTER Project Outline, p. 141). As in Shanmuga Nagar, the architect was not assigned any task at this stage. A team of engineers was assigned responsibility for supervising the quality of construction. A labour contractor was appointed to be in charge of recruiting skilled and unskilled labour, while the procurement and the management of the construction materials was handled by the NGO (e.g. the manager of stores, finance manager, vehicle manager, stores supervisors, the accountant, cashiers, etc.; see Figure 21: Organigram, p. 146). As the houses had been allocated to the villagers prior to construction (a significant difference when compared to Keezhakazakudy-Tsunami Nagar), the villagers were responsible for reporting any problems and deficiencies they observed. Curing was the house owners' responsibility. However, for any other unskilled labour the villagers were appointed only on the basis of their availability. In this phase, moreover, they could carry out the rituals from their building tradition. By the end of 2006, however, the entire project had almost come to a total stand-still, as reconstruction was in full swing throughout the coastal belt of TN, resulting in a scarcity of skilled and unskilled labour. At this stage, the local government wanted to disqualify SIFFS and take over the project to ensure a speedy completion of the construction works. However, the villagers went on the streets to protest as they wanted the NGO to complete the project. In this very tricky situation, SIFFS had to devise a new strategy in order to restart the work, and a 'piece-rate-system' was set-up which involved breaking up the construction process of an individual house into several stand-alone components such as excavation, foundation, wall masonry, pillars, roofing, plastering etc. The smallest component of work was decided on in such a way that a small group of people could finish it in a day's work. This resulted in a fairly complex process, as a single house was divided into approximately 40 components (see CHAPTER The Role and Scope of Work of the Surveyor-Anthropologist; SIFFS 2009: 23–24). However, this system made it possible to revive the works by employing labourers and small builders from within Tarangambadi and its neighbouring villages.

Here is some of the villagers' feedback by project, with regard to the construction phase in general, and the quality of construction in particular.

- Keezhakazakudy-Tsunami Nagar

Fisherwoman: 'We did not know which our house would be. We could not carry out any *pujas*.'

Fisherwoman: 'We saw that the blue metal they used for concreting was too big. You can see the quality is very poor. We informed the NGO, we stressed this issue. But we were not heard.'

Fisherman: 'We reported the poor quality, also after moving in. Nobody has come to do the repair work. We have no money to do it ourselves.'

- Shanmuga Nagar

Irula man: 'We had to learn how to make the bricks. We did not want to do this work. We wanted to continue with our usual livelihood. But we had to.'
Irula woman: 'We would like the houses to be plastered, and the roofs to be repaired. Water enters. We asked the NGO to repair it. They say there is no money left.'

Irula man: 'We can not repair it ourselves, as we used to do, because we don't have the machinery and the money.'

- Tarangambadi-Tsunami Nagar

Fisherwoman: 'The labourers building our house did not speak our language. I think they were from Andhra Pradesh, or thereabouts. Whenever we complained about something, they did not understand.'

Fisherman: 'In our house the concreting was not well done. You can see that on the staircases and on the ceiling, for example. The blue metal they used was too big.'

How did other actors experience this particular phase of the project? What were the most significant challenges and constraints they were faced with? I will now present the voices of the NGO staff, architects, site managers and engineers involved in the three cases studies, but also perspectives from those who have extensive experience in post-disaster reconstruction. I have subdivided, again, their answers into categories, which are: 1) quality and availability of construction materials, 2) availability of local skilled and unskilled labour, 3) cost explosion, 4) construction technologies, 5) management of the construction works, 6) quality supervision, 7) time pressure, and 8) 'small things'.

Quality and Availability of Construction Materials

Arun Menon (engineer): 'The issue of quality of construction materials starts already with the supplier. For example, bricks. In India, bricks are produced in rural areas. It is not an industrially produced material. So, if you want to ensure the use of quality bricks you need to follow up the whole production chain, which starts at the brickyard.'

J. S. Rajasingh (architect): 'On the Andaman and Nicobar Islands we had to import construction materials from the mainland because there the Government had defined how the houses should be constructed [after the Indian Ocean Tsunami of 2004]. So, most of the materials were not available there. We had to ship the materials, which of course affected the cost of the project. But, most important the material was not at all suitable for the local context. We had much discussion with government engineers on that issue, but we did not succeed.'

S. Vasanth (architect): 'The construction market was tight during post-disaster reconstruction. The massive demand resulted in high prices of the materials, and at the same time the quality was not maintained. Bricks in particular. We were strict. We had situations where we had to reject full trucks of bricks, because the quality was so poor.'

Availability of Skilled and Unskilled Labour

PMC (engineer, PMSSS): 'When you think of the years 2006 and 2007, there were so many reconstruction projects going on at the same time. Local skilled and unskilled labour was needed in so many projects. So, the major issue was the screening of good labour in order to be able to construct quality houses. So, even if the contractor's past work performance had been of high quality, in some cases we realised that due to the tight labour market, the builder did not perform as we would have expected.'

Project Manager (SIFFS): 'At one point, our labour contractor was not able to identify local labour anymore. So, he had to get labourers from Orissa [an Indian state]. Then, however, there was a language problem. Direct communication between the villagers and the labourers was not possible anymore. The villagers started to complain.'

J. S. Rajasingh (architect): 'In Andhra Pradesh, we had adopted a different system of a regular housing programme. This could, however, also be a model in post-disaster reconstruction. We used to form groups of villagers. Like ten families in a group. Each group would provide a working member to do the unskilled labour like excavation works, etc. And this we would do for each stage of the project. Unskilled labour from within the family groups, and skilled labour employed by us. We paid a daily salary, so that they have their daily income. For shuttering only we called a contractor, because the masons did not have the necessary materials for that.'

Cost Explosion

Engineer (consultant, Caritas India): 'In any major post-disaster context, a crucial issue is the scarcity of skilled and unskilled labour, and the high demand on basic construction materials such as sand, bricks, cement and steel. This results in a cost explosion of the entire project. In order to keep the labour you need to raise, most likely, the wages. Otherwise, labourers may be hired away. The same thing happens with construction materials. Prices go up when there is a high demand. This needs to be taken into account by the NGO, and budgeted for accordingly. Otherwise, the project may come to a standstill, or even worse, may not be completed at all.'

The voices above suggest that ensuring construction quality is, indeed, tricky. While the quality of construction depends on both the quality of the materials and on the skills of the labourers, the availability of the same is not, at least in a large reconstruction context, assured. Basic construction materials and skilled labourers are scarce, which results in a rise in the project's costs. Even if an NGO is ready (and has the necessary financial resources) to pay higher wages for the labourers and prices for the construction materials, this does not guarantee better quality. In the case of Keezhakazakudy-Tsunami Nagar, for example, additional funds were allocated as a remedy (see page 104). Nevertheless, this strategy did not result, as has been found, in a good quality of construction. Is there a way out of this vicious circle?

The complexity of this problem does not allow for a straightforward answer. A solution to this problem can only be developed from within a specific context, and presupposes, above all, ingenuity and courage. We have seen, for example, that in the case of Tarangambadi the NGO was stuck at one point due to the shortage of construction materials and labourers. As a result, they devised the 'piece rate system' (see page 157; 188) and, in so doing, they were able to both escape this vicious cycle and ensure a better (when compared to the other two projects) quality of construction. The voices below will highlight, however, that there are many other challenges that need to be handled during the construction phase to ensure good quality.

Construction Technologies

Satprem Maini (architect): 'Introducing a new technology is dangerous for various reasons. First, because people may not accept it, adequate labourers are not available locally and because it may not be best suited for the particular purpose. Before even considering the introduction of a new technology you need to find out first if traditional technology would be an option. If so, I advise to implement that, as it is known to the people, and it can be improved. If, however, you opt for an alternative construction technology, then it is essential that you as an architect are well acquainted with the technology, its advantages, its disadvantages and, most important, its specificities. Second, the people need to accept it fully. If they are not convinced about it, and you are not in a position to deliver why this technology would be a better option, then it should not be implemented. Third, you should only implement it if you can ensure that there is adequate labour available that is able to carry out the works with good quality.'

Management of the Construction Works

Site Manager (SIFFS): 'Clearing of bills and the payment of the labourers was done within the same day. This was significant. You can not let them wait. This is important for the pace and the quality of the project.'

Programme manager (Caritas India): 'From the NGO's perspective, there is an advantage when appointing a contractor with regard to the entire management, procurement and accounting procedures. However, we found, that it is also important that the contractor has a good rapport with the people, who will live in the house.'

PMC (architect, PMSSS): 'The management of the reconstruction of entire villages is not only an issue of constructing houses. All the infrastructure need to be provided at the same time, so that at the end of the day, there will be water, roads, electricity. So, in order to manage the project well you also need to have a good rapport and cooperate closely with the government and its engineers, as they are, in most cases, responsible for the provision of these services.'

Project manager (SIFFS): 'Even in the absence of the architect our team of engineers, social workers and local workers were able to manage.'

Quality Supervision

Engineer (consultant, Caritas India): 'There are two issues: quality supervision of the construction works and the quality control of the construction materials. Ensuring the quality of construction works can only be done by those people who have a profound experience of working at construction sites. They need to be very well familiar, of course, with the technology and the materials used. With regard to the quality of construction materials it is a must that they are controlled and tested *before* being stored at the construction site. Also, for this task you need to have people who bring in adequate qualifications.'

Project managger (SIFFS): 'Our experience was that in this case [quality supervision] the people can also play a key role. Because they are the ones who will live in the house, so they want to see that the workers do quality work. We experienced that their reporting of mistakes to the site engineers proved to be absolutely relevant. So, you should not think that they do not know, just because they are not technically trained people.'

Architect (consultant, SIFFS): 'Whether you opt for owner-driven or contractor-driven construction or a mix of both, quality control is an issue of utmost importance, and at the same time one of the most difficult aspects of the project. You need to deploy highly-experienced staff at the construction site that need to be there, in the best case, on a daily basis. Very often, however, funds for skilled personnel are not budgeted for in order to economise. I have argued repeatedly that this is wrong.'

Time Pressure

Architect (team member, SIFFS): 'The construction team was under big pressure. We architects were in charge of finalising and adapting the plans, but they had a lot of pressure. The villagers wanted to move in as soon as possible, the government had a close eye on the project, as it was the biggest in Tamil Nadu, and the donors, of course, wanted to see the houses coming up as quickly as possible.'

Co-founder and executive director (Solidarité, funding agency of BLESS): 'Of course, the pressure comes also from the village level, because people want to get back to a normal life as soon as possible. But the major problem is that the donors define the time frame within which the money has to be spent. Usually, in a post-disaster context, this is a maximum of two years which is of course absurd because especially for a construction project we know that more time is needed. So, what we did, we challenged our donor by saying that we would take the funds only if they granted us four years in total for the project. We succeeded, but this was after the tsunami of 2004 and lots of funds were available.'

Cameron Sinclair (executive director and co-founder of the NGO Architecture for Humanity): 'My donor was very nice. I said, "I am not sure when we are going to finish the project." And the donor said. "OK, that is fine." So I wasn't looking to finish by Christmas or for the annual report. And as a result it was reconstruction on their [the villagers] timeline and not ours. And that has actually become part of our ethos.'

These diverse statements provide additional and profound insights into the many themes of this particular building phase. They highlight the necessity of opting for an appropriate construction technology (which is accepted by the people, which the architect is well versed in and for which skilled labour is available), and the many administrative tasks of this phase (clearing bills, procuring construction materials and labour, cooperating with government engineers, and coordinating teams). Moreover, they stress the importance of assigning qualified personnel to the supervision of the construction works while showing that the people can play, even if they don't have the equivalent educational background, a significant role. Last, but not least, the voices point out that time pressure has a decisive impact on the building process as a whole and its dynamics. Jean-Louis Bato and Cameron Sinclair show, however, that time frames that are too tight and defined by donors don't, necessarily, need to be accepted by the NGO implementing the project(s).

'Small Things'

S. Vasanth (architect): 'When you work with a contractor, it is important that he is one of the team. Like the villagers, and the architect and the engineers. The contractor should not be seen as a third party. This is important because a good relationship with him is critical, not only for the architect, but also for the villagers. They need to experience that the builder is with them, taking seriously their concerns, including their rituals. This is not to romanticise. These are facts.'

Purnima McCutcheon (architect): 'But as the time kept going he [the builder] just kept not performing and then eventually I did the scheduling for him, OK it takes that much time to do the roofing, and I examined him and he told me that it takes so much time to do the painting [...] I would say, look, you have done nothing, you always have excuses; cost of bricks went up, cost of cement bags went up, I don't have labour this time [...] I didn't hold any strings. I couldn't say you are not going to be paid if you don't do this job. I didn't have this sort of relationship with him. It was mostly verbal pressure; I would like to go in there and say I won't pay you if you do not work as agreed.'

Site manager (SIFFS): 'The villagers encouraged the labourers of their houses during construction. They provided them with water, drinks and snacks. They helped whenever there was a need and they had the capacity. And also, they could, if they wanted, provide their own door. Some, for example, did not want to have the door or the tiles that were part of our package. They wanted to have a more decorative door or other tiles. So, they could do that.'

Project manager (SIFFS): 'Transparency is very important. We displayed everything on a notice board in the village, for example, the rate of the materials, the cost of good quality bricks and how much of material is needed. So, these details were also with the people.'

Architect (consultant SIFFS): 'The set up you have in place is critical at all levels and at all stages of the project. By set up I mean the people, their relationships and how they cooperate. You will have teams, so it is important that the various teams work well, and at the same time it is critical that the various teams interact and cooperate well. The ability to listen, accept differences and overcome difficulties are vital qualities.'

In a similar fashion to the planning stage, the voices quoted above show that there are a number of 'small things' that are essential during construction. They range from building up a good relationship between the architect, the villagers and the contractor, holding the purse strings when in charge of controlling the building progress and the quality of the construction work, facilitating a good rapport and cooperation between the labourers and the house owners, being transparent at village level with regard to critical factors such as the cost of construction materials, and, finally, having a good set up of various teams with different skills that cooperate closely.

This chapter set out to outline, first of all, that the construction phase poses a number of challenges, and ensuring the implementation of quality work requires sophisticated approaches, regardless of the mode of construction that has been adopted. The data indicate that even though Tarangambadi-Tsunami Nagar received the highest level of approval (78%), it can not be considered a model case. Construction failures could be identified in all the three case studies, ranging from minor to severe defects. The architects' and engineers' voices quoted above suggest that the issue of quality construction very often does not receive specific attention. Moreover, they emphasise that the assignment of adequately skilled personnel must be a top priority in order to implement good-quality construction. Second, it seems that involving an architect *per se* is not the answer to the many challenges at hand. Rather, it appears to be, once more, a question of the right set-up and the sophisticated interplay of different actors, who bring a range of skills to the project. However, these findings can not be considered conclusive, those from which recommendations can be derived, as in two of the three projects the architect was not assigned any specific task during this phase.[10]

Moreover, the villagers' comments quoted above suggest that there are several questions that remain unacknowledged, even many years after the completion of the projects. Who is liable for the defects? Is it the NGO, the architect, the contractors, the masons or the site supervisors? Who should rectify of the problem, and what is the procedure? What are the villagers' rights? What can they claim?

---

10 | Further research is recommended examining, in particular, the challenges of the construction phase in general, the advantages and disadvantages of different construction modes at the various levels (NGO level and village level), and the skills required for the various actors involved.

At this point, the fifth and final stage, post-occupation, comes into the picture. The importance of devising a strategy for this phase, however, has been neglected in all the three case studies. In Keezhakazakudy-Tsunami Nagar, for example, the contractors' contract included a 'liability clause with a retention of 10% of the project's total cost that should ensure the rectification of the construction defects within two years, starting from the date of completion'.[11] It appeared, however, that the compliance with this clause lacked consistency and transparency at project level.[12]

Thus, the poor quality of construction of many of the houses continues to be of concern for the villagers, particularly for those who are dependent on financial and technical assistance. While some with sufficient financial means were in a position to repair the damage, many households have put up with the situation, and continue to live in houses that have, in a number of cases, severe defects due to gross negligence during construction, and unsettled legal positions regarding liability.[13]

How far are the findings of this research of relevance at an international level? Do the results reflect the themes and questions encountered in other post-disaster contexts? Are there additional key aspects that need to be considered when examining the role of the architect in this particular working context? Or, are there possibly contrary positions, based on practical experience? The following chapter seeks to approach these questions by giving a voice to international architects who have worked extensively in post-disaster reconstruction in various regions across the globe.

11 | Programme manager of Caritas India. Interview on 07.02.2012.

12 | Out of the 40 households interviewed, in 9 cases the contractor rectified the defects. In 5 other cases the house owners did it by themselves. During informal interaction the villagers commented that the contractors rectified the defects only in some houses, but not in others. The reasons could not be elicited. However, the village has not been evaluated as a whole, and it is not known how this issue has been handled in detail. Thus, there are no final data available. Nevertheless, the low degree of satisfaction with regard to the quality of construction suggests that the liability clause has not been enforced consistently.

13 | The issue of liability has not been considered so far in the literature. Further research on this particular subject is recommended.

International Voices: Comparison of the Results of the Three Case Studies

The aim of this chapter is, first of all, to demonstrate the relevance of the findings of this study beyond their specific cultural and post-disaster context. Furthermore, it seeks to broaden the themes encountered in this research by revealing additional ideas and ongoing questions (international) architects have been confronted with repeatedly. The architects selected for the purpose of this chapter differ with regard to their cultural and educational backgrounds. However, over twenty years of work experience in the context of development cooperation, and post-disaster reconstruction, is common to all of them (see APPENDIX A).

Their voices have been placed into two categories: 1) the international relevance of the findings of this study, and, 2) additional subjects and ongoing questions. The latter will be subdivided again into the various themes that emerged during the interviews. Again, given their profound insights and strong messages, which have not been documented elsewhere, I will not comment on or summarise their statements. However, I will take up several of these themes in the final chapter of this study (CHAPTER Conclusion and Recommendations).

International Relevance of the Findings of this Study

Graham Saunders (British architect; Head, Shelter & Settlements; International Federation of Red Cross and Red Crescent Societies): 'The findings of this research are very relevant for us. It resonates very much with our experiences at a global level. Repeatedly, we can only guess why the project did not go well. So, the categories you outline here are very interesting. It is important for us as an NGO and for us architects to know which factors impede success [...] I will give you an example with regard to your category "language/communication". Back in 2001 I worked with CRS [Catholic Relief Services, American NGO] in Gujarat after the earthquake. It is India again; however, it is a different state with a different reconstruction policy, and a different culture [...] We worked in a Muslim village, and we had planned a house with one entrance door only. This, we found out, was a problem. A female social worker sat with the women of the village, and they said that one entrance door would not work out. They needed a second door at the rear, because when the men gather in front of the house, they can not enter. We architects would never have been in a position to find out this, because we were men, did not speak the language, and would probably not have asked the right questions [...] Another experience that might fall into the category that you named "small things": In the 90s, after the Balkan war, I worked in a village where different ethnic groups had lived together before the war. The people returned to their old places but there was a lot of distrust, and the issue of neighbourhood had become a delicate issue. We were also encountered with distrust. So, before even talking about the house a relationship had to be built up. Having coffee in the morning, in the afternoon, talking about many things, planting a tree in the garden, but not touching the topic house was vital before the technical part, the planning could take off. This first part, we architects could not fulfil. We were not "experts" with regard to interacting with the villagers. It is hard for architects to appreciate that they are not central and that they do not have the skills for all the tasks at hand.'

Daniel Schwitter (Swiss architect; Senior Architecture and Settlement Specialist, SKAT)[1]: 'Architects are trained to visualise and draw beautiful plans. My experience repeatedly shows me that presenting two-dimensional plans will not work with lay people. In Sri Lanka, for example, we built a model house in a very simple way. We made a frame of wooden slats which were covered with cloths. Wherever there was a window or a door, the cloth would be cut. The villagers could get a three-dimensional idea of the proportions of the house. Their suggestions were incorporated

1 | The interview with Daniel Schwitter was held in German. Translated by Gertrud Tauber.

when finalising the plans [...] The one who plans the project must speak the language of the people, and most importantly, he/she must cooperate well with other teams, and not work in isolation.'

Sandeep Virmani (Indian architect; Hunnar Shaala–Foundation for Building Technology & Innovation): 'In whatever context we have worked so far, we never had the answers right at hand. It was a process. In Gujarat, Sri Lanka, Indonesia, Afghanistan, Iran. What we did is asking so many questions to so many people. For example, we asked so many questions to artisans. Local artisans have developed habitats and technologies all over the world, and many of their buildings are time-tested for safety and the resources are used in a sustainable way. However, artisans have been relegated in many cases to executing works only, and the prerogative of providing technical answers, the design and artistic content is mainly controlled by architects.'

Vivek Rawal (Indian architect; 'People in Centre' Consulting and 'ODR Collaborative'): 'The architect's role can be important through all the stages of reconstruction after disaster, beginning as and when a relationship between architect and community evolves. The architect has to make effort to build and nurture this relationship. So it is not merely the skills of an architect as designer but more importantly the attitude, perspective and intentions. And it is this aspect that gets most neglected in architecture education.'

Antje Wemhöner (German architect; she has worked for different NGOs, GIZ and KfW)[2]: 'Your findings reflect basically my experiences in different contexts. Communication, for example, is so essential in any context. You need to know *which* themes are discussed, and *how*, within the group of people you are working with. You need to know why you need to ask certain questions, for example, with regard to the location of the bathroom or the toilet. If you don't know that this is a central concern based on the cultural context of the people, you as planner will not ask this question. In Haiti after the earthquake in 2010, for example, I was part of a project team where the communication task was carried out by locals, as they

2 | The interview with Antje Wemhöner was held in German. Translated by Gertrud Tauber.

were part of the local society. They spoke the language, Kreyòl, they had experienced the earthquake themselves, and they knew what the people had gone through. Building up a close relationship with the people was thus much easier. This social team was able to communicate, moderate discussions and to detect shortcomings.'

Sandeep Virmani: 'So, it is not only a social task of getting the people to dialogue. It is a socio-political task where you need to ensure that poorer and less powerful sections of the society will also have a voice. For example, women have to play a major role in decision making, because in many of these rural environments the home is very minutely managed by the woman.'

Additional Subjects and Ongoing Questions

The Relevance of Architects in Post-Disaster Reconstruction

Florian Steinberg (German architect; Senior Urban Development Specialist, Urban Development and Water Division, ADB – Southeast Asia Department): 'Architects are not very essential [...] It seems to me that many other factors of institutional arrangements, the financing and fund flow, the procurement of goods and services, the management of participatory processes, and choices of technologies, are more important than the role or participation of architects.'

Daniel Schwitter: 'Architects are needed. NGOs need architects. One can not say that they are not needed, particularly in the case of large-scale relocation projects. You need to have the skills to make the master plan, to give just one example of a critical task. In an in-situ project, for example, working with the mason or the carpenter may suffice, it may be absolutely appropriate. It depends on the project.'

Antje Wemhöner: 'NGOs, particularly those with no experience of construction in general and of reconstruction in particular, need the support of architects. But, they don't know how to deal with architects. So they also need support to define precisely the roles and the scope of work. The appointment of architects comes along with high expectations from the NGO's, as well as the target group's, side. They expect a particular benefit, a noticeable value. *How* exactly can the architect 'add value' to the project? What can a formally trained professional bring, what can he/she do better than the mason who has always built the houses in the villages? This is the central question. We architects are outsiders and we may possibly never understand the villagers fully, because we are from a different region and have a different background, but at the same time we have know how that might be of relevance.'

Sandeep Virmani: 'NGOs providing housing in such a context require architects. Mostly, the NGOs have no experience with the building industry, and they feel completely at a loss in a post-disaster situation, and they need help. But how would the community ask for an architect? Supposing that the money was given directly to the people how would they choose the agency? Or would they choose an agency? If we start from here, many things become clear because the architects are employed by the agencies, so the architect is accountable to the agency. The architect is responding primarily to the needs and requirements of the agency and not, necessarily, to those of the community. So, if the community had the free choice with whom to construct changes the situation drastically. This does not mean that the community would not choose to work with an architect; probably they would, simply because they are faced with a situation where they have to rebuild from scratch, they feel also lost, and they would like help, because it is not an issue of rebuilding a single house, but an entire settlement. They want their new house to be of a better standard than before. So they want facilitation in that. They want someone who understands technology, materials, and has a sense of history to place the correct questions before them to dialogue and come up with proper suggestions.'

Urban Context

Sandeep Virmani: 'The main difference between urban and rural is that in a rural context, governance is not an issue. Communities come together easily, they will dialogue and they have the power to take action. In a city, one needs to differentiate between middle and high class communities and slum dwellers. In a district with middle and high income households the people are more insular. There are so many tasks that are not within their control. They have also lost the ability to build their own home. So they are much more dependent on architects or engineers. This, however, is not necessarily the case in slums. Many slum communities are very enterprising and far more dynamic and innovative than rural areas because they have seen the world much more. In the case you work with a slum community with a similar background then they come together very well and implement [...]'

Antje Wemhöner: 'In an urban context you are faced with different questions and requirements, such as land tenure, size of plots, infrastructure and agglomeration. Due to the rapid growth of cities you are also confronted with very different and, often, inappropriate construction technologies and qualities. So, the central question becomes, how will the city be rebuilt? It is not like in a village where, very often, traditional technologies have proven to be adequate and may need to only be revised. In a city you need to assess the advantages and disadvantages of various construction technologies.'

Graham Saunders: 'Your findings, I would say, are also relevant for the urban context, but there you are additionally confronted with themes such as transportation, translocation and tenants' rights. Also, land tenure is, in most cities, a very challenging issue.'

Mixed Target Groups

Daniel Schwitter: 'I worked on projects where we had a mix of different religious groups. In one project in Sri Lanka, for example, we had to work with Muslims, Hindus and Catholics. Their very different lifestyles had to be covered by one project. That is very tricky, because you need to know the people you are working with very well, in order to meet their needs. But when you work with a target group with so many different backgrounds, designing the set-up, planning and implementing the project is an enormous challenge. You need good teams that work together closely. This in itself is a project that needs to be managed.'

Inexperienced Architects

Antje Wemhöner: 'Experience is essential. Inexperience and ignorance are a problem for any construction project in any corner of the world. However, inexperience is not negative *per se* because everyone has to start somewhere. It is important that there is guidance and support. Ignorance, however, is fatal [...] NGOs very often can not pay high salaries. So they find it difficult to identify well qualified staff, and the screening of personnel is, very often, *ad hoc*. This is problematic because ultimately it affects the quality of the project.'

Daniel Schwitter: 'I have repeatedly encountered young architects and engineers without any experience in this context. This is very problematic. They were completely lost. They were lost during the planning phase, because they could not anticipate so many things that would ultimately have an impact on the project as a whole, the budget for example, or the execution of the construction work. They were also lost at the construction site, because they had no previous experience of site supervision [...] But we also need to involve young architects and engineers, because they need to learn. However, they need to be guided and helped well. You can not leave them alone.'

Multidisciplinary Cooperation

Sandeep Virmani: 'Typically, sociology and technology are two fields that are uncomfortable with one another in terms of experts. Social workers don't know how to use technologists and technologists don't necessarily respect sociology. So it is very rare to come across an agency that is, for example, primarily technology based and brings in sociologists and social workers to mediate when a disaster happens, or, the other way, where there are many more social agencies that know how to organise the people, but they realise that they need an architect but they don't know how to use an architect. Typically, architects and technologists tend to take on control. I have found in many NGOs, that had brought in an architect, that the staff completely yield to the architect, to whatever the architect was saying, even though they knew the people much better.'

Daniel Schwitter: 'Social workers played a significant role in many projects I was part of; they have the skills to interact with the people. But there is no use having the best social worker if the architect and the social worker can not complement one another.'

Antje Wemhöner: 'In this context you are confronted with a package of tasks. The cultural aspect is particularly difficult for the architects to handle because they have, very often, not the experience with the cultural context they are confronted with. So team work, cooperation with other personnel that complement other capacities and skills are essential.'[3]

International Architects

Graham Saunders: 'Repeatedly architects approach me, asking for an assignment. So I ask them: what do you want to be there, and what can you bring in? Their answer is: well, I know how to plan and to build. I start sharing the many challenges local architects have to face in such a context so that they get an idea. But it is difficult for them to appreciate this.'

Daniel Schwitter: 'I am a Swiss architect. I cannot go to Sri Lanka and do the planning. This would not work. This work must be done by local architects. An international architect mustn't play the role he is used to playing in his/her cultural context. This does not work. *How* a local and an international person cooperate, *how* the tasks are defined, these are the essential questions.'

Antje Wemhöner: 'International architects who are appointed to work in this context are, often, completely unable to cope with the task. The expectations are very high and thus, out of necessity, they make decisions that are not always good, and in doing so, they do harm to the project.'

Sandeep Virmani: 'I will tell you a small story on that. When I was in Aceh, after the tsunami we had an INGOs [international NGOs] coordination meeting, and for two hours there was a discussion going on about the following question: in which American universities can we find good tropical architects? You must imagine, this discussion took place in the middle

3 | See also: Wemhöner 1993.

of Aceh, a city with wonderful architecture all around you, done by local architects, and they are thinking about how to get tropical architects down from America... One problem is that they think that the solution is coming from their own country, but also, because the money is coming from there. Local organisations would not have such a discussion. They would not look for an architect in the United States or in Europe. They would look locally for a sensitive architect. This is because an INGO feels more comfortable working with an architect from the same work culture, because you expect the best efficiency from a certain method of working, which may be American, or German. But this is not necessarily the way other countries work. They have different methods, different work cultures.'

Shortcomings of the Present Architectural Education

Graham Saunders: 'There are many missing pieces that are not given importance in classical training, even though, I would argue that they are very relevant, not only in a post-disaster project but also, for example, in a regular housing project in Britain. An architect from the north of Britain would find it very hard to work in a small village in the south of the same country, to give an example. The "small things" you outlined are relevant everywhere, I guess, but they are not given importance at universities. There are specific courses aiming to equip architects for post-disaster reconstruction. However, also these training courses are too narrow.'

Vivek Rawal: 'Architecture, mostly taught today as an individual pursuit and expression of the designer, does not equip young professionals with skills required for work where the design continues to have a community's ownership of expression. The education at architecture school does not introduce them to vast knowledge resources.'

Antje Wemhöner: 'I studied at the TU Berlin and, back in the 80s, there was a department focusing on building and constructing in so-called developing countries. I attended a number of courses and seminars there. That is how it started in my case [...] I don't think that the training of architects and the discipline of architecture *per se* is inappropriate when dealing iwithn such working environments. But, as you outline in your study, it is very important to define precisely the roles and the tasks.'

Sandeep Virmani: 'Unfortunately, the way architecture is taught at least in this country [India], you are not taught communication skills at all. In fact, even regular architects when they pass they talk and speak a jargon clients can not appreciate or understand. We architects are taught to develop our visual abilities much more than talking abilities. And that is why architects find it very difficult to go into a cultural context and talk to people and try to understand their built habitat through the words and the wisdom of the people and what they value. So many times in the colleges I get them [the students] to do certain rural exercises and they will go to the village and come back after three days without having spoken to anybody. They would have created drawings, beautiful drawings, and I ask them why didn't you talk to the people, did you not feel the need to talk in order to understand? And they would reply: no I was trying to understand through symbolisms that I could see around me. This is valid, but then when you discuss these symbols with the people you will get far more depth into what you are trying to see and understand. One thing is to be able to assess a culture and another thing is that architects say: you know we talk to the people and they say they want a modern house like that in the city. Now, if you are not a student of anthropology or of other social studies you as an architect don't know which questions are relevant to be asked in order to start developing a project which considers their aspirations and which is, at the same time, rooted in their specific cultural context.'

The architects' voices portrayed here suggest that the subject of this research is of relevance at an international level. Moreover, their statements indicate that the findings resonate with their experiences in different post-disaster environments. At the same time, however, they have highlighted that there are a number of additional subjects and questions of concern, such as the specific requirements of the urban context (when compared to the rural), the intricacies of working with target groups of different cultural and/or religious backgrounds, the challenges and requirements when involving inexperienced architects, the importance of multi-disciplinary cooperation, the complexity of assigning international architects, and the shortcomings of the present architect's training in general, and of post-disaster courses in particular. Most importantly, however, the voices imply that the themes outlined in this study, as well as the additional subjects and questions given above, are of great relevance and need to be tackled simultaneously at academic, NGO and project level.

Conclusion and Recommendations for NGOS, Architects and Educational Institutions

The Three Different Roles and Their Implications

This study dealt with a vast and intricate theme, the role of architects in rural post-disaster reconstruction. More precisely, it examined whether the involvement of formally-trained architects has proven to be of positive significance for the realisation of people-oriented housing, as put forward by the NGOs. For that purpose, three case studies were selected that were implemented by local NGOs and planned by local architects.

As a first aim (see CHAPTER NGOs, Architects and Post-Disaster Housing, p. 24), the five building phases of each of the three case studies were analysed to illustrate the intricacies and distinctiveness of a post-disaster working context. What was done by whom and when during the various phases has been outlined, showing that the realisation of such a project involves the participation of a number of different actors with different mandates and powers (the government, the NGO and the villagers). Most importantly, however, the different roles and scope of work of the three architects and the resulting effects at the village level have been illustrated. In so doing, the specifics and the requirements of each project phase, and the skills needed for the various tasks, have been identified and described.

Based on findings obtained in the field, i.e. the villages, the profession of the architect has been deconstructed and the assignment of this professional shown to be problematic in two of the cases, for various reasons.

Firstly, the tasks at hand during the building process, are numerous and multilayered. This requires, above all, sophisticated design of the building process, and the skilful interplay of different actors, roles and skills. However, the two NGOs were ignorant of rural building cultures, their pecularities and capacities, as (post-disaster) housing is not their regular focus of attention. Added to this, the architects assigned for the planning of the projects did not provide the vital skills needed for this specific working context. It has been pointed out that they took on the 'classical roles' of planner-designer-manager (the PMC) and planner-designer (the draftswoman). In doing so, the architects met, primarily, the requirements of the NGOs. At the same time, though, they failed to respond to the basic, yet fundamental, needs of the villagers. As the guidelines issued by the government were adopted wholesale and without question, the project brief was defined in isolation from the villagers and knowledge of the villages' building culture. The expertise of local craftsmen, the village elders and the villagers was excluded from the building process. Moreover, the villagers could not carry out their *pujas* (prayer, worship) at the necessary stages of the project. This is, though, a distinctive feature of their building culture. Furthermore, I have outlined, based on the results of questionnaires at village level and the interviews with NGO personnel, architects and engineers, that along with 'hard facts' come a number of 'soft facts', which have a decisive impact on the degree of success of the project. However, it has been shown that in two of the three case studies neither the NGO nor the architect attached due importance to them. As a consequence, they failed to provide people-oriented housing.

What is, then, the appropriate role for an architect in this particular context, and which skills and attitudes should he/she bring to the tasks at hand? Is it that of the surveyor-anthropologist?

Indeed, this architect has received, thanks to a sophisticated process design and the skilful interplay of various actors, the highest level of approval for all the parameters identified as significant at village level. Moreover, there are a number of creative and courageous measures, as well as distinctive features, that could be seen as inspirational for all those in search of alternative approaches to post-disaster housing. The architect was assigned an unusual role during the building process which could be described as that of a 'searcher' (Easterly 2006: 5). The particular scope of work assigned to him and his team required, though, the application of specific working methods and skills. Nevertheless, not all of these skills were provided by the architect and his team alone. Social workers, NGO staff, engineers, local craftsmen and the villagers contributed significantly during the building process. In this way the project brief was developed from within the village, the guidelines issued by the government were adapted, and the know-how and the skills available within the village and its neighbourhood played a vital role during the building process. This led to a high degree of satisfaction (when compared to the other two cases) at village level. Would this, however, be the justification for naming this process design and this role of the architect as the exemplar in post-disaster reconstruction?

There is no single 'best' approach for the process design and the role of the architect, since the reconstruction process is rooted in a particular socio-politico-economic environment (see Davidson *et al.* 2007: 113). The role and scope of work of the architect (and all the other actors involved) can, therefore, be defined only from within specific post-disaster contexts, which will, inevitably, vary. It will differ with regard to the socio-political, cultural and legal framework, and the financial and the human resource capacities of the public and private actors involved (see also Barakat 2003, Steinberg 2007). Moreover, it will differ with regard to the villagers' building cultures, their skills and needs, and their (past) experiences with public and/or private agencies and outside professionals. Thus, it would be foolish (and naïve) to formulate a single theoretical model for the building process, and a single role for an architect (including the necessary skill-set), and to imply that this results in 'better' projects, 'since there are as many notions of what is "better" as there are participants and as there are contexts' (Davidson *et al.* 2007: 112). At the same time, this study has identified a number of essential abilities and skills, from both the villagers' and the architects' point of view, that could guide the design of the building process and the assignment of the 'right' personnel to the various tasks during the project cycle. The following chapter will outline these findings in more detail.[1]

1 | At this point it is important to emphasise, however, that approaching a post-disaster reconstruction project in this way may be feasible only in a context such as that portrayed in this study, i.e. where NGOs are free to design the process and to develop the project as a whole. This approach may not be possible in a post-disaster environment where the house typology is predefined by the government (as was the case, for example, in the states of Andhra Pradesh, Kerala and the

From Within the Village

The second and third aim of this research is to ascertain the skills and capacities required at project level, and to provide a foundation for NGOs and architects to act more cautiously and prudently when designing and taking on roles during the building process (see CHAPTER NGOs, Architects and Post-Disaster Housing, p. 24). Therefore, this chapter will include, first of all, the voices of the villagers and architects, who have worked extensively in the context of post-disaster housing on the Indian subcontinent and across the globe, and who were interviewed for the purpose of this research. Thereafter, it will emphasise the critical steps and decisions an NGO has to make when providing rural post-disaster housing. Based on the villagers' statements, the ideal skills of 'their architect' can be summarised as follows. He[2] speaks their language, is well acquainted with their (building) culture, interacts intensively (individually) and listens intently, asks questions if he does not know something, and only then develops the project. He cooperates closely with them during *all* the stages of the project. Furthermore, he shows what the house will look like in the end. However, he is able to do this in such a way that the end-product (the house and the new habitat, in the case of relocation) corresponds to what has been discussed (and/or presented) during the planning stage. Finally, he has the ability to build a good-quality house.

Interestingly, the skills outlined by the villagers resonate with the experiences highlighted by the architects. However, the villagers' and the architects' way of reflecting upon this theme differ. While the villagers refer specifically to a person they are familiar with, i.e. the mason, the architects see this issue as about 'outsiders'. How can we (architects) be equipped so that we can receive internal information? How best can we access an unknown context and fit into local dynamics? They argue that it is of utmost importance to become an 'insider' in order to understand the

---

Union Territory of the Andaman & Nicobar Islands after the Indian Ocean tsunami of 2004), or where the rehabilitation process is rigidly controlled by the government and alternative approaches from civil society bodies are rarely accepted. This was the case, for example, in Japan after the tsunami of 2011 (see also: Carrasco 2013).

2 | I use 'he' in this paragraph as I refer to the quotations of the villagers. Both, women and men refer to the qualities of a male person, who is their local mason.

potential and needs of a specific village, and to develop the project from within (see pages 181–185). However, this requires, according to the architects, a number of essential abilities (see CHAPTER International Voices).

First of all, they must concede the argument that formally trained architects are not, necessarily, provided with adequate skills for this working context, and are not 'experts' who have the right answers for the numerous challenges and tasks ahead of them. This is because architecture today is mostly taught as an individual pursuit and expression of the designer. Students are not exposed to the 'real' world, and academic education takes place in self-contained classrooms. Colleges do not teach sensitivity towards local building cultures and 'traditional' construction technologies, and their education does not introduce architects to other knowledge resources of the built environment. Moreover, architects are, primarily, taught to develop their visual but not their communication skills and intercultural competences. Which are, however, vital, as has been shown here, even for local architects working within the Indian subcontinent.

Secondly, architects emphasise that in addition to having a profound knowledge with regard to different construction technologies (including 'traditional' construction technologies) site supervision and project management come a number of skills that this specific working context requires. These include: knowing the people's language; having the ability to build and nurture a relationship with the people; having a keen sense of *how* and *with whom* to interact; understanding *which* and *how* themes are discussed within the group of people you are working with; comprehending *what* type of questions may be relevant and/or essential to ask; having the intuition for *how* to ask the questions; being sensitive (and empathetic) towards the poorer sections of a society and different user groups, and having the capacity (and power) to ensure their participation in decision making; being ready to cooperate with different teams/personnel; having the courage to say 'I don't have the answer right at hand, I need to ask'; and being open to reaching out to other knowledge resources that are fundamental for developing and planning houses (and habitats) that respond to the people's aspirations and are, at the same time, rooted in their culture (see CHAPTER International Voices). These manifold, yet vital, abilities will, most likely, not be provided by formally trained architects, as the present education of architects does not consider these skills and abilities to be important (see Rieger-Jandl 2005, Davis 2006, Latter 2006).

Should, as a consequence, NGOs refrain from appointing architects? This question is valid. Nevertheless, the answer is not a simple yes or no, and thus, I wish to approach it by taking into consideration the 'trivial' steps and decisions an NGO has to make when providing housing in a context such as that portrayed here.

As a first step, the NGO needs to define which type of reconstruction will be undertaken. This may be the repair of damaged houses and the reconstruction of new houses in-situ, this can be a relocation project, or a combination of the two. This decision depends, above all, on the financial standing of the NGO. In the best case, the type of reconstruction will be decided by the NGO and the villagers together. Therefore, the pros and cons of each option need to be assessed thoroughly (see also El-Masri 1997), and discussed with the villagers. Assisting the villagers in taking a decision may require, as we have seen in the case of the surveyor-anthropologist, providing them with vital information. For example, inundation maps were presented to the villagers, highlighting the high-risk zones of the village and its surrounding land. This enabled them to decide whether they wanted to be relocated or stay in the old village. While some of the villagers opted to stay, others opted for relocation. As a result, the NGO supported both relocation and reconstruction in-situ (see SIFFS 2009).

Second, once it has been defined which type of project will be supported, the skills required need to be specified, and it is essential to assess which skills are available at both NGO and village level in order to define who does what, when and why (see Davidson 2010: 108). The NGOs claim to be the other side of institutionalised development policies, to be more flexible, more grassroots-oriented, to have stronger links with the rural poor, and to be more cost effective has already been discussed (Cernea 1988). NGOs have tried to differentiate themselves explicitly from government and to promote the construction of people-oriented housing (see CHAPTER NGOs, Architects and Post-Disaster Housing). Assuming that the NGO takes this goal literally and decentralises its decision making, then it would, logically, as a next step, let the villagers choose 'their architect'. The villagers would, probably, choose to work with their local mason or carpenter, or they would, maybe, choose to collaborate with an architect (because they know one or because a number of architects would be presented to them, for example). Approaching the project in this way could facilitate the process in many ways. First, the villagers could work with the person they trust, a decisive factor in the degree of success of the project, as has been outlined in this study, and the NGO could, thereafter, assign the personnel and/or the teams to complement the abilities of 'their architect' in order to handle the numerous tasks that arise at both NGO and village level. These people may be architects, engineers, social workers, social anthropologists, sociologists, builders, craft cooperatives and/or research institutes. In this way, the project would be developed from within the village, by acknowledging its skills and responding, at the same time, to its needs.

Third, both of the two previous steps require a person (or a team) who has the capacity to oversee and lead the project. Who would best be suited for this task? Should the project management be the responsibility of an architect, an engineer, a social anthropologist, a social worker, a sociologist or a combination of various disciplines?

The skills of the project manager in charge of such a project were described by the NGO personnel and the architects interviewed for this study as follows. He/she has the capacity to comprehend and to oversee the course of the project in its entirety. He/she allocates due importance to all factors – social, cultural, political, architectural, engineering and financial – in order to lead the project holistically. He/she is well aware of his/her own limitations, and will ask for expertise whenever required. He/she has a keen sense of how to identify the 'right' staff and guides the team members skilfully. According to the Indian architect Sandeep Virmani, 'the ideal project leader, in such a context, is philosophical and practical at the same time'.[3]

The findings discussed in this chapter show a challenging reality, and they reveal that there is a crying need for both NGOs that approach rural post-disaster reconstruction cautiously, and for personnel who are adequately qualified and possess the necessary skills for the job. The architect as a professional is called on to take this on board in many ways. Proposals are needed to make the profession of relevance for this working environment. The same holds, nevertheless, for the many other disciplines (engineering, social work, social anthropology, sociology and others) which work in this context. All disciplines participating in such a housing project as that portrayed in this study need to be well trained to interact and cooperate with other disciplines. However, this requires from all disci-

3 | Interview on 09.08.2013 (Internet phone).

plines, as a first step, a rethink of their professional attitudes. This leads to the final, but essential, question: what kind of institutions and course(s) are required to equip professionals for this specific working context? The following chapter proposes changes to the education of architects.

A Challenging Task Ahead: Designing a Specific Training Course for Architects

> [T]here is a big need for architects. However, we are constantly confronted with the fact that architects are not qualified adequately.
> Graham Saunders[4]

> [E]ducational curricula in the UK have become increasingly narrow in focus. Students often come to university without any clear concept of their own culture in any deep sense, let alone with any insight into other world views [...] they are likely to continue their education into a professional elite with more or less uniform values.
> Rosemary Latter 2006: 246

The fourth aim of this study is to provide a foundation for educational institutions for the design of a specific training course for architects who intend to work in the context of (rural) post-disaster housing (see CHAPTER NGOs, Architects and Post-Disaster Housing, p. 24). Thus, this final chapter discusses the idea that a specifically designed course might play a formative role in the education of those architects who will help guide the building of people-oriented housing in (rural) post-disaster environments. The course proposed here should contribute, first of all, to a new kind of professional education that sees the architect as a professional in quite a different way from contemporary architectural education (see Salama *et al.* 2002, Davis 2006). In this new environment architects are

4 | Head, Shelter & Settlments (IFRC) at the 6th International i-Rec Conference on 'Sustainable Post-Disaster reconstruction: From Recovery to Risk Reduction', in Ascona / Switzerland. Date of presentation: 27.05.2013.

humbler, draw their knowledge from the particular situation in which they find themselves (see Janz *et al.* 2008), are familiar with the skills and methods of other disciplines, have deep respect for and are trained to cooperate closely with other disciplines, artisans, builders, clients and members of the communities they are working for (see Woyseth 2002, Davis 2006, Duffy *et al.* 2013, Hughes *et al.* 2013). The formal education of architects has 'traditionally promoted an attitude toward professional expertise that seems opposed to the idea of a shared, embedded knowledge' (Davis 2006: 231). In 'western' societies (Hall 1992), for example, both expertise and control of the building process have been taken away from ordinary citizens, and the building process has been guided, ever since the beginning of the nineteenth century, by formal professionals (see Abbott 1988, Woods 1999). However, rural (and urban) environments in 'non-western' societies do not lack ordinary people with expertise. 'What these communities lack is power which resides in outside institutions like governments, NGOs and banks' (Davis 2006: 232). And it is often 'these institutions that get in the way of the communities ability to use the expertise that already exists within them. Within this view, the people who need appropriate education are not in the settlements, but in these currently unhelpful institutions' (*ibid.*).

Howard Davis (2006), advocating a radical change in the system of architectural education, argues that the pedagogy of present architectural training is based on at least five assumptions that are neither supportive of the healthy vernacular architecture required in the new century, nor of architects in search of alternative roles.[5] The inadequacy of the present academic education of architects when dealing with rural post-disaster housing has been discussed in various chapters of this thesis, and the five assumptions identified by Davis (2006) substantiate the argument put forward here. Therefore, I will briefly summarise them before concluding with my suggestions for the design of a specific course equipping architects for (rural) post-disaster housing.

- Architect's expertise

There is the assumption, taught more implicitly than explicitly, that the architect's expertise is better than that of ordinary people, and that the

5 | See also Janz *et al.* who discuss the importance of a 'postcolonial pedagogy' (2008: 320).

architect must, at all costs, maintain dominance over the craftsmen, the builders, the client and the client's community. This helps educate the architect as someone who is radically opposed to his or her culture, and leads to future professional relationships that cannot foster the kind of sharing of cultural values and habits that characterise 'traditional' building cultures.

- 'Star designer'

There is the assumption that the 'star designer' is more important than other professionals of the built environment, much more than craftsmen, builders and contractors who are not even part of it. This marginalises architecture students who want to be involved with architecture in different ways, and it pushes pedagogy and curricula in ways that marginalise most other roles.

- 'Object building'

There is the assumption (connected to the idea of the 'star designer') that the 'object building' is more worthy of study than the ordinary house. Many design projects in architecture colleges deal with monumental or highly symbolic public buildings (museums, libraries, cultural centres, cinemas, shopping malls) or unusual private buildings (galleries, villas, artists' studios) rather than (informal) housing or rural and urban contexts, and the shops and workplaces of ordinary citizens.

- The past

There is the assumption that architects have little to learn from the past. Architectural history is taught. However, another basic premise of design teaching today is that every problem is new and needs to be solved from first principles, and that the direct use of precedents is to be rejected. This approach is, however, quite different from processes of 'traditional' building cultures. In these, the passing on of know-how and findings from one generation to the next and the repetitive use of designs has helped give coherence to complex, collective configurations like cities and rural habitats.

- Self-contained classrooms

There is the assumption that learning can happen through drawings, away from buildings, construction sites, craftsmen and the people. Learning takes place in the studio in front of the drawing board, the computer and in self-contained classrooms. Abstraction and theory predominate over reality. There are field trips to view construction sites, or study trips to different countries. Still, by and large, the idea that one's own neighbourhoods and present-day reality itself might be the best teacher is not present (Davis 2006: 237–238).

The result of these assumptions, taught implicitly and explicitly at architecture schools today, is a professional that is of no use to NGOs in need of architects who facilitate the realisation of people-oriented housing in a rural post-disaster context. Which could be possible features of a course equipping architects for this very particular working environment? Below, I outline a proposal.

- Paradigm shift

Education should lead to a different professional attitude that respects (and draws upon) the abilities of different actors during the building process. It should guide students in comprehending, and draw their attention to, other sources of knowledge. It should recognise a number of actors involved in the process, ranging from NGO personnel, policy makers and politicians, professionals of other disciplines, craftsmen and communities. In addition, it should teach architects to cope with the inevitability of conflicts and contradictions, and how to comprehend the many different languages spoken by the various actors and to decode their different visions and aspirations. It should build confidence in developing projects together with many different actors out of a given context rather than imposing one's own will onto a situation that is characterised by chaos, conflict and uncertainty. It is also important to equip architects for a working context where there are no easy answers, where there is a need to delve into complex themes and to deal with tedious processes, and it should foster a professional attitude that perceives the architect neither as central, nor as *the* 'expert' in the building process.

- Theoretical content

The course should introduce architects to the nature of (rural) housing, settlements and 'traditional' architecture (see Rapoport 1982, 1983) in 'order to learn from it' (Rapoport 1999: 55); familiarise them with the logics of 'other' societies, their dynamics, values, and complex and vibrant realities; introduce them to the political and economic frameworks of governance in (rural) settlements, the political and economic dimension of post-disaster contexts and these dynamics at a local, national and international level; and it should explore postcolonial discourses on development paradigms, modernity and on the production of space and identity.

- Practical content

The practical part of the course should 'dismiss' the architect from the classroom and expose him/her to 'real' places, i.e. their neighbourhoods (see Latter 2006), and 'immediate settings, [which are] learning venues for all' (Janz *et al.* 2008: 330). Architects should, in partnership with social workers, sociologists and social anthropologists, delve into the nature and the dynamics of the neighbouring villages, and explore the skills available within them and identify the aspirations of the villagers. It should also encourage cooperation with engineers and artisans to examine the 'traditional' construction technologies of both their native region and their place of study. It would also be important to serve an apprenticeship with local artisans in order to experience firsthand the qualities of 'traditional' construction technologies and the skills of craftsmen. They should work at construction sites where the lack of skilled and unskilled labour and construction materials is an issue, so they can learn how to deal with situations characterised by scarcity. It should teach that the building process is not a 'value-neutral, unidirectional, step-wise process towards a finite end-point' (Hillier 2002: 4). Thus, it is also important for them to participate in 'life projects' and develop solutions for the 'real problems' of their neighbourhoods. This should be done in cooperation with actors of different backgrounds (NGO personnel, communities, artisans, politicians, engineers, social workers, etc.) so they are exposed to different languages, logics and paradigms, and experience the dynamics of environments characterised by conflict.

The content proposed here is based on the findings of this study, which has approached the role of the architect in rural post-disaster housing 'from within'. The villagers, the architects, the engineers and the representatives of NGOs all had their say. Their comments were essential to depict the complexity of the subject. Their wisdom, their common sense and their insights have been, among others, the source of inspiration for the possible design of a course. However, the themes – which are far from complete as more (empirical) research is essential – are not as important as the professional attitude which is required in this working environment. This 'new' professional would be equipped to work in contexts where it is necessary to see other worlds as much as possible from the inside and to develop solutions 'from within'. This is 'not only the stance of the anthropologist'

(Davis 2006: 243). This should be the stance of the architect aiming to be of relevance in (rural) post-disaster housing.

At present, numerous courses on international cooperation and disaster management, in different disciplines, are offered at various colleges all over the world. However, there are only two training courses (worldwide) for architects that focus specifically on post-disaster reconstruction. The Centre for Development and Emergency Practice (CENDEP) at the British Oxford Brooks University offers the post-graduate course *Shelter after Disaster.*[6] The Spanish Universitat Internacional de Catalunya Escola Tècnica Superior d' Arquitectura offers a masters course in *International Cooperation and Sustainable Emergency Architecture.*[7]

Nevertheless, the findings of this study suggest that there is a need to do more, to face the complexity of the subject and tackle the root of the problem. Educational institutions are called upon to act. They are faced with the choice of training architects to be of relevance for a working context of increasing importance, or of continuing to perpetuate paradigms, roles and self-perceptions that have fatal consequences for those who do not have the structural power to resist.

6 | http://architecture.brookes.ac.uk/research/cendep/shelter.html (accessed on 28.08.2013).

7 | http://masteremergencyarchitecture.com/program/ (accessed on 28.08.2013).

Appendices

Appendix A: Profile of the Interviewees

NGO REPRESENTATIVES (Case Studies)

Position	Organisation	Date/Place of the Interview
Executive director	BLESS	10.12.2011 / Reddichavady (TN)
Co-founder and executive director	Solidarité	15.12.2011 / Puducherry
(Former) Programme manager	Caritas India	07.02.2012 (Internet phone)
Programme manager	PMSSS	01.02.2012 / Puducherry
(Former) Executive director	PMSSS	12.12.2011 / Neyveli (TN)
Project manager	SIFFS	31.01.2012 / Tarangambadi (TN)
Site manager	SIFFS	31.01.2012 / Tarangambadi

NGO REPRESENTATIVES (Other than Case Studies)

(Former) Executive director (Arul Devadoss)	MSSS	24.01.2012 / Chennai (TN)
Project manager (S. Jeyaseelan)	MSSS	24.01.2012 / Chennai

ARCHITECTS AND ENGINEERS

Name	Organisation/ Firm	Position	Date/Place of the Interview
Ar. P. Anbukarasi (Architect) Puducherry, India	Freelance	Worked as project architect for an NGO	10.12.2011 (Puducherry)
Rajendra Desai (Engineer) Ahmedabad, India	NCPDP	Co-founder and director of the 'National Centre for People's Action in Disaster Preparedness'	22.12.2011 (Internet phone)
Rupal Desai (Architect)	Same as above	Same as above	22.12.2011 (Internet phone)
M.J. Joseph (Engineer) Bangalore, India	Retired (Indian Army Engineering Corps)	Consultant for NGOs	20.01.2012 (Chennai)
S. L. Karunakaran (Engineer) New Delhi, India	Retired (CPWD – Central Public Works Department)	Consultant for NGOs	15.01.2012 (Chennai)
Benny Kuriakose (Architect) Chennai, India	Kuriakose Architecture	Worked as project architect for different NGOs	11.01.2012 (Chennai)
Satprem Maini (Architect) Auroville, India	Auroville Earth Institute	Director	08.02.2012 (Auroville)
Purnima McCutcheon (Architect) Ulaanbaatar, Mongolia	Worked for different architecture firms and for 'Architecture for Humanity'		01.08.2011 (Internet phone)

Arun Menon (Engineer) Chennai, India	Indian Institute of Technology, Madras	Assistant professor, Department of Civil Engineering	04.02.2012 (Chennai)
J.S. Rajasingh (Arch.) Chennai, India	Kingsway Consultants	Founder and director; worked for different NGOs	26.01.2012 (Chennai)
Viwek Rawal (Architect) Ahmedabad, India	'People in Centre' and 'ODR Consulting'	Works with these two organisations	16.06.2013 (Email)
K. Sakti (Architect) Puducherry, India	Siva & Sakti Architecture	Worked for different NGOs and agencies	05.01.2012 (Puducherry)
S. Siva (Engineer)	Same as above	Same as above	05.01.2012 (Puducherry)
Graham Saunders (Architect) Geneva, Switzerland	IFRC	Head, Shelter & Settlements	31.07.2013 (Phone)
Daniel Schwitter (Architect) St. Gallen, Swizterland	SKAT	Senior Architecture and Settlement Specialist	06.08.2013 (Internet phone)
Cameron Sinclair (Architect) San Franscico, USA	Architecture for Humanity	Co-founder and executive director	18.07.2011 (Internet phone)
Florian Steinberg (Architect) Manila, Philippines	ADB	Urban Development Specialist / Department South-East Asia	01.08.2013 (Email)
S. Vasanth (Architect) Chennai, India	Quadrant Architects, Chennai	Founder and director; worked as project architect for an NGO	11.01.2012 (Chennai)
Sandeep Virmani (Architect) Bhuj, India	'Hunnar Shala' (Foundation for Building Technology & Innovation)	Director	09.08.2013 (Internet phone)
Antje Wemhöner (Architect) Berlin, Germany	Freelance architect and consultant	Works for different NGOs, GIZ and KfW	08.08.2013 (Internet phone)

Appendix B: Parameters Affecting the Cost of the House

Table 19: Parameters affecting the cost of the house

	Keezhakazakudy-Tsunami Nagar (200 Houses)	Shanmuga Nagar (62 Houses)	Tarangambadi (including Tarangambadi-Tsunami Nagar) (1091 Houses)
Position			
Field-survey / Habitat mapping			x
Architect	x	x	x
Poor quality of land	x		x
Land filling	x		x
Land levelling	x		x
Increased height of foundation	x	x	x
Cost explosion of labour	x		x
Cost explosion of construction materials	x		x
Time span of construction			x

Appendix C: 'Traditional' House Typologies in Pattanavar Villages (Coromandel Coast/TN)

Picture 17: Thatched house with palm leaves; classified as unserviceable kachcha[1]

Picture 18: Brick walls with straw-thatched roof; classified as semi-pucca

1 | For definitions see CHAPTER The Revised Policy.

Picture 19: Brick walls and palm leaves (thatched roof); classified as semi-pucca

Picture 20: Brick walls with tiled roof; classified as pucca

Picture 21: Flat-roofed house: reinforced cement concrete (RCC) framed structure with brick infill and concrete roofing; classified as pucca

Appendix D: 'Traditional' House Typologies in Irula Villages (Villupuram and Cuddalore District/TN)

Picture 22: Mud (walls) and leaves (roof); classified as serviceable kachcha

Source: Picture 22 and 23 courtesy of Justin P. H.

Picture 23: Mud (walls) and palm leaves (roof); classified as serviceable kachcha on the left and unserviceable kachcha on the right

Glossary

Language

Adivasi (HINDI: ādivāsī)	Umbrella term for a heterogeneous set of ethnic and tribal groups claimed to be the aboriginal population of India.
Anganwadi (HINDI: āṅganvāḍī)	'Courtyard shelter': they were started by the Indian government in 1975 as part of the Integrated Child Development Services program to combat child hunger and malnutrition. A typical *anganwadi* centre also provides basic health care in Indian villages.
Balwadi (HINDI: bālvāḍī)	Indian pre-school, run in rural areas and for economically weaker sections of the society, either by government or NGOs.
Bhoomi puja (HINDI: bhūmi pūjā)	Ceremony performed to inaugurate a new site for the construction of a building. Literally it means 'worship of the soil'.
Cuddalore	District in Tamil Nadu
Grahapravesam (TAMIL: krahapravēśam)	Ceremony performed upon completion of the house. Literally it means: house entry.

Irula	Adivasi community
Kallāram	Beach in front of (and along) the village (see Bharati 1999: 266).
Karaikal	District in Karaikal (Union Territory of Puducherry)
Katumaran (TAMIL: kaṭṭumaram)	Literally 'tied wood'; a boat used by artisanal fishers, c.f. catamaran.
Kaveri	River in Tamil Nadu
Koil (TAMIL: kōyil/kōvil)	Temple
Koyi (TAMIL: kōrai)	Sedges and bullrushes (used for thatching).
Kuppam (TAMIL: lit. fishers' village)	Village
Kachcha/kutcha (HINDI: kaccā, lit. 'raw')	Officially used by the Government of India to define houses built out of local construction materials.
Manaj puja (HINDI: maṇaj pūjā)	Ceremony performed when construction actually starts. Literally it means the worship of the floor level.
Metu (TAMIL: mēṭu)	Slightly elevated (hilly)
Mukkavar	Caste specialising in fishing (southern-most part of Tamil Nadu).

Nagapattinam	District in Tamil Nadu
Nagar (TAMIL: nakaram)	City area
Panchayat (HINDI: pañcāyat)	Along the Coromandel Coast, almost every village has a *panchayat* of nominated members or elected members who represent the various lineages, headed by a man called the *chettiyar* or *naddar*. This council, which consists wholly of adult males, is closely tied into a system of village membership and decision-making. Important matters are decided upon consensually in the context of the village meeting (Bavinck 2003: 650). The traditional (nominated) *panchayat* plays a crucial role in *Pattanavar*-dominated villages. Nothing can be done without their consent.
Paravar	Caste, specialising in fishing (Palk Strait region).
Pattanavar	Caste, specialising in fishing (Coromandel Coast).
Pompay	Grass (used for thatching).
Pucca (HINDI: pukkā)	Officially used by the Government of India to define houses built out of industrially produced construction materials.
Puja (HINDI: pūjā)	Prayer or worship
Swami (HINDI: svāmī)	Priest or holy man

Taluk (HINDI: tālūkā)	Generally, a *taluk* (South India) or *tehsil* (North India) consists of a city or a town that serves as its headquarters, possibly additional towns, and a number of villages. As an entity of local government, it exercises certain fiscal and administrative power over the villages and municipalities within its jurisdiction. It is the ultimate executive agency for land records and related administrative matters. Its chief official is called the *tehsildar* or less officially the *talukdar* or *taluka muktiarkar.*
Tehsildar (HINDI: taḥsīldār)	Chief official at *taluk* level (*talukdar* or *taluka muktiarkar)*

Measuring Units

1 sq ft = 0.0929m²

1 cent = 40.467m²

1 acre = 4046.9m²

Lakh (HINDI; lākh)	A unit in the South Asian numbering system equal to one hundred thousand and written as 1,00,000. It is widely used in both – official and unofficial – contexts in India, Pakistan, Bangladesh, Nepal, Sri Lanka and Myanmar. 1 Lakh = 100,000 Indian Rupees.

List of Figures, Pictures and Tables

List of Figures

List of Pictures

All pictures Gertrud Tauber unless otherwise specified

List of Tables

Bibliography

Abbot, Andrew. 1988. *The Systems of Professions: An Essay on the Division of Expert Labor.* The University of Chicago Press, Chicago.

Alvesson, Mats/Sköldberg, Kaj. 2000. *Reflexive Methodology*. SAGE Publications Ltd London.

Aquilino, Marie J. (ed.). 2011. *Beyond Shelter. Architecture and Human Dignity.* Metropolis Books, New York.

Arce, Alberto/Long, Norman. 1992. The Dynamics of Knowledge. Interfaces between Bureaucrats and Peasants. In: Long, Norman/Long, Ann. *Battlefields of Knowledge. The Interlocking of Theory and Practice in Social Research and Development.* Routledge, London and New York: 211–246.

Asian Development Bank (ADB). 2005. *India Post-Tsunami Recovery Program Preliminary Damage and Needs Assessment.* Available under: http://www2.adb.org/documents/reports/tsunami/india-assessment-full-report.pdf (accessed on 10.06.2010).

— 2008. *Tsunami Recovery in India. 3 Years On.* Asian Development Bank, Manila.

Asian Development Bank Institute (ADBI). 2005. *Post-Tsunami Recovery: Issues and Challenges in Sri Lanka.* Available under: http://www.adbi.org/files/2005.10.dp39.tsunami.recovery.srilanka.pdf (accessed on 10.01.2013).

— 2007. *Adjustment and Recovery in Thailand. Two Years after the Tsunami.* ADB Institute Discussion Paper No. 72. Available under: http://www.adbi.org/files/dp72.thailand.tsunami.adjustment.recovery.pdf (accessed on 10.01.2013).

Asquith, Lindsay/Vellinga, Marcel (eds.). 2006. *Vernacular Architecture in the Twenty-First Century. Theory, Education and Practice.* Taylor & Francis, London and New York.

Asquith, Lindsay. 2006. Lessons from the Vernacular. Integrated Approaches and New Methods for Housing Research. In: Asquith, Lindsay/Vellinga, Marcel (eds.). *Vernacular Architecture in the Twenty-First Century. Theory, Education and Practice.* Taylor & Francis, London and New York: 128–144.

Auroville Building Centre, Development Alternatives. 1997. *Code of Practice for Production and Use of Ferro-cement Roofing Channels.* Auroville, New Delhi.

Balaji, G. 2007. *Tribes of Nilgiris. Arts and Crafts of the Kotas, Krumbas, Irulas and Pjiyas.* The C.P. Ramaswami Aiyar Foundation, Chennai.

Barakat, Sultan. 2003. *Housing Reconstruction after Conflict and Disaster.* HPN Network No. 43. Overseas Development Institute, London.

Bavinck, Maarten. 2003. The Spatially Splintered State: Myths and Realities in the Regulation of Marine Fisheries in Tamil Nadu, India. In: *Development and Change* 34(4): 633–57.

Beck, Ulrich. 1992. *Risk Society. Towards a New Modernity.* Sage, London.

Betke, Friedhelm/Grunewald, Matthias/Weitekämper, Johannes. 1978. *Partner, Pläne und Projekte. Die personelle Hilfe der Bundesrepublik Deutschland in West Malaysia.* Breitenbach, Saarbrücken.

Bhatia, Gautam. 1991. *Laurie Baker. Life, Works & Writings.* Penguin HUDCO Book, New Delhi.

Bharathi, Bhakthavatsala S. 1999. *Coromandel Fishermen. An Ethnography of Pattanavar Subcaste.* Pondicherry Institute of Linguitics and Culture, Pondicherry.

Boano, Camillo/Garcia, Marisol. 2011. Lost in Translation? The Challenges of an Equitable Post-Disaster Reconstruction Process: Lessons from Chile. In: *Environmental Hazards* 10: 293–309.

Boano, Camillo/Hunter, William. 2012. Architecture at Risk(?): The Ambivalent Nature of Post-Disaster Practice. In: *Architectoni.ca* 1: 1–13.

Boen, Teddy/Jigyasu, Rohit. 2005. *Cultural Considerations for Post-Disaster Reconstruction. Post-Tsunami Challenges.* Available under: http://www.adpc.net/irc06/2005/4-6/Tbind01.pdf (accessed on: 10.03.2012).

Bortz, Jürgen/Döring Nicola. 2006 [1984]. *Forschungsmethoden und Evaluation für Human- und Sozialwissenschaftler.* Springer, Heidelberg.

Bourdieu, Pierre. 1977. *Outline of a Theory of Practice*. Cambridge University Press, Cambridge.

— 2005. The Berber House. In: Carsten, Janet/Hugh-Jones Stephen (eds.). *The Anthropology of Space and Place. Locating Culture*. Blackwell Publishing, Oxford: 131–141.

Bourdieu, Pierre/Wacquant, Loïc, J.D. 1992. *An Invitation to Reflexive Sociology*. Polity Press, Cambridge.

Briand, Michael. 1999. *Practical Politics*. Urbana, University of Illinois.

Burgess G. Robert/ Pole J. Christopher/ Evans, Keith/Priestley, Christine. 1994. Four Studies from One or One Study from Four? Multi-site Case Study Research. In: Bryman, Alan/Burgess G. Robert (eds.). *Analyzing Qualitative Data*. Routledge, Oxford and New York: 129–145.

Carrasco, Sandra. 2013. *International NGOs' Competences towards Reconstruction of the Built Environment in the Region of Tohoku, Japan*. Paper presented at the 6th International i-Rec Conference: *Sustainable Post-Disaster Reconstruction: From Recovery to Risk Reduction*, May 2013. Ascona, Switzerland.

Caritas India. 2005a. *Tsunami Rehabilitation Shelter Programme for Tamil Nadu and Puducherry by Caritas Network*. Unpublished document. Courtesy of Caritas India.

Caritas Internationalis. 2007. *Safe. Sustainable. Shelter*. Folder for the International Workshop on Shelter. 19–21 July, Chennai.

Carsten, Janet/Hugh-Jones, Stephen. 1995. *About the House. Lévi-Strauss and Beyond*. Cambridge University Press, Cambridge.

Cernea, M. Michael. 1988. *Non-Governmental Organizations and Local Development*. World Bank Discussion Paper No.40. Washington D.C.

Chambers, Robert. 1997. *Whose Reality Counts? Putting the First Last*. Intermediate Technology, London.

Chandhoke, S. K. 1990. *Nature and Structure of Rural Habitations*. Concept Publishing Company, New Delhi.

Clarke, Matthew/Fanany, Ismet/Kenny, Sue (eds). *Post-Disaster Reconstruction. Lessons from Aceh*. Earthscan, London.

Cuny, Frederik 1983. *Disasters and Development*. Oxford University Press, New York.

Davis, Howard. 1999. *The Culture of Building*. Oxford University Press, Oxford.

— 2006. Architectural Education and Vernacular Building. In: Asquith, Lindsay/Vellinga, Marcel (eds.). *Vernacular Architecture in the Twenty-*

First Century. Theory, Education and Practice. Taylor & Francis, London and New York: 231–244.

Davidson, Colin/Johnson, Cassidy/Lizarralde Gonzalo/Dikem Nese/Sliwinski Alicia. 2007. Truths and Myths about Community Participation in Post-Disaster Housing Projects. In: *Habitat International* 31: 100–115.

Davidson, Colin. 2010. Multi-actor Arrangements and Project Management. In: Lizzaralde, Gonzalo/Johnson, Cassidy/Davidson, Colin (eds.). *Rebuilding after Disasters: From Emergency to Sustainability.* Taylor & Francis, New York: 88–109.

Desai, Rajendra/Desai Rupal. 2011. Citizen Architects. In: Aquilino, Marie (ed.). *Beyond Shelter - Architecture and Human Dignity.* Metropolis Books, New York: 88–93.

Diekmann, Andreas 2010 [1995]. *Empirische Sozialforschung. Grundlagen, Methoden, Anwendungen.* Vierte Auflage. Rowohlt Verlag, Hamburg.

Duffy, Francis/Rabeneck, Andrew. 2013. Professionalism and Architects in the 21st Century. In: *Building Research and Information*, 41(1): 115–122.

Duyne-Barenstein, Jennifer. 2006. *Housing Reconstruction in Post-Earthquake Gujarat. A Comparative Analysis.* HPN Network No. 54. Overseas Development Institute, London.

— 2007: *Post-Disaster Housing Reconstruction: Current Trends and Sustainable Alternatives for Tsunami affected Communities in Coastal Tamil Nadu.* Available under: http://www.chs.ubc.ca/archives/files/Post-disaster%20housing%20recounstruction%20current%20trends%20and%20sustianable%20alternatives.pdf (accessed on: 21.01.2012).

— 2010. Who Governs Reconstruction? Changes and Continuity in Policies, Practices and Outcomes. In: Lizzaralde, Gonzalo/Johnson, Cassidy/Davidson, Colins (eds.). *Rebuilding after Disasters: From Emergency to Sustainability.* Taylor & Francis, New York: 149–176.

— 2011a. The Home as the World: Tamil Nadu. In: Aquilino, Marie, J. (ed). *Beyond Shelter. Architecture and Human Dignity.* Metropolis Books, New York: 184–195.

— 2011b. Housing Reconstruction in Tamil Nadu. The Disaster after the Tsunami in India. In: Miller Demond/Shondell, Rivera/Jason, David (eds.). *Community Disaster, Recovery and Resiliency – Exploring Global Opportunities and Challenges.* Taylor & Francis, Boca Raton Florida: 343–362.

Easterly, William. 2006. *The White Man's Burden. Why the West's Efforts to Aid the Rest Have Done So Much Ill and So Little Good*. Oxford University Press, Oxford.

Edwards, Michael. 1999. *Future Positive: International Co-operation in the 21st Century*. Routledge, London.

Elliot, Philip. 1972. *The Sociology of the Professions*. Macmilan, London.

El-Masri, Souheil. 1997. Learning from the People: A Fieldwork Approach in War-Damaged Villages in Lebanon. In: Awotona, Adenrele (ed.). *Reconstruction after Disaster. Issues and Practices*. Ashgate Publication, Aldershot Brookfield USA: 57–72.

Escobar, Arturo. 1995. *Encountering Development. The Making and Unmaking of the Third World*. Princeton University Press. Princeton, New Jersey.

Evetts, Julia. 2003. The Sociological Analysis of Professionalism: Occupational Change in the Modern World. In: *International Sociology*, 18(2): 395–415.

Fathy, Hassan. 1973. *Architecture for the Poor. An Experiment in Rural Egypt*. The University of Chicago Press, Chicago and London.

Gardner, Katy/Lewis, David. 1996. *Anthropology, Development and the Post-Modern Challenge*. Pluto Press, London.

Giddens, Anthony. 1990. *The Consequences of Modernity*. Stanford University Press, Cambridge.

Glaeser, Bernhard. 1995. *Housing, Sustainable Development and the Rural Poor. A Study of Tamil Nadu*. Sage Publications, New Delhi.

Goldstein, Howard. 1994. Ethnography, Critical Inquiry and Social Work Practice. In: Sherman A. Edmund/Reid, William James (eds). *Qualitative Research in Social Work*. New York, Columbia University Press: 42–51.

Government of Puducherry. 2005a. *Progressive Report*. Available under: http://www.pon.nic.in/tsunami/dmg1002.htm (accessed on 3.05.2012). Government of Puducherry, Puducherry.

— 2005b. *Government Order on Construction of Permanent Housing*, G.O.Ms.No. 29 issued on 15.03.2005. Available under: http://www.pon.nic.in/tsunami/tsunaminew.htm (accessed on 7.05.2012).

— 2006. *Village-wise Summary of Rehabilitation of Tsunami affected Villages* as on 2.02.2006. Available under: http://www.pon.nic.in/tsunami/villagewise_summary_of_rehabilit.htm (accessed on 11.05.2012).

Government of Tamil Nadu. 2005a. *Government Order: G.O.Ms.No. 25.* (13.01.2005). Government of Tamil Nadu, Chennai.

— 2005b. *Government Order: G.O.Ms.No. 172.* Dated: 30.03.2005. Government of Tamil Nadu, Chennai.

— 2005c. *Tiding over Tsunami - Part 1.* Published by the Government of Tamil Nadu. Government of Tamil Nadu, Chennai.

— 2005d. *Guidelines for Reconstruction of Houses Affected by Tsunami in Tamil Nadu.* Part I. Revenue Administration, Disaster Management & Mitigation Department, New Dehli.

— 2008. *Tiding over Tsunami – Part 2.* Published by the Government of Tamil Nadu. Available under: http://www.tn.gov.in/tsunami/digital-library/ebooks-web/TOTPART2/TidingoverPART2.pdf (accessed on 10.01.2013).

Grønseth, Kristian. 2007. *A Little Piece of Denmark in India.* Master Thesis at the Universtiy of Oslo, Faculty of Social Anthropology. Available under: https://www.duo.uio.no/bitstream/handle/10852/16719/Completexxversionx6.1xxmedxinnholdsfortegnelse.pdf?sequence=1(accessed on: 10.01.2013).

Guha-Sapir, Debby/Vos, Femke/Below, Regina/Ponserre, Silvain. 2012. *Annual Disaster Statistical Review 2011: The Numbers and Trends.* CRED, Brussels. Available under: http://reliefweb.int/sites/reliefweb.int/files/resources/2012.07.05.ADSR_2011.pdf (accessed on 03.09.2013).

Guijt, Irene/Shah Meera Kaul. 1998. *The Myth of Community. Gender Issues in Participatory Development.* Practical Action, London.

Hall, Stuart. 1992. The West and the Rest: Discourse and Power. In: Hall, Stuart/Gieben, Bram (eds.). *Formations of Modernity.* Polity Press, Cambridge: 185–227.

Harris, Victoria L. 2011. The Architecture of Risk. In: Aquilino, Marie J. (ed.). *Beyond Shelter – Architecture and Human Dignity.* Metropolis Books, New York: 12–22.

Harris, Simon. 2006. Disasters and Dilemnas: Aid Agency Recruitment and H.R.D. in Post-Tsunami Sri Lanka. In: *Human Resource Development International* 9(2): 291–298.

Hartenberger, Ursula/Lorenz, David/Lützkendorf Thomas. 2013. A Shared Built Environment Professional Identity through Education and Training. In: *Building Research and Information*, 41(1): 60–76.

Harvey, Paul. 2005. *Cash Vouchers in Emergencies.* HPN Networkd Paper No. 21. Overseas Development Institute, London.

Hernández, Felipe. 2010. *Bhabha for Architects.* Routledge, Oxford and New York.

Hillier, Jean. 2002. *Shadows of Power. An Allegory of Prudence in Land-Use Planning.* Routledge, London.

Hobart, Mark (ed). 1993. *An Anthropological Critique of Development. The Growth of Ignorance.* Routledge, London and New York.

Hoffman, Susanna M. 1999. The Worst of Times, the Best of Times: Toward a Model of Cultural Response to Disaster. In: Oliver-Smith, Anthony/Hoffman, Susanna M. (eds.). *The Angry Earth: Disaster in Anthropological Perspective.* Routledge, New York: 134–155.

Hosagrahar, Jyoti. 2005. *Indigenous Modernities. Negotiating Architecture and Urbanism.* The ARCHI*TEXT* Series. Routledge, London and New York.

Hughes, Will/Hughes, Cathy. 2013. Professionalism and Professional Institutions in Times of Change. In: *Building Research and Information,* 41(1): 28–38.

Hüsken, Thomas. 2010. Outside the Whale: The Contested Life and Work of Development Experts. In: *Journal für Entwicklungspolitik* XXVI 3: 14–28.

Ifthekar, Ahmed. 2011. An Overview of Post-Disaster Permanent Housing Reconstruction in Developing Countries. In: *International Journal of Disaster Resilience in the Built Environment,* 2(2): 148–164.

International Federation of Red Cross (IFRC). 2003. *Guidelines for Post-Disaster Housing* (Version 1). Available under: http://www.ifrc.org/PageFiles/95751/B.d.03.%20Guidelines%20for%20Post%20Disaster%20Housing%20%20version%201_OXFAM%20GB.pdf (accessed on 30.08.2012).

— 2009. *Tsunami Five Year Progress Report*: 2004–2009. Available under: http://www.ifrc.org/Global/Publications/disasters/tsunami/IFRC-Tsunami-5Yrs-Report-Final-Web.pdf (accessed on 13.10.2012).

— 2011. *Federation-wide Tsunami 6.5-Year Progress Report.* Appeal No. 28/2004. Available under: http://www.ifrc.org/docs/appeals/04/FWR10.pdf (accessed on 13.10.2012).

Janz, Wes/Gray, Timothy/Mulvihill, Thalia. 2008. A New Village in Sri Lanka. Learning Lessons There, Sharing Lessons Here. In: *Property Management.* Volume 26 (5): 319–330.

Jigyasu, Rohit. 2002. *Reducing Disaster Vulnerability Through Local Knowledge and Capacity. The Case of Earthquake Prone Rural Communities in*

India and Nepal. Doctoral dissertation at the Faculty of Architecture and Fine Art Department of Town and Regional Planning. Norwegian University of Science and Technology, Trondheim.

— 2006. Structural Adaptation in South-Asia: Learning Lessons from Tradition. In: Bosher, Lee. *Hazards and the Built Environment*. Routledge, London and New York: 74–95.

— 2010. Appropriate Technology for Post-Disaster Reconstruction. In: Lizzaralde, Gonzalo/ Johnson Cassidy/Davidson Colins (eds.). *Rebuilding after Disasters: From Emergency to Sustainability*. Taylor & Francis, Oxford and New York: 49–69.

Karunasena, Gayani/Rameezdeen, Raufdeen. 2010. Post-Disaster Housing Reconstruction: Comparative Study of Donor vs Owner-Driven Approaches. In: *International Journal of Disaster Resilience in the Built Environment*. Vol. 1 (2): 173–191.

Khosla, Romi. 1980. Architecture of Rural Housing: Some Issues in India. In: *Lotus*, 32 (1): 56–60.

Lachenmann, Gudrun. 1991. *Systems of Ignorance. Alltags-/Expertenwissen. Wissenssoziologische Aspekte im Kulturvergleich*. Sozialanthropologische Arbeitspapiere Nr. 38. Hans Schiller, Berlin.

Lamnek, Siegfried. 2010 [1988]. *Qualitative Sozialforschung*. Beltz Verlag, Weinheim, Basel.

Latter, Rosemary. 2006. Educating Architects to Become Culturally Aware. In: Asquith, Lindsay/Vellinga, Marcel (eds.). 2006. *Vernacular Architecture in the Twenty-First Century. Theory, Education and Practice*. Taylor & Francis, London and New York: 245–261.

Lewis, David/Kanji Nazneen 2009. *Non-governmental Organisations and Development*. Routledge, New York.

Lizzaralde, Gonzalo/Johnson, Cassidy/Davidson, Colins (eds.). 2010. *Rebuilding after Disasters: From Emergency to Sustainability*. Taylor & Francis, Oxford and New York.

Lloyd-Jones, Tony (ed.). 2009. *The Built Environment Professions in Disaster Risk Reduction and Response. A Guide for Humanitarian Agencies*. MLC Press, London.

Lyons Michal. 2009. Building Back Better: The Large-Scale Impact of Small-Scale Approaches to Reconstruction. In: *World Development*, 37(2): 385–398.

— 2010. Can Large-Scale Participation be People-Centred? Evaluating Reconstruction as Development. In: Lyons, Michal/Schilderman, Theo/

Boano Camillo (eds.). *Building Back Better. Delivering People-Centred Housing Reconstruction at Scale.* Practical Action Publishing: 39–62.

Luig, Ute (ed.). 2012. *Negotiating Disasters: Politics, Representation, Meanings.* Peter Lang GmbH, Internationaler Verlag der Wissenschaften, Frankfurt am Main.

Marchand, Trevor H. J. 2009. *The Masons of Djenne.* Indiana University Press, Bloomington & Indianapolis.

Mathur, Hari Mohan (ed.). 2006. *Managing Resettlement in India. Approaches, Issues, Experiences.* Oxford University Press, New Delhi.

McNeill, Desmond/St Clair Auncion Lera. 2013. The World Bank's Expertise. Observant Participation in the World Development Report 2006, Equity and Development. In: Mosse, David (ed). *Adventures in Aidland. The Anthropology of Professionals in International Development. Studies in Public and Applied Anthropology.* Berghahn Books, New York and Oxford: 103–122.

Meding, Jason/Oyedele, Lukumon/Cleland, David. 2009. Developing NGO Competencies in Post-Disaster Reconstruction: A Theoretical Framework. In: *Disaster Advances* 2(3): 36–45.

Mosse, David (ed.). 2013. *Adventures in Aidland. The Anthropology of Professionals in International Development.* Studies in Public and Applied Anthropology. Berghahn Books, New York and Oxford.

Naimi-Gasser, Jasmin. 2012. The Remembered Trees: Contractor-Driven Reconstruction and Its Consequences in Communities' Well Being in Coastal Tamil Nadu. In: Duyne-Barenstein, Jennifer/Leemann, Esther (eds.). *Post-Disaster Reconstruction and Change. Communities' Perspective.* CRC Press. Francis & Taylor Press, New York and London: 137–156.

National Buildings Organisation (NBO) and UN Regional Housing Centre ESCAP. 1984. *Handbook of Housing Statistics 1982–83.* Nirman Bhawan, New Delhi.

Okley, Judith. 2011. Retrospective Reading of Field notes. Living on Gypsy Camps. In: *BEHEMOTH: A Journal on Civilisation.* Volume 4(1): 18–42.

Oliver, Paul. 1999. *Vernacular Architecture in the Twenty-First Century.* Hepworth Lecture. Prince of Wales Institute, London.

— 2003. *Dwellings: The Vernacular House World View.* Phaidon, London.

Oliver-Smith, Anthony. 1991. Success and Failures in Post-Disaster Resettlement. In: *Disasters* 15(1): 12–24.

Ortiz, Enrique. 2002. Self-determined Housing Approaches and the Role of Architects in Post-Disaster Strategies. In: *Trialog* 73 (2). Disaster Relief / Katastrophenhilfe: 14–19.

Oxfam. 2009. *Final Report.* Available under: http://www.oxfam.org/en/pressroom/pressrelease/2009-12-22/oxfam-closes-final-elements-its-tsunami-aid-programme (accessed on 29.03.2013).

PMSSS. 2005. *Project Documentation – Keezhakazakudy-metu: About the village.* Unpublished project document. Courtesy of PMSSS.

Rapoport, Amos. 1982. An Approach to Vernacular Design. In: Fitch, James Marsten (ed.). *Shelter: Models of Native Ingenuity.* Katonah, New York, Katonah Gallery: 43–49.

— 1983. Development, Culture Change and Supportive Design. In: *Habitat International* 7(5/6): 249–268.

—1999. A Framework for Studying Vernacular Design. In: *Journal of Architectural and Planning Research* 16(1): 52–64.

Rieger-Jandl, Andrea. 2005. *Living Culture in the Himalayas. Anthropological Guidelines for Building in Developing Countries.* WUV Universitätsverlag, Vienna.

Salama, M. Ashraf/O'Reilly, William/Noschis, Kaj. 2002. *Architectural Education Today. Cross-Cultural Perspectives.* Comportements and Authors, Lausanne.

Sanderson, David. 2010. Architects are often the last People needed in Disaster Reconstruction. In: *The Guardian.* 3rd March 2010. Available under: http://www.guardian.co.uk/commentisfree/2010/mar/03/architects-disaster-reconstruction-haiti-chile (accessed on 17.09.2012).

Schaur, Eda. 1991. *Ungeplante Siedlungen – Unplanned Settlements.* IL 39, Stuttgart.

Schutz, Alfred/Luckmann, Thomas. 1973. *The Structures of the Life-World.* North-Western University Press, Illinois. Republished 1974, Heinemann, London.

Sharma, Anura. 1997. Profession as Agent: Knowledge Asymmetry in Agency Exchange. In: *Academy of Management Review,* 22: 758–798.

SIFFS. 2009. *Rebuilding Habitats – Process Document.* SIFFS, Trivandrum, Kerala.

SKAT. 2008. *Tsunami Housing Reconstruction Program, Nagapattinam, Tamil Nadu, India.* Available under: http://www.skat.ch/publications/prarticle.2005-09-29.1982292338/skatpublication.2009-04-21.6029201534 (accessed on: 15.08.2011).

Sökefeld, Martin. 2012. The Attabad Landslide and the Politics of Disaster in Gojal, Gilgit-Baltistan. In: Luig, Ute. *Negotiating Disasters: Politics, Representation, Meanings.* Peter Lang GmbH, Internationaler Verlag der Wissenschaften, Frankfurt am Main: 175–204.

Srinivas, M. N./Shah, A.M./Ramaswamy, E. A. (eds). 1979. *The Fieldworker and the Field: Problems and Challenges in Sociological Investigations.* Oxford University Press, Delhi.

Steinberg, Florian. 2007. Housing Reconstruction and Rehabilitation in Aceh and Nias, Indonesia – Rebuilding Lives. In: *Habitat International*, 31: 150–166.

Steinberg, Florian/Smidt, Pieter (eds.). 2010. *Rebuilding Lives and Homes in Aceh and Nias, Indonesia.* Asian Development Bank, Manila.

Subramanian, Ajantha. 2009. *Shorelines – Space and Rights in South India.* Stanford University Press, Stanford.

Tauber, Gertrud. 2005. Die 'Campi Nomadi' oder Wo beginnt die Planung? In: Tauber, Elisabeth (ed.). *Sinti und Roma. Eine Spurensuche.* ARUNDA 67, Schlanders: 174–191.

— 2013. *Can Architects Contribute to Making a Difference? Post-Disaster Housing and the Role of Architects: A Case Study in Rural South India.* Paper presented at the 6th International i-Rec Conference: *Sustainable Post-Disaster Reconstruction: From Recovery to Risk Reduction,* May 2013. Ascona, Switzerland.

— 2014 (in press). Architects and Rural Post-Disaster Housing: Lessons From South India. In: *International Journal of Disaster Resilience in the Built Environment.*

Tauber, Elisabeth/Tauber, Gertrud. 2012. *Die Zeit und das Holz. Der Zimmermann Josef Tauber.* ARUNDA 82 and Verlag *Bibliothek* der Provinz, Schlanders and Weitra.

Telford, John/Crossgrave, John. 2007. The International Humanitarian System and the 2004 Indian Ocean Earthquake and Tsunamis. In: *Disasters*, 31(1): 1–28.

Tendler, Judith. 1982. *Turning Private Voluntary Organisations into Development Agencies: Questions for Evaluation.* Program Evaluation Discussion Paper 12: United States Agency for International Development, Washington DC.

Tvedt, Terje 1988. *Angels of Mercy or Development Diplomats? NGOs and Foreign Aid.* James Currey Ltd Oxford.

The Hindu. 2005a. *Pondy Guidelines for Private Parties to Build Houses for Tsunami Victims.* Available under: http://www. thehindu. com/2005/03/17/stories/2005031707620100.htm (accessed on: 3.05.2012).

— 2005b. *Dalits, Irulas were also badly affected by tsunami.* Available under: http://www.hindu.com/2005/03/21/stories/2005032108540100.htm (accessed on: 28.06.2012).

— 2006. *Bill to rename Pondicherry as Puducherry passed.* Available under: http://www.hindu.com/2006/08/22/stories/2006082207481000. htm (accessed on: 3.05.2012).

Turner, John F.C. 1972. The Reeducation of a Professional. In: Turner, John F.C./Fichter, Robert (eds.). *Freedom to Build: Dweller Control of the Housing Process.* Coller MacMillan, New York: 122–147.

— 2009 [1976]. *Housing by People. Towards Autonomy in Building Environments.* Marion Boyars Publishers, London.

Turner, Stephen. 2004. *Liberal Democracy 3.0. Civil Society in an Age of Experts.* Sage, London.

Twigg, John. 2000. The Age of Accountability? Future Community Involvement in Disaster Reduction. In: *The Australian Journal of Emergeny Management,* 14(4): 51–58.

UNTRS (United Nations Team for Tsunami Recovery Support). 2006a. *Building Back Better for our Children – How the Tsunami changed the Lives of Irula Communities in Cuddalore District, Tamil Nadu* (Report). Available under: http://www.recoveryplatform.org/assets/publication/ Tsunami%20Reocvery/india-tsunami-recovery.pdf (2.07.2012).

— 2006b (April). *Quarterly Report. Tsunami Recovery. A Joint UN Report. India.* UNTRS, Chennai.

— 2008. *Tsunami India – Three Years After.* UNTRS, Chennai.

Waterson, Roxana. 1990. *The Living House. An Anthropology of Architecture in Southeast Asia.* Oxford University Press, New York.

Waqabaca, Jokatama/Panko, Mary/Potangaroa, Regan. 2013. *Community Engagement: Rebuilding Samoan Fale post 2009 Tsunami.* Paper presented at the 6th International i-Rec Conference: *Sustainable Post-Disaster Reconstruction: From Recovery to Risk Reduction,* May 2013. Ascona, Switzerland.

Wemhöner, Antje. 1993. Diseño Participativo – Entwurf unter Nutzerbeteiligung. In: *Trialog* 39: 34–37.

Wilson, Gordon. 2006. Beyond the Technocrat? The Professional Expert in Development Practice. In: *Development and Change*, 37(3): 501–523.

Woyseth, Dunin Halina. 2002. Making-Based Knowledge: Between Identity and Change. In: *Architectural Education Today. Cross-Cultural Perspectives.* Comportements and Authors, Lausanne: 17–24.

Wood, Geof, D. 1998. Projects as Communities: Consultants, Knowledge and Power. In: *Impact Assessment and Project Appraisal*, 16(1): 54–64.

Woods, Mary N. 1999. *From Craft to Profession: The Practice of Architecture in Nineteenth Century America.* University of California Press, Berkeley.

Woods, Ngaire 2006. *The Globalizers: The IMF, the World Bank and their Borrowers.* C.A.: Cornell University Press, Ithaca.

Wu, Jy/Lindell, Michael K. 2004. Housing Reconstruction after Two Major Earthquakes: The 1994 Northridge Earthquake in the United States and 1999 Chi-Chi Earthquake in Taiwan. In: *Disasters*, Volume 28(1): 63–81.